Growing Up in a
Korean
Kitchen

❀ ❀ A Cookbook ❀ ❀

Hi Soo Shin Hepinstall

Ten Speed Press
Berkeley / Toronto

I humbly dedicate this book to all generations of Korean women, especially to my grandmother and mother.

Ten Speed Press
Box 7123
Berkeley, California 94707
www.tenspeed.com

Distributed in Australia by Simon & Schuster Australia, in Canada by Ten Speed Press Canada, in New Zealand by Southern Publishers Group, in South Africa by Real Books, in Southeast Asia by Berkeley Books, and in the United Kingdom and Europe by Airlift Book Company.

Cover and book design by Jeff Puda
Copyediting by Jackie Wan
Photographs by Hi Soo Shin Hepinstall
Photograph on page 248 by Pat Benic
The romanization of Korean in this book generally follows the McCune-Reischauer System.

Some of the recipes in this book include raw eggs, meat, or fish. When these foods are consumed raw, there is always the risk that bacteria, which is killed by proper cooking, may be present. For this reason, when serving these foods raw, always buy certified salmonella-free eggs and the freshest meat and fish available from a reliable grocer, storing them in the refrigerator until they are served. Because of the health risks associated with the consumption of bacteria that can be present in raw eggs, meat, and fish, these foods should not be consumed by infants, small children, pregnant women, the elderly, or any people who may be immunocompromised.

Library of Congress Cataloging-in-Publication Data
Hepinstall, Hi Soo Shin.
Growing up in a Korean kitchen: a cookbook / Hi Soo Shin Hepinstall.
p. cm.
ISBN 1-58008-281-5
1. Cookery, Korean. I. Title.

TX724.5.K65 H47 2001
641.59519—dc21   2001027322
First printing, 2001
Printed in Canada

1 2 3 4 5 6 7 8 9 10 — 05 04 03 02 01

Contents

Side Dishes 113

Fresh Salad and Vegetable Dishes 115

✿ Foreword by Sonya Hepinstall

Food has always played an important part in my mother's life, whether she was in Asia, Europe, or the U.S. It was in Europe that her real adventure with food began, as my parents dined at the great restaurants of the continent. There, my mother first realized that she could unite three passions—writing, a love of the culinary arts, and the desire to introduce the world to Korean culture and food—in a book filled with recipes and memories. The result is a work that is both a loving reconstruction of a time-honored way of life and a guide to traditional Korean cooking.

My mother's book will be useful to all readers, Korean and American. Fewer young Koreans make their own kimchi these days, let alone toenjang paste, and how many could say what goes into the making of soy sauce? The sights, smells, and tastes of food are inextricably bound up with a way of life, and this book goes a long way toward making sure we don't lose our understanding of Korea's version altogether.

In the case of my mother and me, one was brought up as a second-class citizen (as a woman) in a deeply Confucian society nearly destroyed by occupation, natural disaster, and war, and the other was American through and through, a girl brought up free in an era of great prosperity for the United States, deliberately raised to believe no goal was too lofty. My mother left behind in South Korea a career as a celebrated novelist, a family, and a protected life and became just another Asian immigrant at a time of little real understanding or interest in Asia and its culture or people. My mother had the right to expect that her daughter, at least, would try to understand, but I was often found siding with those who didn't want to bother. This book is a testimony to the fact that she never gave up on me or all those who needed encouragement to recognize the value of things Korean. For that, thanks Mom.

(above) A wedding ceremony in traditional attire (author's sister-in-law, nephew, his bride, and author's elder brother)

❋ Returning to My Childhood Home

It warms my heart whenever I remember the happy days of my childhood. In my fond memories, I often go back home to the place where I was born and raised. Our great-grandfather built our house about 160 years ago. Having but an only son (our grandfather), and again only one grandson (our father), he dreamed that he would have many great-grandsons; they would fill his big house and carry on the family tradition with honor and prosperity.

Like many others in Asia during those years, *pugwi tanam* (may our family be wealthy, noble, and have many sons) was every Korean's daily prayer. Our great-grandfather's dream for his family was half-fulfilled in my father's time: our family was blessed with six boys, and six girls came along as extras, rounding out our family register to a full dozen children.

It was our grandmother's law that we girls must not step outside our enclosed yard. But when I was five or six years old I'd take a most daring adventure now and then and climb the hill behind our house, a special off-limits place. From the top of the hill I had a sweeping view of our village surrounded by low mountains. I could see people coming and going on winding dirt roads. I could hear the distant sounds of children playing, barking dogs running in small alleys, bicycles, and a few old trucks. Now and then I could catch sight of a bus creeping along the road, coughing and trailing black smoke and huge clouds of dust.

On my right was the primary school with a small playground that I was to attend later. I could see part of downtown Ch'ŏngju. There was the poplar tree–lined dirt road that led to the short main street, the only asphalt road in town. Beyond that was our town's landmark, a stream named Musim Ch'ŏn, "the stream of no desire." The name came from one of Buddha's teachings: "Empty your mind, and depart from earthly desires." Across the stream lay two bridges, like a pair of chopsticks. One, made of

(above) Confucian school gate

(opposite) Park in Kyŏngju, the ancient capital of the Silla Kingdom (57 B.C. to A.D. 936)

concrete, was for pedestrians, buses, trucks, and carts; the other was a railroad crossing. It was fascinating to watch the train cross the bridge and glide through the rice fields like a dark caterpillar. I loved to follow it as it made its funny *ch'ik-ch'ik p'ok-p'ok* sound—the sound of a steam engine to Korean ears—as it puffed spirals of white smoke. My eyes would linger long after the train's tail disappeared behind the hill.

Whenever I made an escape to my perch on the hill, I'd never fail to notice our house below. I could see the shining jet-black tin roof of the main living quarters. It looked like a letter F, with the bottom part hidden from view in summer by drooping persimmon tree branches. On the other side, partially covered by our big old tree, were four smaller, thatched roofs among the vegetable plots and flower gardens. The compound was neatly bundled by what looked like a semicircle of straw-braided rope, which, in fact, was the rice straw roof on top of our mud and rock wall.

My paternal and maternal grandmothers, grandaunt, and father at Dimond Mountain, now North Korea, circa 1930

I loved the way the world around our house looked with the change of seasons. In winter everything was so gray and gloomy. There was nothing much to see except bare trees and frozen roofs with long icicles. It was biting cold. In spring, I could see pink azalea bushes and chick-yellow forsythia in full bloom through the hazy, soft air. When I would hear magpies and noisy locusts from the fragrant acacia groves that cast long shadows all the way down to our *changdokdae*, the sauce crock pad where our giant pot-bellied sauce crocks were kept, I'd know it was summer. Under the blazing sun the flowers and leaves would droop, the tin roof would glisten and crackle. In no time, there would be bright flaming-yellow persimmons hanging everywhere on the tree branches, and it was autumn. Under the azure blue sky, the surrounding mountains would be ablaze with autumn colors.

Looking back, it's the merry times around our house that stand out in my memory, the times when it was as if some magical spell had been cast where usually there was a frightfully austere and regimented daily life. A feast day was coming! I could tell. The grown-ups were talking about food preparation. It might be an occasion for someone's sixty-first birthday, or a very important ancestral ceremony, or better yet, a wedding.

Several weeks in advance our kitchen would have more traffic—busy with extra help from distant relatives, aunts nearby, our neighbors, and others. Soon the sights, sounds, and smells of good food would be floating everywhere around the house. When the special day was almost upon us, there would be more relatives from faraway places. As is customary, we would provide them rooms to stay for a day or a week, or as long as they wished. Our house would end up resembling a bustling village market. Everyone seemed so happy and content. This was that rare time when grown-ups, with unbelievable generosity, would say, "Eat all you want," in an incredibly amiable tone of voice. Perhaps it was on these occasions that I began to learn how good food makes everyone feel. Even our dogs seemed to be wagging their tails happily with excitement. At the gate, the beggars would be treated better than usual, getting something extra besides plain rice and bean paste soup. They gave extra bows in return.

All in all, those were the happiest times in my little world at the age of five. At this merry feast time, our family's *kŏnnŏbang*, the room across from the central hall, was turned into a temporary pantry. We children knew that the most delicious and sweet-tasting desserts were all stored in that large room. Everything would be neatly and prettily arranged in many boxes, large storage dishes, jars, trays, and baskets of various sizes made of wood, bamboo, brass, earthenware, porcelain, and some silver. Very rare items were stored in a covered silver bowl: honey-candied ginseng roots, lotus root wheels, candied ginger, crystallized chrysanthemums, sweet rice flower pancakes, and others. Everything was covered with silk patchwork cloth padded with oiled mulberry paper.

Grandmother's most precious jellied ox hoof, a favorite with rice wine, was placed in a wooden pan in the corner of the room. Another tray had pancakes made from green onions, mung beans, and summer squash. A tray of pan-fried thin meats and vegetable strips skewered on bamboo picks was in another corner. Pork cold cuts were pressed under a pair of heavy grinding stones. Nearby, on a large flat bamboo tray, were pieces of tasty coin-sized beef and bean curd patties. The goodies prepared by our family for the special occasion were endless: all kinds of rice cakes, honey-dipped rice cookies, semisweet paste made from powdered nuts or beans and stamped in many pretty patterns, rice taffy, and all sort of nuts, seed cakes, dried fruits, flowers, and many, many more. I'd tiptoe in, just for a peek at the dazzling array of good food, to admire and inhale the roomful of mixed

aromas so indescribable and so beautiful a visual feast, as I'd say to myself. But in truth, I confess, I was there to sneak a bite or two on each visit.

Our kitchen became an unimaginable place of absolute madness at feast time, when more than 100 people might be served. But the truth of the matter is, even on ordinary days it was a riot at our house. All the kitchen folks, women of all ages, labored frantically in the Korean kitchen of the 1940s, sweating in the hot summer and freezing in the winter. Almost every day they cooked and served more than thirty family members, including revered houseguests. Looking back on those times, our family kitchen was like the kitchen of a small, exclusive restaurant—one in which only men could be members with the sole exception of our grandmother, a strong-willed woman and the undisputed head of our clan. They were very demanding and fastidious guests.

In the Korea of my childhood, preparing good food, serving it with care and love, and enjoying the pleasures of eating was an all-consuming daily activity. However, as an adult I came to realize with sadness that the richness of traditional Korean cuisine was little known, not only to the outside world, but until recently, even to modern Koreans, as each culinary tradition has rarely been shared outside each Korean province or the tightly knit circle of one's clan or family. Good food was prepared only for one's ancestors, descendants, friends, and guests. Family recipes were handed down by word of mouth, from one generation to the next.

After living for more than thirty years in America, Europe, and elsewhere in Asia, and enjoying and learning to cook international cuisines, I came to realize there was great interest in Korean food and that it was a near-perfect answer to our modern quest for a healthy, low-fat, delicious diet. When I returned to Korea in the 1980s, I was determined to discover the hidden culinary treasures that existed only in my vague memory and to help make better known Korea's variety of robust and subtle dishes and its long tradition in pickling and cooking with garlic and hot peppers. But something made me wince: In our Confucian-Buddhist family ethic, it is absolutely forbidden to talk about one's family to others, good or bad. If you praise yourself or your family, you are branded as a *p'albulch'ul*, an imbecile with at least eight reasons for being absolutely useless. Worse, to criticize your family is like *nuŏsŏ ch'imbaet'ki*, spitting into the air while lying on one's back. If my grandmother were living now and heard about my plans, would she denounce me? After further

Growing Up in a Korean Kitchen

reflection, I came to believe that she would give me a typically silent gesture of approval by simply looking away.

The recipes I introduce in this book, for the most part, have been handed down orally within our family for generations. Allow me to explain the influence of royal cuisine in our family kitchen. Our Shin family clan belongs to one of the Yangban-literati families in the heartland of South Korea. Since Korean family law forbade marriage within the same clan, throughout Korean history the royal and upper-class clans and families were related by marriage and, naturally, so was their kitchen culture. In fact, women from upper-class clans were in charge of the royal kitchen and its cuisine was mostly their creation. Yangban family recipes, especially in our province close to Seoul, naturally had a flair and refinement comparable to those of royal cuisine, but possibly with more variety.

The chapters are arranged according to traditional categories: main dishes, side dishes, and desserts and beverages. Rice, soup, kimchi, and sometimes stew are considered main dishes and are served in individual bowls and placed in front of each guest. About seven to ten side dishes *(panch'an)* are served either in individual dishes or family style and include not only vegetables and salads but also meat and fish—what are considered entrees on most Western menus. They also include the more elaborate dishes made for ceremonies, feasts, and other special occasions.

My family, around 1947 (my mother, grandmother, and father in the middle; I'm standing second from the left)

The Korean Kitchen

At Home

During most of my childhood, the food for our kitchen came from our own land—fresh vegetables from our backyard and rice and grain from our fields in the countryside. Every harvest, ox-drawn carts (and, in later years, trucks) lined up at our outer gate. Our tenants would unload and carry huge sacks to the storerooms in our house. The grain would nourish us for the rest of the year.

Our yard was always decked with flowers, vegetables, and herbs according to the season. They grew by themselves, like that incredible beanstalk in the fairy-tale, or so I thought as a child, not realizing how much labor it took. Our wide sliding doors were open all summer long; maybe that's why we didn't need flowers on the table.

Now, older than our grandmother was then, I cannot help but remember those years with her in her garden. I feel it was only yesterday, with me standing beside our grandmother, who'd be busy gardening with a shovel, a hoe, or some other tool in her hand. I was there to assist her in her labor of love: aerating, mulching, seeding, collecting seeds, planting, transplanting, the work seemingly never ending. Gardening was one of her passions and she worked tirelessly, rain or shine. Probably, for this reason, I have a habit of calling the gardens around our house "Grandmother's gardens."

Our home was one of the largest, if not the largest, traditional house in our town. During the Korean War, the North Koreans used it as its military headquarters for Ch'ŏngju City. Allied planes tried to bomb it, but it was spared because we were protected by our hill in the back. In the middle of the compound, our tin-roofed main house stood on a two-foot-high stone foundation. It had six rooms, plus a kitchen and a pantry. A three-foot-wide parquet porch *(maru)* surrounded most of the house. Our father's straw-roofed house was across the inner courtyard.

(above) Outside a traditional home kitchen

(opposite) Traditional Korean gate

He had two rooms and a library, plus his own entrance gate. Next to his house were two more storerooms and our bathroom containing a large, sunken cast-iron tub. Our water well and pump were at the far end of the courtyard, near our servant family's two-room house. It had its own kitchen, courtyard, and vegetable patch. Nearby, our manservant lived in a one-room gatehouse.

On the other side of the main house, toward the hill, was a semidetached two-room storehouse. In one room, three huge crocks for winter kimchi were buried in the cement floor up to their necks and capped with straw-lined covers. In the center of the backyard, a few steps from the kitchen's back door and surrounded by flowerbeds and terraced vegetable gardens, was a raised stone platform *(changdokdae)* where we kept twenty or so large and small crocks for storing the three basic sauces: soy sauce, fermented soybean paste, and hot red pepper paste.

The huge tree we loved to climb was at the base of the hill. Nearby, we had a barn for hay and pigsties. Beside caged rabbits, there were other animals running around the yard: egg-laying chickens, dogs, stray cats, and wild weasels. Between the barn and the house was a tin-roofed room-size rice chest. At the far side, by a mud fence, we had an apricot tree and a stocky sour plum tree. Each autumn, we would harvest the fruit, most of which my grandmother made into plum-flavored liqueur. The rest of the backyard and the hill was a green blanket, except when covered with snow. As the seasons turned, it was splashed in colors of wild flowers and herbs—white clover, violet pansies and pasques, dandelions, shepherd's purse, mugwort, wildly perfumed chrysanthemum, and day lilies.

Our family kitchen *(puŏk)* and separate pantry *(ch'anbang)* were at the corner of the L-shaped main house, dividing the boys' quarters (two rooms) from the women's quarters (two rooms), the high-beamed, parquet-floored great hall *(taech'ŏng maru)* open to the elements and a guest room *(kŏnnŏbang)* at the far end. The unusually large clay-floored kitchen, about ten by twelve feet, was four feet below the floor level of the pantry and the rest of the house and two feet below ground level. A long working bench with a chopping block, knives, and cooking utensils along the wall divided the kitchen and pantry. Between the two was an opening large enough for passing trays back and forth. A trap door to the cellar was below the bench. In the pantry, one whole wall had two built-in storage chests—one for dishes, crystal bowls, and glasses and the other for ready-made food. The women in the kitchen passed hot food to those in the pantry, where the several individual tables were set and then carried to family members and guests.

Along the other interior wall was a raised cement counter (*put-tumak*), in which was permanently sunk three evenly spaced cast-iron cauldrons, each with a wood-burning oven (*agungi*) underneath. I remember well how the kitchen was an arctic zone in winter, except when the *agungi* were blazing bright. Then it was warm and cozy and I would perch between the cauldrons with my short legs dangling over the edge above the kitchen floor. The grown-ups would let me watch them cook. They always told me to be mindful of the water storage jar buried in the corner; it was so gigantic I could easily have drowned in it. Two more cauldrons sat idle, their chimneys facing outside, to be used during the summer to spare us from the hot *ondol* floors and the sweltering kitchen. Then we did most of the cooking outside over makeshift wood fires and the several clay charcoal braziers that in winter stood in the corner of the kitchen.

The *agungi* served two purposes, for cooking the family meals and for heating the floor of the house. The flue from the stove wound through the clay *ondol* floor and out the chimney on the other side of the house, creating one of the earliest systems of radiant heating. To retain the heat, the flues were covered with shale and paved and sealed with a mixture of clay and straw. Then multiple layers of heavily oiled mulberry paper were pasted over the floor and several coats of soybean oil were applied to the paper. The result was a room with a pale yellow floor that kept us snug and comfortable through the harsh winters.

Our house, as with most traditional Korean homes, was simplicity itself. One might even say austere. The Korean interpretation of Confucian philosophy at the end of the Yi Dynasty (1392–1910) stressed modesty, simplicity, and naturalness. Open spaces, straight lines, rectangles, and minimum ornamentation were the basic architectural elements. Natural imperfections were admired, as was asymmetry. Rooms were multifunctional: they were our living rooms as well as where we ate and slept. Furnishings were kept to the minimum. We did not use chairs and instead sat on cushions on the floor. Every morning we folded our *ibul* and *yo*, our individual comforters and cotton-stuffed sleeping pads, and put them in the corner or hid them in built-in closets or in plain wooden chests. We returned the eating tables to the pantry after meals. Coming in from the courtyard, we left our shoes under the parquet porch, opened the lattice-shuttered door, and then slid open the sliding doors into our room. Colors were subdued. The floors were soft yellow and walls were white and rarely had hanging pictures. Whenever possible, we kept our doors and windows open. Our ideal was an open, uncluttered, almost empty room.

The Family Meal

In our house, there were few differences in the food we ate for breakfast, lunch, and supper. Instead, the contrasts at mealtime were within the household: differences in table arrangements, utensils, food, and presentation.

In the pantry, maids arranged the food on individual meal tables (about 12 inches high and 27 by 20 inches across) and then dispatched them first to our grandmother, then a single table to our father's house (plus additional tables for each of his precious guests) and three two-person tables to the boys' room (or more, depending on the number of country cousins who were studying at the local high school). As for the girls, we helped the maids carry trays to the upper room in the women's quarters, where six or seven of us ate with our mother around a huge round table made from a tree trunk. (It was the only table that was not taken away after meals. We used it for homework and our mother kneaded dough and made noodles on it.) After we were finished, the maids served our manservant in the gatehouse and then quickly ate their meal in the pantry or kitchen. A tray was always prepared for the beggars who invariable visited our gate in the morning.

Each table was different and had its own dinnerware and dishes. Our grandmother's oblong table with gracefully curved legs was made of resin-coated paulownia wood, as was our father's and the tables of his precious guests. The tables had a simple but elegant matte finish with a faint reddish tint, exactly to our grandmother's taste. "I don't allow gaudy, shiny mother-of-pearl lacquerware in my house!" she used to say with disdain. Their dishes would be mostly porcelain in summer and brassware in winter. Each had his or her own personal cloisonné-tipped silver spoon and set of chopsticks. Their ringing sound at the slightest touch to the dishes was very pretty to our ears, but it sounded like a warning too because we had to be careful not to break their mood by placing their flatware incorrectly when we set the table. The boys ate from porcelain dishes and used nickel spoons and chopsticks, while we girls and servants had earthenware dishes and wooden or brass spoons and chopsticks.

According to traditional Korean table etiquette, there were five types of table settings, according to the number of side dishes. All the dishes were set on the table at the beginning of the meal. Without counting the fixed main dishes (steamed rice, soup, and kimchi, plus sauces) there were tables of three, five, seven, nine, or twelve. Ordinary households prepared tables of three or five, while only upper-class households could afford seven or nine. The table of twelve (*sipi chʻŏp sang*) was strictly reserved for the royals.

In our home, there were clear differences in the type and quality of food offered in each world. The standard fare on every table included steamed rice, soup, and three kinds of kimchi. At the minimum, a stew and a preserved dish would be part of the standard table. Our grandmother, father, and the boys would have a fish or beef stew and special preserved dishes, while the girls would have something simple such as fish head stew and a preserved dish. For our grandmother and the males there would also be a pancake dish, some seaweed, and a braised dish or a grilled dish. In season, our grandmother always had her favorite, spiced dandelions, and our father had eggplant kimchi, plus there would always be an extra-special dish or two. The manservant and maids ate rice, soup, and kimchi. Our manservant had a very special menu, his favorite: a mound of whole garlic and fresh hot peppers, plus a bowl of hot red pepper paste as a dip.

Even the ambiance was different. For us girls, mealtime was like an hour of silent prayer, except for the habitual clang of dishes and chopsticks and spoons touching china. The womenfolk, dead serious, kept their faces buried in their rice bowls. The kitchen folk scurried around like shadows. Only the swishing sounds of their skirts could be heard. Out of our father's quarters, convivial conversation flowed freely. But one thing was similar among the worlds—the smacking sounds and slurps when the soup was hot and spicy. Here we kids were allowed to join in because it was not impolite, but rather a sign that one appreciated the tasty food.

Earthenware sauce crocks, Kyŏngbok Palace, Seoul

Our ancestors were and still remain an important part of our family life. Each year, on their ceremonial day (*chaesa*), we honor those in our family that have departed in the last four generations. We also hold Confucian ceremonies (*chʻasa*) for the four great Korean national holidays. Our family, even today, has nearly a ceremony a month. These solemn ceremonies, held at midnight, are much to do about food. The best-quality food obtainable and prepared according to strict rules is central to the ceremonies. The ceremonial altar is a grand assembly of the most authentic traditional Korean cuisine. Every cooking step must be executed in a highly formal and disciplined way, according to set rules. For example, boiled beef must be in perfect squares; braised chicken must be butterflied; every slice must be symmetrical. Fruit are stacked whole, with the minimum touch of a knife. The placement of red fruit on the east side and white and pale fruit on the west and fish on the east and meats on the west has to be strictly observed. Preparing food for each ceremony literally takes days. (Each family has passed down and modified its own family ceremonial rules. Recently, for example, I hear our family is performing the ceremonies at suppertime, a revolutionary innovation for us.) In my childhood it seemed as if most ceremonies were held in the dead of winter, when we had to open all the doors to let the spirits in. To me, the ceremonies meant good food, but as I grew older they meant hard labor rather than food. Through these rigorous family drills and moral lessons, I unwittingly caught a glimpse of traditional Korean food, allowing me to write about it. It is the most reverent way that I have to remember and pay homage to our ancestors.

Today most Korean families are downsized to four or five members and they have their meal together. Even at our mother's still hierarchical household in Seoul, all of us, including the women, eat at one round table, exchanging convivial conversation. We even watch television together. There is still the obligatory steamed rice, soup, and three kimchi, of course, plus several other dishes, sometimes including a Western-style steak, hamburger, or pizza. While the variety of food has changed considerably, the family cooking tradition remains strong because family Confucian rituals continue.

✳ Ingredients, Equipment, and Techniques

When asked about the taste of their food, Koreans eagerly recite the phrase *Hanguk ŭmsikŭn saek'om, dalk'om, maek'om hago ŏlk'ŭn, tchabtchal, ssŭbssŭl, kkosohan masida:* Korean food is pleasingly sour, sweet, hot, burning hot, salty, bitter, and nutty. It is a happy marriage of intriguing tastes, often in subtle harmony, sometimes in surprising contrasts. Sourness *(saek'om)* derives mainly from grain vinegar, herbs, and certain fruit. From honey, grain syrup (before sugar was widely used in Korea), and fruit like pears and jujube comes its sweetness *(dalk'om)*. Sweet and spicy hotness *(maek'om)* gives the food its aggressive exuberance, originating from Korean hot peppers. "Deliciously burning hot" *(ŏlk'ŭnham)* is the ultimate expression of delight for Korean hot pepper aficionados, signifying a spiciness so explosive it can make the diner break into a sweat. Soy sauce or other salty seasoning gives just the right touch of salt *(tchabtchalham)*. The agreeable bitterness *(ssŭbssŭlham)* comes from ginger, ginseng, berries, seeds, and certain vegetables and herbs. Finally, nuttiness *(kkosoham)* comes from a variety of indigenous nuts and seeds, including pine nuts, chestnuts, walnuts, gingko nuts, sunflower seeds, pumpkin seeds, and sesame seeds.

The three quintessential ingredients in Korean cooking are garlic, green onions, and hot peppers. For centuries these ingredients have been a vital part of the Korean kitchen. Most recipes are lost without them. To Koreans, they are no less important than the very air they breathe. They play many roles: as basic flavorings, side dishes, garnish, and folk medicines.

(above) A variety of Korean beans

Acidulated Water

To make acidulated water for blanching vegetables, add 1 tablespoon distilled white vinegar and a pinch of salt to 4 cups of water and bring to a boil. Blanching time varies according to the ingredient. Start counting from the time the water comes back to a boil. To stop the cooking, plunge the vegetables into ice cold water, then drain.

Acorn Curd (Tot'ori Muk)

This chocolate-colored curd, one of several grain-starch curds or jellies, has a rather wobbly texture and pleasant nutty flavor. It can be found in Korean markets packaged in plastic bags. Stored in water, it will stay fresh in the refrigerator for about 1 week.

Anchovies (Myŏlch'i)

Dried anchovies and salted anchovies are used throughout this book. Dried anchovies come in 1- or 2-pound containers in Korean markets. Salted anchovies (myŏlch'i chŏt) are sold in jars and often labeled "anchovy paste or sauce." However, most Korean brands are not pastes but salted, tiny, whole anchovies. The Korean variety is less salty and pungent than many of its Asian counterparts. Store both dried and salted anchovies in the refrigerator. They will stay fresh for 1 year at least.

Aralia Roots (Tŏdŏk)

Bittersweet wild aralia roots are one of Korea's most exotic herbal roots. Dark brown and with a rough skin, they are crunchy and fibrous, and their milky white pulp has an explosive aroma and incredible flavor. Both fresh and dried aralia roots can be found at Korean and Asian markets; fresh ones are better but are less available.

Bamboo Baskets and Steamers

Very handy around the kitchen, bamboo baskets can be used for draining vegetables and straining noodles. Although they are not as aesthetically pleasing, metal steamers do a good job and they are easy to clean.

Bamboo Shoots (Chuksun)

Fresh and canned bamboo shoots are available in Asian markets. Before using fresh bamboo shoots, trim them as you would artichokes. Simmer for about 15 minutes and then immerse in cold water. They will stay fresh for 1 week in the refrigerator.

Barley Malt (Yŏtkirum)

Barley malt, a grain syrup made from toasted barley sprouts, is a sweetening agent in Korean cooking. It is available in Korean markets and natural food stores.

Bean Curd (Tubu)

Nutritious bean curd (also known as tofu) is widely available in supermarkets and Asian markets. It comes in different levels of firmness: silky, soft, medium-firm, firm, and extra-firm. Fresh bean curd can also be bought loose, stored in buckets full of water. Bean curd must be absolutely fresh. Before buying, I always sniff the water, which should have a pleasant bean scent. Store bean curd in a tightly sealed container filled with cold water in the coldest spot in the refrigerator. A daily change of water keeps it fresh for about 2 weeks. Chilled bean curd is easier to slice. Deep-fried bean curd is also available at Korean markets.

Beans, Dried (K'ong)
Dried beans are a Korean staple. I always keep a variety of beans on hand, including yellow soybeans, black beans, mung beans, and red beans. In autumn, Koreans love to eat fresh baby soybeans (haet k'ong).

Bellflower Roots (Toraji)
A widely used herbal root in Korean cooking, it is milky white, 4 to 5 inches long, and faintly sweet and crunchy, with a somewhat celery-like flavor. Both fresh and dried roots are found year-round in Korean markets (prepackaged shredded roots are also available).

Braiser Pan
A braiser pan with two handles, sloping sides, and a domed lid is excellent for fish stews, hot pot cooking, and sautéing.

Burdock (Uŏng)
These flavorful roots resemble thin, long carrot sticks, but in a dark brown color. They can be found in Asian and Korean markets. Select firm stalks and use soon after buying. Peel them before using.

Cast-Iron Skillet (12-inch)
This workhorse does wonders, although it takes stamina to lift. Season it well before using.

Chives, Korean (Puch'u)
Chives are the most perishable among the green onion family. It is best to purchase them on the day of use. Wrap them in a paper towel and store in the refrigerator.

Chŏch'ŏng (Grain Syrup)
Also called mul yŏt in Korean markets, this bottled grain syrup is a traditional sweetener in Korean cooking. Corn syrup is a good substitute.

Ch'ŏngju (Rice Wine)
Similar to Japanese sake, this semisweet rice wine is very suitable for cooking. I like to recommend dry white vermouth as a substitute.

Coral Mushrooms (Ssari Pŏsŏt)
These rich, delightfully chewy mushrooms are often compared to beef. They are available in autumn in specialty markets.

Clay Pots
Both functional and attractive, a number of clay pots are good to have in the kitchen. As a porous clay pot breathes, it helps keep kimchi crisp and pleasantly sweet and sour. Clay pots are deemed to be the most suitable for storing Korean sauces (glass jars are the next best choice).

Crown Daisies (Ssukgat)

Crown daises resemble chrysanthemum leaves. They make refreshing salads and are used as a garnish. Buy a bunch at a time and use within a few days. They can be found in Asian markets.

Cutting Boards

I recommend having two wooden cutting boards, one for meat and fish and the other for vegetables, and one plastic cutting board for slicing kimchi.

Cutting Meats and Vegetables

Korean meats and vegetables are thoughtfully sliced into various shapes and sizes. Different cuts bring out subtle differences in texture, flavor, and even color. Most of all, cutting is done with presentation and the convenience of guests in mind. There are traditional rules, depending on the recipe. Among them are: diagonal cuts (for green onions and hot peppers), domino shapes (for radishes, summer squash, potatoes, and bean curd), ribbon cuts and diamonds (for egg garnish), strip cuts (for meats and vegetables in stews), matchsticks or julienne (for salads), and slivers, threads, and strings (for salads and garnishes). Meats and fish are usually cut across the grain; however, in some recipes they are cut along the grain into thin strings to prevent them from breaking up into bits and pieces. Chapchae, beef tartare, and raw seafood are good examples.

Day Lilies (Wŏnch'uri)

Dried day lilies (also called golden needles in Chinese) are regarded as both a medicinal herb and a cooking ingredient for their delicate flavor. The tender, high (about 2-inch) sprouts are picked in the springtime. Available in Asian markets, they should be soaked before using.

Dumpling Skins (Mandu P'i)

Fresh and frozen dumpling skins are sold in Asian markets and supermarkets. They are labeled "wonton wrappers," "wonton skins," or "Shanghai-style wraps" and are usually made with wheat flour, egg, and water. Some Korean brands add sweet rice flour for its chewy texture. They come in various thicknesses, about 100 sheets to a pack. They can also be made fresh.

Fatsia Shoots (Turŭp)

These wild, seasonal delicacies are a highly prized ingredient in Korean cooking. Not commonly found in the U.S., they may be available in some Korean markets.

Fermented Soybean Paste, Korean. *See* Toenjang.

Fernbracken (Kosari)

Fernbracken is a favorite mountain vegetable, similar to fiddlehead ferns, with a long stem (up to 7 inches) and a tip divided into three smaller stems with unfurled fronds. It is available in Asian markets and must be boiled and rinsed before cooking, to remove bitterness.

Garlic (Manŭl)

Choose healthy whole garlic with white skins, firm to the touch and with as few cloves as possible. Buy a pound or two and store in a cool and dry place, never in the refrigerator. However, leftover peeled and chopped garlic may be kept in a doubly tight container, to ensure freshness and to seal in its strong smell. Store in the refrigerator for a few days. When a recipe calls for garlic juice, grate the cloves and squeeze through a garlic press. About 5 fresh cloves make 1 tablespoon juice.

Ginger (Saenggang)

Most ginger roots have many knobs, so try to find fresh-looking roots with smooth skin. As the roots easily dry out and lose their strength, buy only a few at a time. Do not store in the refrigerator. Ginger powder is a poor substitute. When a recipe calls for ginger juice, grate the peeled ginger and squeeze through a garlic press. Always use freshly squeezed ginger juice. Two ounces of fresh ginger makes 1 tablespoon juice. An equal amount of grated ginger may be used in place of the juice.

Gingko Nuts (Ŭnhaeng)

Gingko nuts have semihard white shells. When cracked and toasted in oil, their yellow meat turns forest-green and are as chewy as minced meat. It is best to buy unshelled gingko nuts; however, they are also sold shelled, in cans. *See also* Toasting Seeds and Nuts.

Ginseng (Insam)

When I was little, I got to see and taste it because our granduncle was one of the prosperous ginseng planters. At that time, ginseng was very rare and its use was limited to tonics and medicine. Today it is more affordable and also widely used in cooking: in soups, side dishes, and desserts. Korean ginseng is reputed to be of superior quality. A variety of ginseng is available in Asian markets and natural food stores.

Gourds (Pak)

Gourds resemble pumpkins, but they are pale green. Mysteriously, their white flowers bloom only at night, like the pear tree. Their stunning white pulp is made into soups, side dishes, and candied sweets.

Green Onions (P'a)

Three kinds of green onions are displayed at Korean markets: large sweet green onions (tae p'a or kol p'a), thread green onions (sil p'a), and regular green onions (tchok p'a), also called scallions and spring onions. (Thread green onions are found only in Korean markets and only in season.) Select the tenderest ones you can find. As soon as you buy green onions, wash them under cold running water, paying attention to the root ends. Trim the wilted and browned leaves, cutting off the roots and discarding them. Cook the white and pale green part and use the less tender tops for soup or stock. To store for later use, deliberately leave on some of the root ends so the leaves will stay fresh. Lay the green onions on a clean kitchen towel to dry. Before they wilt,

place in one layer on a paper towel and loosely roll them up. Place in large plastic bags and store in the refrigerator. They can stay fresh for a few weeks.

Hot Peppers, Red and Green Korean (Koch'u)

The best-quality hot peppers are about 3 inches long, with straight and smooth lustrous skin, tapered ends, and clear yellow-green stems. They resemble Anaheim or New Mexico Reds in their color and shape and are packed with sweetness and explosive heat. As hot peppers do not keep fresh for long, buy them only as needed. After buying, wash the peppers in cold running water, pat dry with a clean kitchen towel, and lay in one layer on a paper towel; roll up and seal in a plastic bag in the refrigerator.

Hot Red Pepper Paste, Korean. *See* Koch'ujang.

Hot Red Pepper Powder, Korean. *See* Koch'u Karu.

Hot Red Pepper Threads, Korean. *See* Sil Koch'u.

Innards, Beef and Pork

Innards include heart, liver, lung, tripe, tendons, kidneys, tongue, and intestines. They are important in Korean cooking and can be found neatly prepared at Korean meat counters and in frozen food sections.

Insam. *See* Ginseng.

Jujube (Taech'u)

Also called dried red dates, semisweet jujube can be found packed in small, plastic bags in the dry food section of Asian markets. Store them in a cool, dry place. Be sure to pit jujubes before using: hold between the thumb and finger and rotate while cutting away the fruit with a paring knife.

Kelp (Miyŏk)

Both dried and fresh kelp are sold at Korean markets. To rehydrate dried kelp, soak 3 ounces of kelp in 5 quarts of warm water for 5 minutes. It will swell into well-packed 6 cups and turn a dark green. Kelp can be reused several times. Kelp has a nutty mushroom flavor and fragrance.

Kim. *See* Laver.

Kimchi

There is nothing like homemade kimchi, but you can find an array of good kimchi on refrigerator shelves in Korean markets. Some packaged kimchi may contain MSG, so check the ingredients label before purchasing.

Knives

A 7-inch chef's knife, 6-inch utility knife, paring knife, and cleaver are essential equipment. Although I have a prized set of knives from cooking school, my crude Korean carbon-steel knives work best for me. Of course, they must be cleaned and sharpened often.

Koch'u. *See* **Hot Peppers, Red and Green Korean.**

Koch'u Karu (Korean Hot Red Pepper Powder)

The Korean variety is one of the hottest, sweetest, and most flavorful pepper powders found anywhere. The good powder should be a brilliant, flaming red, pungent, and sweet smelling. Usually, three grades of the pepper powder are sold in the market: fine ground for cooking and making koch'ujang, coarse ground for making kimchi, and crushed flakes (like the Western kind) for cooking and garnish. Store in a tightly covered jar or plastic bag in the refrigerator. It stays fresh for several months. Once it loses pungency and the luster fades, it is useless.

Koch'ujang (Korean Hot Red Pepper Paste)

Pure Korean koch'ujang does not have artificial coloring, cornstarch, vinegar, or other additives. Do not confuse this paste with similarly named sauces or pastes from other countries. There is no substitute. Most Korean brands are excellent, but some contain MSG so check the ingredients label before purchasing. Wrap the jar tightly with plastic wrap and store in the refrigerator. It will stay fresh indefinitely.

Kudzu (Ch'ik)

Invasive kudzu vines and roots have many uses in the Korean kitchen. The strong vines are used in basket and rope making, like bamboo. Koreans make noodles with its starch. It is a very popular drink in summer.

Laver (Kim)

Laver (also known as nori, or dried seaweed) is sweet and nutty in flavor. Rich in calcium, minerals, amino acid, and iodine, it is made by pressing seaweed flakes into paper-thin sheets. It is available in Asian markets.

Lotus Roots (Yŏnkŭn)

In Asian markets, lotus roots are sold either whole, about the size of long yams, or peeled and sliced. Cook them as soon as possible. To store, place in a screw-top jar of water in the refrigerator. They will stay fresh for a few days.

Meju (Korean Fermented Soybean Paste Block)

The basic ingredient for making the three essential Korean sauces and pastes: koch'ujang, toenjang, and kanjang. Store-bought meju comes in various shapes and sizes; some are sold in convenient pea-size pellets or in powder form in Korean markets. Although it is best to use meju as soon as possible, it will stay fresh in the refrigerator for a few months.

Minari. *See* Watercress, Korean.

Mortar and Pestle

These ancient tools are as handy today as in the past. Keep them nearby for crushing small amounts of black pepper, garlic, and other spices. When Korean children look at a full moon, they see the image of two rabbits pounding rice cake in a mortar and pestle.

Mugwort (Ssuk)

Mugwort resembles tiny chrysanthemum leaves and is used extensively in Korean cooking: in rice cakes, a variety of invigorating soups, and many others. To the Korean mind, the August moon festival (Chusŏk) and pine needle–scented and celadon-green mugwort rice cakes (ssuk song p'yŏn) are inseparable.

Multi-Cooker, Four-Piece

A versatile multi-cooker (at least an 8-quart heavy stockpot with colander and steamer insert) is a good investment. It can be used for stewing, boiling, steaming, smothering, braising, and even sautéing.

Mung Bean Curd (Nokdu Muk)

Looking somewhat like bean curd, it is sold in Korean markets packaged in plastic bags. Immersed in water and stored in the refrigerator, mung bean curd will stay fresh for about 1 week.

Mung Bean Sprouts (Nokdu Namul)

These are usually found alongside soybean sprouts in Korean markets. Mung bean sprouts are smaller and more common. They must be absolutely fresh. Check carefully and discard any with brown spots.

Mustard, Hot Yellow (Kyŏja)

For its intensity and flavor, Colman's mustard powder is what I use. Mix the powder with enough water to make a smooth paste.

Napa Cabbage (Paech'u)

This is one of the most important vegetables in the Korean pantry. Choose healthy, firm, and heavy heads. Napa cabbage has a relatively long shelf life. After purchasing, peel off several outer leaves (use them in soups) and trim and discard the roots. Wash in a pan with a few changes of water. For later use, wash the tightly closed inner cabbage in cold running water. Pat dry with a kitchen towel. Split oversized cabbages in half lengthwise. Wrap in paper towels and store in sealed gallon-size plastic bags in the refrigerator. It will stay fresh for a couple of weeks.

Nonreactive Utensils

In the Korean kitchen, nonreactive utensils are a must. Herbs, hot peppers, red beans, and kimchi tend to react with utensils. Stainless steel is fine, but clay pots are best. Always use rubber or plastic gloves when handling hot red peppers.

Noodles, Korean (Kuksu)

There are many varieties of fresh and dried noodles in Korean and Asian markets. I buy fresh Korean noodles (kal kuksu) from the frozen food section, and I keep several kinds of dried noodles on my shelf: regular wheat noodles, sweet potato starch noodles, mung bean noodles (cellophane or bean thread noodles), and buckwheat noodles.

Nuts

Nuts are widely used in Korean cooking. I always keep a pound or so of walnuts and pine nuts in the refrigerator. Other nuts, such as chestnuts and gingko nuts, I buy as needed. Store in a tight container in the refrigerator. Nuts, like oil, must be as fresh as possible. *See also* Toasting Seeds and Nuts.

Oil, Cooking

The recipes in this book call for vegetable oil. Corn, canola, and sunflower oil seem best suited for Korean cooking. You can also use a mixture of soybean oil and olive oil for cooking and keep sesame oil as a flavoring.

Oyster Mushrooms (Nŭt'ari Pŏsŏt)

Most oyster mushrooms found in today's markets are cultivated on mushroom farms. The natural ones grow on old tree stumps in deep shade and are picked from spring until frost appears in the fall. Select the freshest possible, avoiding any wilted or discolored ones, and use as soon as possible. They will stay fresh for only a few days. Store in a tightly sealed container in the refrigerator.

Par-Cooking

Adding hot water to stiff flour dough, such as sweet rice flour and buckwheat flour, makes it more pliable and easier to make into noodles and dumpling wrappers.

Pear, Korean (Naju Pae)

Also known as Asian pear or apple-pear, this delicious fruit is available in Korean and Asian markets and some supermarkets.

Pepper, Mild Green (Kkoari Koch'u)

These tiny, wrinkled green peppers are about $1^1/2$ inches long. If you can't find them at Korean markets, substitute the mildest green peppers you can find and slice them into short pieces.

Persimmons (Kam, Kkotkam, and Hongsi)

All variety of persimmon are sold in the markets. In Korea, hard ones are called kam; sundried like raisins, they are kkotkam; and when mature and soft and sweet as custard, they are called hongsi.

Pickles, Korean (Changatchi)

Store-bought pickles are fine, but usually they are cured in heavy salt in the traditional way. Soak in cold water to reduce saltiness and then liven up their flavor by adding minced green onions, sesame oil, toasted sesame seeds, and a pinch of hot red pepper flakes. They are tasty appetizers and side dishes. Keep refrigerated.

Piji (Bean Curd Dregs)

Piji is the residue after the soybean juice is extracted from boiled and ground soybeans when making bean curd. It resembles Middle Eastern hummous and can be purchased at Korean markets.

Pine Needles (Sol Ip)

These are the same pine needles found on a Christmas tree. Pluck the live needles, wash, pat dry, and store in the refrigerator. They will stay fresh indefinitely.

Pine Nuts

Pine nuts are found in most markets. They should be crispy and have a sandy white color. Dark, oily ones are no longer fresh. The brown tips can be easily removed with your fingers and a little patience. *See also* Toasting Seeds and Nuts.

Pine Pollen (Songwha)

Rare pine flower pollen is an important ingredient for making marzipan-like cookies called sonwha tasik.

Pomegranates (Sŏkryu)

A favorite subject in Oriental poems and paintings, pomegranates resemble persimmon, but with leathery skin and a tiny crown. They crack open by themselves when ripe, revealing tiny clusters of bright red seeds. Its sweet and sour kernels are used in fruit soup and flavorful drinks. They are sold at supermarkets.

P'yogo Mushrooms (P'yogo Pŏsŏt)

P'yogo mushrooms are one of the most popular, affordable, and flavorful among all mushrooms in Korea. These brown forest mushrooms also grow in China and Japan and have become known as shiitake. Both fresh and dried p'yogo are sold in Asian and Korean markets. To rehydrate the dried ones before cooking, simply rinse them once in cold water and soak in warm water for 30 minutes, or until soft. Use 1 cup of water for every 2 ounces of dried p'yogo and reserve it to add to soup stock or stews. Because they grow naturally in oak stumps, they are also called oak mushrooms (ch'amnamu pŏsŏt).

Radishes, Korean (Mu)

Korean radishes are grown in various shapes and sizes. Chubby ones, about the size of rugby balls, with pale green tops, are used primarily in cooking and in making kimchi. Korean radishes are crispy, sweet, and tangy. Select smooth and unblemished ones. After purchasing, immediately scrub-wash them with a vegetable brush and pat dry. To use them later, wrap them in a paper towel with the skin still on, seal in a plastic bag, and store in the refrigerator. They will stay fresh for 1 month. In some cases, daikon may be substituted.

Radish Greens (Mu Ch'ŏng)

The leafy parts of young radishes are considered to be more nutritious than full-grown radishes (mu). Radish greens are sold by the bunch, usually next to green onions, in Korean markets.

Red Bean Paste (P'at Komul)

Red beans, also known as azuki or adzuki beans, are first boiled and mashed into a paste and then dried over very low heat until it becomes a moist, powdery paste. It can be found in Asian markets.

Rice (Ssal)

Many brands of rice are sold in the Korean market, with the short-grain variety the most favored. Short-grain rice produced in America and imported from Korea are available in Korean markets, sold in

2- to 50-pound bags. Although the labels usually indicate that no washing is needed, I wash the rice at least once. Stored in a cool, dry place, the rice should be used within a few months.

Rice, Brown (Hyŏnmi)
This unpolished short-grain rice was once neglected by Koreans because of its rough and sandy texture. Recently it has become a much-respected health food.

Rice, Sweet (Ch'apssal)
Sweet rice is used mainly in making desserts. When cooked, its original chalky color turns clear, almost translucent, and the texture becomes chewy and sticky. Hence, it is also called "glutinous rice" and "sticky rice." Because of its stickiness, sweet rice is always steamed, not boiled. Sweet rice is more expensive than short-grain rice. It is available in Korean and Asian markets in 1- to 5-pound plastic bags.

Rice Cake Sticks (Ttŏk Karae)
This traditional Korean food, made from short-grain rice, comes frozen in 5-pound bags, usually already sliced. Keep in the refrigerator.

Rice Flour (Ssalgaru)
Regular short-grain rice flour is available in Korean markets. Store in a tightly sealed container in the refrigerator. I usually keep about 1 pound of both regular and sweet rice flour on hand. Like regular wheat flour, it should be used within a year.

Rice Flour, Sweet (Ch'apssal Karu)
This is used for sauces and desserts. Store in a tightly sealed container in the refrigerator. I usually keep about 1 pound of both regular and sweet rice flour on hand. Like regular wheat flour, it should be used within a year.

Rice Wine. *See* Ch'ŏngju.

Rocamboles, Wild (Tallae)
Wild rocamboles belong to the onion family and resemble tiny, thin green onions. They are sold in the Korean market in season.

Salt (Sogŭm)
Two kinds of sea salt are used in the Korean kitchen: coarse salt (kulgun sogŭm) and refined salt (kkot sogŭm), or "flowery salt." Purified coarse salt, without its bitterness, is ideal for making kimchi and Korean sauces. It is also used in salting seafood and vegetables. Refined salt is low-sodium Korean table salt that is highly soluble in water. It is identical to kosher salt. (Koreans also use iodized table salt.) Both salts are available in Korean markets.

Salted Shrimp (Saeu Chŏt)
Tiny salted shrimp (salted krills) are one of the vital ingredients in making kimchi. The best are considered to be sweet and pink shrimp caught in June, called yuk chŏt. Salted shrimp should not be confused with the more salty and pungent Southeast Asian shrimp paste. Korean

markets carry salted shrimp in 1- and 2-quart glass jars in the refrigerated section. Juice can be extracted from salted shrimp that has been finely chopped and pushed through a strainer.

Salting

Salting is a common preliminary step in Korean cooking. An excellent method for preserving food, it extracts water, locks in flavor, and firms up texture. Good candidates for salting are vegetables with high water content, such as napa cabbage, cucumbers, and summer squash. Fish are also prepared with a light salting to draw out excess water, firm the flesh, and enhance flavor.

Seaweed

Korean cooking utilizes many different forms of this edible plant from the sea. Clusters of seaweed leaves can be sold fresh as green seaweed (chŏnggak) or dried in plastic bags as dried seaweed threads (sil myok). Both are available in Korean markets and some Asian markets. *See also* Kelp *and* Laver.

Sesame Seeds (Kkae)

I keep three kinds of sesame seeds in my pantry: sandy-white (ch'amkkae), black (kŏmunkkae) and wild, or brown (tŭlkkae). Toasted straw-white sesame seeds are for everyday use. Both fresh and toasted are available at the market. For maximum strength and freshness, I buy only 1 pound at a time and toast my own. Korean brands are superior, but not easy to find. Black and wild sesame seeds are only sold fresh at Korean markets. Store sesame seeds in airtight containers in the refrigerator. They will stay fresh for several months. Use a mini grinder or blender to make ground sesame seed paste (tul kkaejup). Tahini may be substituted as a last resort. *See also* Toasting Seeds and Nuts.

Sesame Oil (Ch'amgirŭm)

There are many excellent brands of sesame oil in Korean and Asian markets. I buy 100 percent pure Korean sesame oil, not a blended kind, and only a 1-liter bottle at time. It should be as fresh as possible. After opening, store the bottle in the refrigerator.

Shepherd's Purse (Naengi)

Shepherd's purse, a plant related to mustard, is one of the popular field greens and herbal remedy ingredient in Korea. With a sweet and earthy aroma, it can be found in Korean and Asian markets.

Sil Koch'u (Korean Hot Red Pepper Threads)

A traditional component of the five-color garnish, these burgundy-red threads resemble saffron and smell sweet like raisins. They add a colorful elegance and zest to any dish. Dried hot red peppers are cut by machine into hair-thin threads and sold in 1-ounce packages. Double-wrap and store in the refrigerator. It will stay fresh for several months.

Soaking in Cold Water

This method is used for preparing meats, innards, and bones for making stock and soups. Soaking in cold water draws off blood and

Growing Up in a Korean Kitchen

washes away strong flavors. The water must be ice cold. Heavily salted vegetables are also soaked in cold water to wash away their saltiness.

Soaking in Warm Water
This is a way to reconstitute dried ingredients. Dried grains, beans, herbs, meats, shellfish, and many others are rehydrated in warm water to soften their texture before further cooking. Soaking time varies, depending on the ingredient. To retain nutrition and flavor, do not use hot water.

Steaming
After blanching, steaming is the next preferred choice, but it takes longer. Steaming brings the best result when cooking soft, pulpy vegetables, such as eggplants. It is an ideal method to retain an ingredient's attractive appearance.

Soy Sauce (Kanjang)
There are many excellent Korean and Japanese brands of soy sauce sold in Korean and Asian markets. There is no need to store soy sauce in the refrigerator. It stays fresh indefinitely. Both light and dark soy sauce can be used in Korean cooking.

Soybean Powder (K'ong Karu)
In the market, near the rice flour section, this yellow powder is sold in 1-pound plastic bags.

Soybean Sprouts (K'ong Namul)
These are usually found alongside mung bean sprouts in Korean markets. Sprouts must be absolutely fresh. Check carefully and discard any with brown spots. Store soybean sprouts loosely in a tightly sealed container and use within a day or two.

Stone-Ear Mushrooms (Sŏgi Pŏsŏt)
Jet-black with a mossy look, these rare mushrooms, which grow precariously between the crevices of Korean cliffs, are used primarily as a garnish. Since they are currently unavailable in the U.S., any dark-colored mushrooms may be substituted.

Summer Squash
The Korean variety is usually round. It is seedless and sweet and can even be eaten raw. Some have a chubby eggplant shape and some resemble zucchini in size, color, and flavor.

Toasting Seeds and Nuts
To toast sesame seeds, wash and drain the seeds. Heat a skillet over medium-high heat until hot. (Cooking oil is not necessary, since the sesame seeds shed their own oil during toasting.) Add seeds and stir with a wooden spoon until dry. Decrease the heat to medium and toast, stirring constantly, for about 20 minutes, until they turn golden, plump, and fragrant, with a crackling sound. Be careful not to burn. Toast no more than 2 cups at a time for their freshness. Cool and store in a tight container in the refrigerator.

Pine nuts, gingko nuts, and almond slivers are toasted in the same way but with different cooking times. It takes 7 minutes for 2 cups of pine nuts and less than 5 minutes for slivered almonds. To toast 1 cup of cracked gingko nuts, first soften in 1 cup water with 1 tablespoon of salt. Toast over medium heat with 1 tablespoon vegetable oil for about 20 minutes, or until fragrant. Transfer to a brown paper bag and rub between the palms to peal the skin. They will be shiny and bright green. Walnuts should be blanched, then carefully peeled with a toothpick.

Toenjang (Korean Fermented Soybean Paste)

There are many excellent brands in Korean markets. Some markets also sell traditional toenjang made from naturally fermented soybean powder (meju), which I prefer. As toenjang is salty, you may omit salt from the list of ingredients. Japanese miso is not a substitute for toenjang. Wrap the container tightly with plastic wrap and store in the refrigerator. It stays fresh indefinitely.

Toraji. *See* Bellflower Roots.

Tree Ear Mushrooms (Mogi Pŏsŏt)

Tree ear mushrooms, also known as cloud ear mushrooms, can be found in Korean and Asian markets. They are dried and packed in plastic bags and look like dark confetti with a lighter-colored lining. They have a crunchy texture similar to button mushrooms when reconstituted. *See also* Soaking in Warm Water.

Tripe, Beef (Yang)

Tripe is beef stomach that consists of four chambers. The lining of each chamber has a different look and texture; they are called Turkish towel, honey comb, bible or ten thousand leaves, and blanket. You can find them in the frozen food section of most Korean markets, all scrubbed and ready to cook, or ask your butcher. *See also* Innards, Beef.

Vinegar (Ch'o)

Korean cooking requires a lot of vinegar. I buy distilled white vinegar by the gallon because I use it in both cooking and pickling. In the pantry, I also keep some flavorful grain vinegar (rice vinegar) for cooking meat dishes and apple cider vinegar for making salad.

Watercress, Korean (Minari)

Korean watercress is water-cultured. Its pale-green leaves somewhat resemble Western watercress, but with a long, slender, and knotty stem similar to bamboo. Its assertive, refreshing herbal fragrance can be compared to that of celery or parsley. It is an important ingredient in kimchi-making and is one of the three-color garnishes. Sold in bunches, watercress is usually displayed alongside parsley and cilantro. It must be absolutely fresh. If it must be kept for a few days, loosely wrap the watercress (without washing) in a paper towel in a tightly sealed container in the refrigerator. There is no substitute for this ingredient in cooking, but Western watercress leaves may be substituted as a garnish.

Wheat Flour, All-Purpose (Mil Karu)

All-purpose wheat flour in the Western kitchen can be substituted whenever the Korean recipe calls for regular rice flour, sweet rice flour, or cornstarch.

Wild Sesame Plants (Tŭlkkae)

Wild sesame plants, also called perilla, is a Korean garden staple. The leaves, pods, and seeds are used. They are easy to grow. Every Korean market sells wild sesame seeds and sesame powder. Sesame leaves are sold year-round in packs of ten or a dozen.

Yŏngji Mushrooms (Pulnoch'o)

Called "the mushroom of eternal youth," this rare and expensive mushroom is revered almost as much as ginseng for its medicinal property.

Yuja (Asian Citrus)

Yuja are probably the rarest and most precious fruit among all Korean fruits. They look like tangerines but have an explosive fragrance. They also grow in China and Japan. They can be found in Korean and Asian markets.

✤ Essential Sauces and Pastes

There are three essential Korean sauces: soy sauce (kanjang), fermented soybean paste (toenjang), and hot red pepper paste (koch'ujang). They are primarily responsible for the character and unique flavor of Korean food. Traditionally, the sauces were made once a year and stored in a dozen or more large and small earthenware crocks placed on the backyard *changdokdae* (sauce-crock pad), a standard feature of every Korean home.

The basic ingredient in creating Korean sauces and pastes is a dry block of fermented soybean paste, called meju. Making meju was a major annual undertaking, as important as preparing kimchi. Today, meju may be purchased in stores, but Koreans still believe that meju made from traditional methods is the best.

Soy sauce (kanjang) is the first important sauce. Today, of course, excellent ones can be found everywhere. The family recipe in this chapter merely demonstrates how conventional Korean soy sauce was made. Soy sauce combined with rice wine, green onions, garlic, and sesame oil creates a base seasoning called mit'gan; almost all Korean meat or fish dishes begin with this simple, important seasoning. Many of the recipes in this book include variations on this basic preparation.

The two other important sauces are uniquely Korean creations. Fermented soybean paste (toenjang), a protein powerhouse, was traditionally created as a by-product of soy sauce. But today, both homemade and factory-made versions are fortified with pure meju, skipping the traditional soy sauce–making stage. Good-quality fermented soybean paste is available in Korean markets in America, although more contemporary Koreans insist on making their own.

Traditionally, hot red pepper paste (koch'ujang) was made around the first day of spring by the lunar calendar *(ipch'un)*, but today it is mostly factory made and available year-round. For those ambitious few who may wish to create their own pure koch'ujang, the classic recipe is presented here.

Homemade Soy Sauce and Fermented Soybean Paste

Kanjang and Toenjang

Makes 10 gallons
About 2 months to prepare

3/4 bushel coarse sea salt

10 gallons sterilized water

4 blocks meju

3 pieces oak wood charcoal, 3 to 4 inches long, plus several smaller pieces

1 gallon white choch'ung (grain syrup)

10 toasted jujubes

5 dried hot red peppers

Soy sauce before it is aged is called ch'ŏngjang (clear soy sauce) or Chosŏn kanjang (Korean soy sauce), a plain and somewhat salty light brown sauce used mostly in base seasonings and clear soups. To produce chin kanjang, a superior thin, syrupy, jet-black soy sauce (similar to the dark soy sauce found in today's market), our grandmother would submerge a large-mesh cloth pouch containing black beans, p'yogo mushrooms, and kelp strips to the ch'ŏngjang and simmer over low heat for an hour or so. The longer it aged, the mellower it became and the color and flavor intensified.

Here is the traditional way our family made soy sauce and fermented soybean paste, before the store-bought versions became a common product. This recipe makes a year's supply, enough for a Korean family of five.

❁ ❁ ❁

In a large vat, add the salt to the water. Stir to dissolve and let settle for 2 to 3 days. Strain through a fine-mesh sieve or a bamboo basket lined with a fine-mesh cloth. With a stiff brush, clean the meju, removing any materials that may have lodged on the crust during drying. Wash the block briefly under running water and let sun-dry.

With long fire pokers, place a few pieces of burning red-hot oak charcoals in a large, sterilized earthenware crock. Pour the choch'ung over the burning charcoal. As it sizzles and becomes fragrant, add meju and salt water. The oak charcoals do not dissolve, but later bob to the top. Add the jujubes, hot peppers, and a few pieces of charcoal to float on the top. Cover the crock with a mesh or gauze cloth and tightly tie a string around the neck. Today, we have a salt gauge, but in my childhood my mother used finger tasting and the bounce of an egg or a bean to test saltiness.

During the maturing period, let the crock stand in the open without a lid; cover when it rains. After about 60 days, the meju blocks will have crumbled into soft lumps of oatmeal-like paste floating on the liquid's surface. Transfer the paste to a bamboo strainer and strain the liquid back into its original crock. (At this stage, there are two sauces: one is fermented soybean paste, toenjang, the residue collected in the strainer, and the other is soy sauce, the liquid in the crock. Pack the soybean paste into another sterilized crock and sprinkle a thin layer of coarse salt on top.)

Pour the soy sauce liquid into a cauldron. Bring to a boil and let simmer over low heat until it is reduced to one-third of its original volume. Adjust saltiness by adding more salt or sterilized water. Both the fermented soybean paste and the soy sauce are ready to be aged.

Homemade Hot Red Pepper Paste

Koch'ujang

Makes 4 cups
1 hour to cook
and 1 to 3 months to mature

1¹/₂ cups fine barley malt powder

5 cups sterilized water

2 cups sweet rice flour

2 cups koch'u karu (hot red pepper powder)

1 cup fine meju powder

1 cup coarse sea salt or kosher salt

¹/₂ cup soy sauce

There are several varieties of koch'ujang made from regular or sweet rice, barley, millet, and so on. Each has its own subtle and distinctive flavor. Sunch'ang koch'ujang, from the town of Sunch'ang in Chollanamdo, is reputed to be Korea's best. During the Yi dynasty (1392–1910), the town supplied the royal palace kitchen in Seoul. It is said that their secret was in the locally grown koch'u karu, clean mountain spring water, sweet rice powder, and a superior quality soy sauce. Finally, the koch'ujang was aged for at least 6 months.

Most people conveniently buy koch'ujang from the market these days, but the classic homemade recipe is here for those seeking to create an authentic Korean kitchen.

In a bowl, combine the malt powder and water. Stir to dissolve. Let stand overnight in a warm place or keep warm in an electric rice cooker. Strain into a heavy stockpot, add the sweet rice flour, and dissolve well. Bring to a boil and simmer over low heat until its volume is reduced by one-third to one-half. Cool and set aside. In a large bowl, combine the koch'u karu, meju powder, rice and malt paste, ¹/₄ cup salt, and soy sauce. Mix thoroughly with a wooden spoon. (If too little salt is added, the koch'ujang will turn sour and mold may grow.) Let stand overnight.

Sprinkle half of the remaining salt on the bottom of a sterilized jar. Transfer the koch'ujang paste to the jar and sprinkle the remaining salt on top. Leave 2 inches or more of space at the top. Cover with a mesh or gauze cloth and tightly tie a string around the neck. Cover with a lid. Sun-dry every day and cover with an earthenware top at night. It may be used right away, but for best results allow the koch'ujang to mature for about 30 days. Store in a tight container in the refrigerator. It will stay fresh indefinitely.

Korean hot red pepper market

Growing Up in a Korean Kitchen

Cooked Hot Red Pepper Paste

Pokkun Koch'ujang

Makes 2 cups
1 hour to cook

1 tablespoon vegetable oil

4 ounces beef ground round

$^1/_4$ cup corn syrup, or
  3 tablespoons sugar

$^1/_4$ cup finely chopped walnuts,
  pine nuts, or toasted sesame
  seeds

2 cups koch'ujang (hot red pepper
  paste)

Cooked hot red pepper paste is a Korean favorite. The basic koch'u-jang flavor is enhanced by adding honey or syrup, pine nuts, and ground meat. During cooking, the color turns a richer, wine-red color. Adding cooked hot red pepper paste to a bowl of rice makes a perfect one-dish meal for people on the run.

In a heavy stockpot, heat the vegetable oil over medium-low heat until hot. Add the beef and sauté for about 2 minutes, or until the beef is cooked through, breaking the beef into fine crumbs with a wooden spoon. Pour out and discard any fat that may have accumulated in the pot. Decrease the heat to low and add the corn syrup. Add the walnuts and koch'ujang and cook over low heat for 1 hour, stirring constantly with a wooden spoon. Remove from the heat and let cool. Store in a jar with a tight-fitting lid. It will stay fresh in the refrigerator indefinitely.

Instant Fermented Soybean Paste

Makjang

Makes 5 cups
30 minutes to cook and
10 days to mature

2 cups steamed sweet rice
  (page 226)

5 cups meju powder

1 cup coarse sea salt or kosher salt,
  or $^1/_2$ cup salt and $^1/_2$ cup soy
  sauce

5 cups sterilized water

This sauce is fresher and nuttier than the basic fermented soybean paste (toenjang). Although called "instant," it actually takes about 10 days to mature. It is very easy to make.

In a bowl, combine the steamed rice and meju powder and mix well. Cover with a kitchen towel and let sit at room temperature overnight.

In a bowl, dissolve the salt and soy sauce in the water and strain through a sieve. Add it to the rice. Transfer to a ceramic jar with a tight-fitting lid. Let mature at room temperature for about 10 days. Stored in the refrigerator, it will stay fresh indefinitely.

Allspice Sauce

Kajin Yaknyŏmjang

Makes ¹/₂ cup
5 minutes to prepare

---

3 tablespoons soy sauce

1 tablespoon ch'ŏngju (rice wine)
or vermouth

1 tablespoon sugar, corn syrup,
or honey

1 green onion, white and pale green
part only, finely minced

2 cloves garlic, crushed and finely
chopped

1 tablespoon toasted sesame seeds

1 walnut half, finely chopped

1 tablespoon sesame oil

¹/₂ tablespoon koch'u karu (hot red
pepper powder)

¹/₂ teaspoon salt

1 teaspoon freshly ground black
pepper

Korean allspice sauce is similar to the base seasoning (mit'gan) found in recipes throughout this book, but with several additional spices. It is a basic for dressing vegetables and for marinating meat and fish. It is also one of the most popular dipping sauces.

In a small bowl, combine all the ingredients and mix well. Store leftovers in a tightly sealed container in the refrigerator. It will stay fresh for at least 1 week.

Vinegar Soy Sauce

Ch'o Kanjang

Makes ¹/₂ cup
5 minutes to prepare

---

2 tablespoons soy sauce

2 tablespoon ch'ŏngju (rice wine)
or vermouth

2 tablespoons rice vinegar or apple
cider vinegar

1 tablespoon sesame oil

2 tablespoons freshly squeezed
lemon juice

Pinch of salt

1 tablespoon coarsely chopped pine
nuts or toasted sesame seeds

Pinch of freshly ground black
pepper

This simple and refreshing sauce, along with Allspice Sauce (above), are the two basic Korean dipping sauces.

In a bowl, combine the soy sauce, ch'ŏngju, rice vinegar, sesame oil, lemon juice, and salt and mix well. Before serving, sprinkle the pine nuts and black pepper on top. Store leftovers in a tightly sealed container in the refrigerator. It will stay fresh for at least 1 week.

Roasted Hot Peppers in Soy Sauce

P'utgoch'u Yaknyŏmjang

Makes 1 cup
10 minutes to prepare

---

4 Korean hot green peppers or jalapeño peppers

4 Korean hot red peppers or other hot red peppers

3 tablespoons soy sauce

1 tablespoon ch'ŏngju (rice wine) or vermouth

1 green onion, white and pale green part only, finely minced

2 cloves garlic, crushed and finely chopped

1 tablespoon toasted sesame seeds

1 walnut half, finely chopped

1 tablespoon sesame oil

$1/2$ teaspoon salt

1 teaspoon freshly ground black pepper

This robust sauce is a customary and delightful companion to many Korean dishes. Its temperament may remind one of Mexican salsa or Thai siracha sauce.

Wash the hot peppers and pat dry. Roast the peppers under a broiler or on the stovetop until all sides are broiled and blistered, but not charred. Discard the stems and chop into $1/4$-inch rounds, seeds and all. In a small bowl, combine all ingredients and mix well. Store leftovers in a tightly sealed container in the refrigerator. It will stay fresh for at least 1 week.

Variation: For extra flavor, stir in 2 tablespoons cooked ground round. It makes an excellent spread for Vegetable Wrapped Rice (page 53).

Vinegar and Hot Red Pepper Sauce

Ch'o Koch'ujang

Makes $1/2$ cup
5 minutes to prepare

---

2 tablespoons Cooked Hot Red Pepper Paste (page 27)

1 tablespoon soy sauce

1 tablespoon ch'ŏngju (rice wine) or vermouth

2 tablespoons apple cider vinegar or distilled white vinegar

2 tablespoons freshly squeezed lemon juice

1 tablespoon sugar

1 tablespoon chopped pine nuts or toasted sesame seeds

Pinch of freshly ground black pepper

This is another delicate vinegar dipping sauce. Use it as an alternative whenever a recipe calls for Vinegar Soy Sauce (page 28).

In a bowl, combine the pepper paste, soy sauce, ch'ŏngju, vinegar, lemon juice, and sugar. Mix well with a pair of chopsticks or a spoon. Sprinkle the pine nuts and pepper on top just before serving. Store in a tightly sealed container in the refrigerator. It will stay fresh for 1 week.

Hot Red Pepper Sauce

Yaknyŏm Koch'ujang

Makes ³/₄ cup
5 minutes to prepare

- 2 tablespoons Cooked Hot Red Pepper Paste (page 27) or koch'ujang
- 1 tablespoon koch'u karu (hot red pepper powder)
- 1 tablespoon soy sauce
- 2 tablespoons ch'ŏngju (rice wine) or vermouth
- 2 tablespoons corn syrup
- 1 tablespoon sugar
- 1 green onion, white and pale green part only, finely minced
- 2 cloves garlic, crushed and chopped
- 1 tablespoon freshly squeezed lemon juice
- 1 tablespoon freshly squeezed ginger juice
- 1 tablespoon sesame seed oil
- 1 tablespoon toasted sesame seeds
- ¹/₂ teaspoon salt
- 1 teaspoon freshly ground black pepper

The true quality of a family's food depended on its meju, hence the Korean saying "One can judge a housewife's cooking skill by tasting her meju and sauces."

This riotously hot sauce is used most often as a marinade for barbecue meat, but it also goes well with seafood, even with delicate fish.

In a bowl, combine all the ingredients and mix well. Store leftovers in a tightly sealed container in the refrigerator. It will stay fresh for about 1 week.

Fresh Hot Red Pepper Sauce

P'utgoch'ujang

Makes 1¹/₂ cups
15 minutes to prepare

5 cloves garlic

10 hot red Korean peppers, coarsely chopped, or 1 cup hot red pepper flakes

3 tablespoons saeu chŏt (salted shrimp)

¹/₂ cup ch'ŏngju (rice wine) or vermouth

¹/₄ cup sesame oil

¹/₄ cup vegetable oil

This sauce is made with fresh peppers and garlic, not with fermented koch'ujang. It is an excellent topping for soups and noodles. It also makes a refreshing salad dressing. Probably the sweetest and hottest Korean pepper sauce, some may compare it to Tabasco sauce, Sichuan hot bean paste, or Thai papaya salad dressing.

In a mortar, add the garlic and mash well with a pestle. Add the peppers and pound into a paste. Transfer to a bowl and add the saeu chŏt, ch'ŏngju, sesame oil, and vegetable oil. With a wooden spoon, mix into a coarse paste. Store leftovers in a tightly sealed container in the refrigerator. It will stay fresh indefinitely.

T'ang Soybean Paste

T'anggukjang

Makes 2 cups
30 minutes to prepare and
3 hours to cook

2 cups freshly harvested dried soybeans or regular soybeans

¹/₄ cup hot red pepper flakes or other variety

¹/₄ cup sea salt or kosher salt

This is the best tasting soybean paste among all toenjang. The secret is yellow soybeans at their prime in autumn—newly harvested, toasted, and freshly fermented. That was the time when we children used to pick the green bean stalks that grew along the banks of the rice fields and bake them over a bonfire. We called these snacking expeditions *haet kongttŏri*, "fleecing of the fresh bean stalks."

Wash the soybeans in cold water and drain. In a skillet, add the soybeans and toast over medium-high heat for about 30 minutes (no oil is necessary). Let cool a bit. Place the soybeans in a paper bag and run over with a rolling pin, to remove the skins. Discard the skins.

In a stockpot, add the soybeans and 6 cups of cold water. Bring to a boil over high heat and immediately decrease the heat to medium. Gently boil for about 3 hours, or until the soybeans become tender. Transfer the soybeans to a bamboo basket lined with hemp cloth. Cover loosely with several layers of dry leaves and keep in a very warm place to ferment for about 5 days. In a mortar, combine the fermented beans, hot red pepper flakes, and salt. Coarsely mash together. Transfer the fermented beans to a ceramic jar with a tight-fitting lid. After mellowing for a few days, they are ready to be used. Store in a tightly closed container in the refrigerator. They will stay fresh for a few months and then slowly turn into regular toenjang.

Fermented Soybean Paste with Garlic and Bean Curd

Ssamjang

Makes 2 cups
10 minutes to prepare

8 ounces medium-soft bean curd, mashed

1 tablespoon vegetable oil

5 cloves garlic, crushed and finely chopped

1 green onion, white and pale green part only, finely minced

4 ounces beef ground round

1 cup Instant Fermented Soybean Paste (page 27) or mild toenjang (fermented soybean paste)

2 tablespoons Cooked Hot Red Pepper Paste (page 27) or koch'ujang (hot red pepper paste)

Probably the tastiest soybean paste made in the Korean kitchen. It is commonly used in the popular Korean summer fare, Vegetable Wrapped Rice (page 53).

Wrap the bean curd in a kitchen towel and squeeze out as much liquid as possible. Set aside. In a skillet, heat the vegetable oil over medium heat until hot, but not smoking. Add the garlic and sauté for 2 minutes, until fragrant. Add the green onion, beef, and mashed bean curd and sauté for 5 minutes, breaking the beef into fine crumbs. Let cool. Transfer to a bowl, add the fermented soybean paste and pepper paste, and mix well. Store leftovers in a tightly sealed container in the refrigerator. It will stay fresh for about 2 weeks.

Koch'ujang ingredients, clockwise from top: barley malt, barley flour, sweet rice porridge, koch'u karu, meju powder, and salt.

❋ Garnishing

Garnishing, *komyŏng*, is taken very seriously in the traditional Korean kitchen. There are rules for ingredients, color, size, and shape, and yet the food arrangements should appear natural, like gardens left unattended.

Vibrant, bright-colored ingredients are favored for garnishing, and they are crucial elements in creating the traditional Korean three-color garnish and five-color garnish. To make a three-color garnish, one must use yellow, white (egg yolks and egg whites), and green (Korean watercress). Red and black are added to complete the five-color garnish.

Red is traditionally created by adding sil koch'u (hot red pepper threads). Today, precut threads may be conveniently purchased at Korean markets. Homemade threads are easy to make, although the cuts may be irregular (except when sliced by the master hands of veteran Korean cooks, including our mother). Here is an easy technique: Select a few healthy dried hot red peppers. Wearing gloves, wipe the peppers clean with a damp paper towel. With a pair of scissors, split the peppers and remove the seeds and ribs. Flatten them and lay in one layer on a paper towel. Wrap with a damp towel and let sit for 1 hour. Stack the peppers on top of each other, then roll up like a cigar. With a sharp knife, slice into threads.

Jet-black stone-ear mushrooms are the fifth component of the five-color garnish. Since they are currently not available in the U.S., another dark-colored mushroom may be substituted (however, in Korea, for special ceremonies stone-ears are a must).

(above) Eggs in straw cartons

Today's busy Koreans no longer follow the strict rules for garnishing, except for ancestral ceremonies, weddings, and very formal dinners. For the final visual touch, they go creative by using almost any ingredient that strikes their fancy: gingko nuts, almonds, walnuts, pine nuts, chestnuts, fresh garlic or ginger slivers, toasted seaweed crumbles, toasted sesame seeds, green onion rings, parsley, lemon wedges, and edible flowers. All are used as stylish decorations at the top of many delicious dishes.

Yellow and White Egg Garnish

Kyeran Chitan

Makes 2 pancakes
5 minutes to prepare
and 7 minutes to cook

2 eggs, separated

Pinch of salt

Pinch of freshly ground white
  pepper

1 tablespoon vegetable oil

Cooked eggs make some of the most important Korean traditional garnishes, either as ribbons (kyeran chitan), threads (kyeran chitan ch'ae), diamonds, or flakes. It is a rigid custom to use them on ceremonial soups, noodles, braised dishes, and stews, for example.

Place the egg yolks and egg whites in separate bowls and beat. Season each with salt and pepper. Set aside. In a skillet, heat $^1/_2$ tablespoon vegetable oil over medium heat until hot. Pour the egg white into the skillet and quickly coat the bottom with a thin layer (similar to crepe batter). Decrease the heat to medium-low and cook for about 2 minutes, or until the egg sets firm, but is not dry. Flip over and cook for 1 minute. Do not overcook. Transfer to a tray to cool. Repeat with the remaining oil and egg yolks, making 2 pancakes, each 8 inches in diameter.

To make egg ribbons or diamonds, cut the pancakes into $^1/_2$-inch-wide strips, then cut each straight or diagonally to make ribbons or diamond shapes. To make egg threads, roll the pancake tightly like a cigar, then with a sharp knife slice crosswise into $^1/_8$-thick threads.

Variation: To make Egg Flakes, boil 1 egg for 12 minutes and separate the yolk from the egg white. With the back of a spoon, press each through a sieve onto the prepared dish.

Hard-boiled whole quail eggs also make an attractive garnish.

Grandmother used to say,
"Garnishing is like placing a
beautiful long-stemmed flower
on brocade."

Korean Watercress Ribbons

Minari Chitan

Makes 1 pancake
10 minutes to prepare
and 4 minutes to cook

---

1 bunch Korean watercress,
stems only, cut crosswise into
7-inch-long pieces

2 bamboo skewers, 7 inches long

1 tablespoon all-purpose wheat
flour

1 egg, lightly beaten

Pinch of salt

Pinch of freshly ground black
pepper

1 tablespoon vegetable oil

Korean watercress teams with yellow and white egg to make the traditional three-color garnish. For simple presentations, fresh watercress may also be cut into short pieces, sautéed, and used as a garnish.

Skewer each end of the watercress stems on 2 bamboo skewers, making a flat, rectangular sheet. On one plate, add the flour; on another plate, lightly stir together the egg, salt, and pepper. Lightly dredge both sides of the watercress in the flour, then coat both sides with the egg. In a skillet, heat the vegetable oil over medium-low heat until hot. Add the watercress and cook for 2 minutes per side, or until the egg sets and the color turns bright green. Turn only once. Be careful not to burn. Transfer to a bamboo tray to cool. Remove the skewers. On a cutting board, slice the pancake into $1/2$-inch strips, then into $1/2$ by 2-inch ribbons.

Variation: Although considered second-best to Korean watercress, green onions and chives are common ingredients that can be substituted in the above recipe to make Green Onion Ribbons (P'a Chitan) or Chive Ribbons (Puch'u Chitan).

Stone-Ear Mushroom Slivers

Sŏgi Komyŏng

Makes $1/4$ cup
10 minutes to prepare and cook

---

10 dried stone-ear mushrooms

$1/2$ teaspoon sesame oil

Pinch of salt

Stone-ear mushrooms have a strikingly jet-black color and are rare and quite expensive. Parchment-dry mushrooms are sold as bits and pieces in small packages. Except for ceremonial use, any dark-colored mushroom may be substituted.

Wash each mushroom piece by scrubbing between the palms until the lining becomes clean and sky blue. Pat dry and stack on top of each other. Roll up tight like a cigar and slice crosswise into thin slivers. In a small skillet, heat the sesame oil over medium heat until hot. Sauté the slivers briefly, until fragrant and the color turns bright. Season with the salt and a drop of sesame oil.

Main Dishes

✳ Rice and Cereals

In Korea, rice is called *pyo* when it is growing in the field, *ssal* after it is husked, and *pap* when it appears, cooked, on the meal table. Even today, Koreans greet each other by bowing and saying, "Did you eat your pap?" instead of "Good morning" or "How are you?" The ups and downs of the Korean commodity market is referred to in general as "the price of rice." Rice is synonymous with Korean livelihood.

In today's industrialized Korea, more than half of the farmers are still devoted to rice cultivation. With the help of modern technology, rice farming has never been more efficient, and twenty men can now do what once took two hundred men to do. Korean farmers are producing good harvests year after year; even in 1989 they had a bumper crop, despite a typhoon and major flooding. Some years there are even surpluses.

Rice is valuable not just as a food staple. After the harvest, the leftover material—the dry husks and straw—are put to good use: for cooking fuel, for making rope and rice sacks, and, most important in past days, for making thatched roofs for village houses. (Nowadays, tin and tile have replaced the old thatched roofs, but to me, the sight of straw always takes me back to my childhood home and our barn where I used to play hide-and-seek with my friends. We rolled in and out of those haystacks like a pack of mice, forever giggling.)

Rice remains the single most important grain to the Korean people. It is the ingredient with which a myriad of Korean dishes are magically transformed—from appetizers to desserts, and countless dishes in between. Rice is even turned into teas, soft drinks, wines, and spirits—the list seems to go on forever. In fact, Koreans boast that rice can be made into more than 700 great dishes. Among the many varieties of rice, Koreans favor short-grain white rice, which has a nutty fragrance and a tender yet chewy texture.

(above) Kosabap (offering to the three gods of childbirth)

(opposite) Ceremonial offering of rice, unhusked and cooked

Steamed White Rice

Pap

Serves 4
30 minutes to soak
and 30 minutes to cook

2 cups short-grain rice

2 cups hot water

I cannot help remembering the special white rice, kosabap, that our mother used to make for our house spirit, placed in an earthenware pot, a small, dark-gray replica of a large cooking cauldron. Under a flickering sesame oil lamp, she prayed with a humble offering of rice and a bowl of sweet, fragrant seaweed soup. Sometimes she added a piece of dried pollack. In hard times, the offering was only a bowl of rice and a bowl of clear water, because that was all she had for an offering. As an adult I no longer drool over thoughts of that steaming, snow-white, clay-fragrant rice, but the prayer she whispered as she rubbed her palms in perpetual motion still echoes in my mind: *"Chebal! Aedul i kŏngang hagiman!"* ("Please, Holy Spirit! I invoke you for the sake of our children's health and well-being!")

Cooking rice seems easy, but cooking rice perfectly is no simple matter. In modern kitchens, just about everyone uses an electric rice cooker. But Koreans still believe that the nuttiest and most fragrant rice is made in a cast-iron cauldron (*pabsot*) or in an earthenware pot, fired by dry pine needles or soybean husks. Though it is not necessary, rice may be washed once or twice before soaking (the water can then be used for making soups). Soaking the rice speeds up the cooking time, but do not soak longer than 30 minutes, or the rice will lose its nutrients and flavor. (Rice cooked in an electric cooker does not need to be soaked.)

Other delicious dishes can be created from this basic recipe just by stirring an added ingredient or two into the rice halfway through cooking: spinach (page 42), mushrooms (page 43), shredded radish and baby oysters (page 44), soybean sprouts (page 44), seaweed (page 45), and kimchi (page 46) are just a few of the possibilities. Be sure to use a pot, not an electric rice cooker, for these recipes.

Our mother could conjure up several dishes from her gigantic rice cauldron. When the rice was nearly cooked, she would carefully spread a damp hemp cloth on top of the rice and lay on it fresh vegetables from our garden: eggplant, summer squash, squash blossoms, wild sesame leaves—whatever was plentiful at the time. The most coveted items to appear from Mother's cauldron were steamed eggs studded with bright green onion rings, pollack roe, and tiny earthenware dishes of meat and fish that had been nestled on top of the steaming rice.

❀ ❀ ❀

Soak the rice in lukewarm water for 30 minutes. Drain the rice in a colander. Add the rice and hot water to a heavy 3-quart pot with a tight-fitting lid. Cover and bring to a boil over medium-high heat. Immediately decrease the heat to medium and boil gently for 10 minutes, or until the rice has absorbed all the liquid, occasionally stirring and scraping the bottom with a wooden spoon. Cover, decrease the heat to low, and cook the rice for 10 minutes more. (This is a crucial point in making soft, chewy rice.) The pot must remain tightly covered throughout the cooking process, except when stirring. Decrease the heat to very low and let rest for 10 minutes.

Fluff the rice with a wooden spoon. (Always fluff the rice when it is still hot, or it will cake together). Serve steaming hot in a serving bowl or in individual dishes.

Note: The cooking time and amount of water needed may vary slightly, according to the variety of rice. Try not to make more than needed for one meal, though leftover rice can be stored in the refrigerator for a few days and reheated in a saucepan with a little water, or sautéed in a skillet with a drop of light vegetable oil.

Five-Grain Rice

Ogokbap or Chapgokbap

Serves 6
45 minutes to cook

$^1/_2$ cup dried black soybeans

$^1/_2$ cup millet

$^1/_2$ cup sticky Italian millet

$^1/_2$ cup red beans

1 cup short-grain rice

$^1/_2$ cup sweet short-grain rice

$^1/_2$ teaspoon salt

Korea's farmers grow a variety of grains, including wheat, rye, corn, millet, Italian millet, oats, buckwheat, soy beans, sunflower seeds, and barley. To encourage people to eat grains other than rice, President Park Chung-hee in the 1960s resorted to a nationwide campaign that required families and restaurants to mix additional grains with their daily rice. Born to a poor tenant farmer, President Park wanted to help the farmers sell all the grains they produced. We obliged, but grudgingly. There is no grain as nutty, fragrant, and with as silky a texture as snow-white rice, in most people's opinion, mine included. But gradually, Koreans have come to terms with the lesser grains, realizing that those unappealing dark, sand-papery grains are packed with nutrition. Now I know why our grandmother relished her chapgokbap. As our mother said, those high-fiber grains were very good for Grandmother's digestion.

It is an old Korean custom to eat this dish on the fifteenth day of the first month of the lunar year. On this day, twelve varieties of mountain greens and several kinds of fruits and nuts are always served with the rice. Our ancestors believed that this balanced grain treat would ward off sickness during the rest of the year.

To prepare this dish, the red beans need to be precooked and the other grains should be soaked in separate containers. Then all are combined for the final cooking. Allow 4 hours to soak the black beans, during which time the red beans can be cooked. Italian millet, which resembles tiny couscous, can be found at specialty markets.

❀ ❀ ❀

In one bowl, soak the black soybeans in hot water for 4 hours. Drain and set aside. In another bowl, soak the millet in cold water for 1 hour. Using your hands, scrub the millet (this removes its bitterness); drain and set aside. In a third bowl, soak the sticky Italian millet in cold water for 1 hour. Drain and set aside. Place the red beans in a stockpot with 3 cups of cold water and bring to a boil. Pour out and discard the water, add 3 cups fresh cold water, and boil for 50 minutes, or until the beans are tender. Drain, reserving 1 cup of the cooking liquid. Transfer the black and red beans to a heavy 5-quart stockpot with a tight-fitting lid and set aside. In a fourth bowl, combine the rice and sweet rice and soak in lukewarm water for 30 minutes. Drain.

Add all the ingredients, except the sticky millet, to the stockpot with the beans. Dissolve the salt in 2 cups water and combine with the reserved bean cooking liquid; add this to the pot. Cover and bring to a boil over medium heat, occasionally stirring and scraping the bottom with a wooden spoon to prevent the grains from sticking. Spread the sticky millet on top, cover, and boil gently for 15 minutes over medium-low heat until the rice has absorbed all the liquid. Decrease the heat to low and cook for another 15 minutes. Decrease to very low and let rest for 10 minutes.

Fluff the grains with a wooden spoon. (It will have a much stickier texture than regular rice.) Serve steaming hot in individual dishes.

Spinach with Steamed Rice

Sigŭmch'ibap

Serves 4
30 minutes to prepare
and 35 minutes to cook

2 cups short-grain rice

1 pound spinach, leafy part only

2 cups hot water

This is a refreshingly delicious one-dish meal. It also works nicely as a side dish with fish and other entrees.

Soak the rice in lukewarm water for 30 minutes. Meanwhile, in a stockpot, make 4 cups acidulated water (page 10) and bring to a boil. Add the spinach and blanch for no more than 10 seconds, until the spinach is barely wilted and turns bright green. Plunge it into ice water to stop the cooking, then drain in a colander. Using a paper towel, squeeze out as much liquid as possible. Finely chop the spinach and set aside.

Drain the rice. Add the rice and hot water to a heavy 3-quart pot with a tight-fitting lid. Cover and bring to a boil over medium-high heat. Immediately decrease the heat to medium and cook for 10 minutes, or until the rice has absorbed all the liquid, occasionally stirring and scraping the bottom with a wooden spoon. Add the spinach to the rice and stir in well. Cover, decrease the heat to low, and cook for 15 minutes more. Decrease the heat to very low and let rest for 10 minutes.

Fluff the rice with a wooden spoon. Serve hot in a serving dish or in individual bowls with Vinegar Soy Sauce (page 28) on the side.

Ox-drawn grain husking stone

Growing Up in a Korean Kitchen

Mushrooms with Steamed Rice

Pŏsŏtbap

Serves 4 to 6
10 minutes to prepare
and 40 minutes to cook

---

2 cups short-grain rice

8 ounces fresh p'yogo (shiitake) mushrooms or other mushrooms, finely diced

1 tablespoon vegetable oil

5 cloves garlic, crushed and finely chopped

1 tablespoon soy sauce

1 tablespoon sesame oil

2 cups hot water

This recipe is one way to bring out the most from mushrooms and rice. The mushrooms are first sautéed in garlic and added to steaming rice. The two are then steamed together, lightly mingling into a subtle and succulent mushroom-infused rice dish. This is a quick, easy, and delicious one-dish meal; it makes a nice side dish, too.

❀ ❀ ❀

Soak the rice in lukewarm water for 30 minutes. Meanwhile, wrap the mushrooms in a clean, dry kitchen towel and squeeze out as much liquid as possible. Heat the vegetable oil in a skillet over medium heat until hot. Add the garlic and sauté for 2 minutes, or until fragrant. Add the mushrooms and soy sauce and sauté for 6 minutes, or until the mushrooms are cooked through. Add the sesame oil, mix well, and set aside.

Drain the rice. Add the rice and hot water to a heavy 3-quart pot with a tight-fitting lid. Cover and bring to a boil over medium-high heat. Immediately decrease the heat to medium and cook for 10 minutes, or until the rice has absorbed all the liquid, occasionally stirring and scraping the bottom with a wooden spoon. Evenly spread the mushrooms on top of the rice. Cover, decrease the heat to low, and cook for 10 minutes more. Decrease the heat to very low and let rest for 15 minutes.

Fluff the rice with a wooden spoon. Serve hot in individual bowls with Vinegar Soy Sauce (page 28) on the side.

Shredded Radish and Baby Oysters with Steamed Rice

Mubap

Serves 4 to 6
10 minutes to prepare
and 45 minutes to cook

2 cups short-grain rice

1 pound Korean radish or daikon,
peeled and shredded into
2-inch-long threads

2 cups hot water

8 ounces small fresh oysters,
coarsely chopped

This dish is a happy union of seafood and fresh radishes. One of the most delicate and fragrant rice dishes, it is very easy to make.

Soak the rice in lukewarm water for 30 minutes; drain. Arrange the radish in one layer on the bottom of a heavy 3-quart pot with a tight-fitting lid. Carefully add the rice and hot water. Cover and bring to a boil over medium-high heat. Immediately decrease the heat to medium and cook for 15 minutes, or until the rice has absorbed all the liquid. Decrease the heat to low and add the oysters in one layer on top of the rice. Cover and cook for 15 minutes more. Fluff the rice with a wooden spoon. Decrease the heat to very low and let rest for 15 minutes.

Serve hot in individual bowls with Vinegar Soy Sauce (page 28) on the side. Cucumber Salad (page 118) makes a refreshing companion.

Variations: Use minced shrimp, squid, clams, scallops, or octopus in place of the oysters. Smoked salmon is a rich and elegant choice. Or try a combination. When combinations of seafood are cooked together with rice, it is called Haemulbap.

Soybean Sprouts with Steamed Rice

K'ongnamulbap

Serves 4
10 minutes to prepare
and 45 minutes to cook

2 cups short-grain rice

8 ounces soybean sprouts, rinsed,
tails removed, and cut into
1/2-inch pieces

2 cups hot water

Although I ate soybeans so often in my childhood that I thought I might turn into a soybean sprout, this dish was extra special, even for me. It was always served with wonderful roasted hot peppers in soy sauce.

Soak the rice in lukewarm water for 30 minutes; drain. Arrange the soybean sprouts in one layer on the bottom of a heavy 3-quart pot with a tight-fitting lid. Carefully add the rice and hot water. Cover and bring to a boil over medium-high heat. Immediately decrease the heat to medium and cook for 15 minutes, or until the rice has absorbed all the liquid. (Do not open the lid during cooking, or a raw bean taste will develop.) Decrease the heat to low and, with the lid on tight, cook for 10 minutes more. Decrease the heat to very low and let rest for 15 minutes.

Fluff the rice with a wooden spoon. Serve hot with Roasted Hot Peppers in Soy Sauce (page 29).

Seaweed with Steamed Rice

Miyŏkbap

Serves 6 to 8
10 minutes to prepare
and 45 minutes to cook

2 cups short-grain rice

$^1/_2$ ounce dried kelp, rehydrated
(page 14)

3 cups hot water

Salt

Freshly ground black pepper

$^1/_2$ tablespoon hot red pepper
flakes, for garnish

If you haven't eaten much seaweed, this recipe is a good introduction to it. You'll be pleasantly surprised by its pleasant color and aroma and refreshing flavor. As an added bonus, this tasty dish is very nutritious as well.

Soak the rice in lukewarm water for 30 minutes. Meanwhile, pat dry the kelp with a paper towel, cut it into $^1/_2$-inch pieces, and set aside.

Drain the rice. Add the rice and hot water to a heavy 3-quart stockpot with a tight-fitting lid. Bring to a boil over medium-high heat. Stir in the kelp, cover, and decrease the heat to medium. Cook gently for 15 minutes, or until the rice has absorbed all the liquid. (The kelp will expand a little more.) Decrease the heat to low and cook, covered, for 10 minutes more. Decrease the heat to very low and let rest for 15 minutes.

Fluff the rice with a wooden spoon or chopsticks. The rice should have a pale forest green color and a seaweed fragrance. Adjust the seasoning with salt and pepper. Serve hot in individual bowls with a pinch of pepper flakes on top and Vinegar Soy Sauce (page 28) on the side. Cucumber Salad (page 118) is a perfect companion dish.

Kimchi with Steamed Rice

Kimchibap

Serves 4 to 6

10 minutes to prepare
and 45 minutes to cook

---

2 cups short-grain rice

1 tablespoon vegetable oil

1 clove garlic, crushed and finely chopped

1 tablespoon finely chopped green onion

4 ounces lean ground pork or ground chicken breast

2 cups finely diced Whole Cabbage Kimchi (page 97), stem part only and without stuffing

1 tablespoon sesame oil

Pinch of salt

Pinch of freshly ground black pepper

2 cups hot water

$^1/_2$ cup fresh or frozen green peas

This is a uniquely Korean dish. It has a robust, feisty flavor thanks to the happy marriage of tastes between the nutty rice and the fresh, well-pickled cabbage kimchi. This well-loved dish comes in various degrees of pungency, depending on the temperament of the kimchi, from fiery hot to refreshingly pale and delicate.

This recipe calls for whole cabbage kimchi, either homemade or store-bought. Since only the stem part is used, the remaining stuffing and leaves can be saved for other uses, for instance to make Stuffed Dumplings (page 90).

Soak the rice in lukewarm water for 30 minutes. Meanwhile, heat the vegetable oil in a skillet over medium heat until hot. Add the garlic and green onion and sauté for $1^1/_2$ minutes, until fragrant. Add the pork and sauté for 5 minutes. Add the kimchi and sauté for another 5 minutes. Add the sesame oil, salt, and pepper and immediately remove the skillet from the heat.

Drain the rice. Add the rice and hot water to a heavy 3-quart pot with a tight-fitting lid. Cover and bring to a boil over medium-high heat. Add the kimchi mixture to the rice and stir well. Cover, decrease the heat to medium, and cook gently for 15 minutes, or until the rice has absorbed all the liquid, occasionally stirring and scraping the bottom with a wooden spoon. Decrease the heat to low and sprinkle the green peas on top of the rice. Cover and cook for 10 minutes more. Decrease the heat to very low and let rest for 15 minutes.

Fluff the rice with a wooden spoon and serve piping hot in individual bowls. With its robust kimchi flavor, this rustic one-dish meal does not need to be accompanied by any other sauce.

Rice with Red Beans

P'atbap

Serves 4 to 6
10 minutes to prepare
and 1 hour to cook

1 cup dried red beans

5 cups hot water

3 cups short-grain rice

There are few dishes simpler than this bean and rice dish. Rich in protein, it makes an ideal side dish. It has a velvety soft texture and a beautiful purplish hue.

Add the beans and 3 cups hot water to a heavy 3-quart pot with a tight-fitting lid and bring to a boil. Pour out the water. Add 3 cups of cold water, bring to a boil, and simmer gently over medium heat for 45 minutes, until tender. While the beans are cooking, soak the rice in lukewarm water for 30 minutes; drain.

Drain the beans, reserving 1 cup of the cooking liquid. Return the beans to the pot along with the rice, 2 cups hot water, and the reserved bean liquid.

Cover and cook gently over medium-high heat for 15 minutes, or until the rice has absorbed all the liquid, occasionally stirring and scraping the bottom with a wooden spoon. Decrease the heat to low and cook, covered, for 10 minutes more. Decrease the heat to very low and let rest for 5 minutes.

Fluff the rice with a wooden spoon. Serve hot.

Fried Rice with Chicken

Pokkŭnbap

Serves 4
30 minutes to prepare
and 15 minutes to cook

---

3 cups short-grain rice

3 green onions, white and pale green part only

½ tablespoon soy sauce

1 tablespoon ch'ŏngju (rice wine) or vermouth

4 cloves garlic, crushed and finely chopped

2½ tablespoons sesame oil

Pinch of salt

Pinch of freshly ground black pepper

6 ounces boneless, skinless chicken breast or shelled and deveined shrimp, finely diced

2 tablespoons vegetable oil

2 walnut halves, finely chopped

8 ounces medium-firm bean curd, finely diced

½ pound napa cabbage, firm stem part only, finely diced

½ pound soybean sprouts, washed, tails removed, and finely chopped

6 ounces oyster mushrooms or other white mushrooms, finely diced

1 hot green Korean pepper, or jalapeño pepper, seeded, deribbed, and finely diced

1 hot red Korean pepper or ½ red bell pepper, seeded, deribbed, and finely diced

1 cup Whole Cabbage Kimchi (page 97), stem part only, rinsed, squeezed, and finely diced, or 2 Pickled Hot Peppers (page 110) seeded, deribbed, and finely diced

1 tablespoon toasted sesame seeds, for garnish

To me, pokkunbap without kimchi is not pokkunbap. It's the tangy and tasty bites of kimchi that make the dish so special. This one-dish meal is a refreshing harmony of tastes and delightful textures. Shrimp is a wonderful alternative to the chicken in this recipe.

❀ ❀ ❀

Cook the rice in an electric rice cooker according to the manufacturer's directions. Meanwhile, prepare the seasoning for the chicken: Finely chop 2 of the green onions and place them in a bowl. Slice the remaining green onion into thin rings, and set it aside for garnish. Add the soy sauce, ch'ŏngju, 1 clove garlic, ½ tablespoon sesame oil, salt, and pepper to the bowl, and stir to combine. Add the chicken and stir to coat the pieces evenly. Set aside.

When the rice is done, heat 1 tablespoon of the vegetable oil in a large skillet over medium-high heat until hot. Add the remaining 3 cloves of garlic and walnut pieces and sauté for 1½ minutes, or until the garlic is fragrant. Add the bean curd and sauté for about 5 minutes, or until it firms and turns a light gold color. Add the cabbage, soybean sprouts, mushrooms, and peppers and sauté for about 2 minutes. Transfer to a bowl and set aside. In the same skillet, heat the remaining 1 tablespoon of vegetable oil over medium-high heat until very hot. Add the chicken and kimchi. Sauté for 2 minutes, or until the chicken is cooked through to medium doneness. Return the vegetables to the skillet along with the rice. Decrease the heat to medium-low and add the remaining 2 tablespoons of sesame oil. Gently toss all together for about 2 minutes. Taste and adjust the seasoning.

To serve, divide the fried rice into 4 large, deep bowls. Sprinkle green onion rings and sesame seeds on top. Serve with Spinach and Clam Soup (page 64) and a fresh salad such as Leaf Lettuce Salad (page 116).

Growing Up in a Korean Kitchen

Sautéed Rice Cake with Meat and Vegetables

Ttŏk Pokki

Serves 4 to 6
1 hour to prepare
and 30 minutes to cook

2 green onions, white and pale green part only

4 tablespoons soy sauce

1 tablespoon chŏngju (rice wine) or vermouth

3 cloves garlic, crushed and finely chopped

1½ tablespoons sugar

6 ounces lean beef tenderloin, sliced into thin, 2-inch-long strips

3 tablespoons vegetable oil

8 fresh p'yogo (shiitake) mushrooms, sliced into thin, 2-inch-long strips

½ tablespoon freshly ground black pepper

10 ounces napa cabbage, stem part only, sliced into strips 1 inch wide and 2 inches long

2 large sweet green onions, or 4 green onions, white and pale green part only, halved and cut diagonally into 2-inch-long pieces

2 walnut halves, finely chopped

12 ounces small rice cake sticks, ½ inch in diameter and 2 inches long

1 tablespoon sesame oil

1 tablespoon toasted sesame seeds

Pinch of salt

4 tablespoons Beef Stock (page 58)

Pinch of sil koch'u (hot red pepper threads), for garnish

1 tablespoon pine nuts, coarsely chopped, for garnish

This classic dish adorns the ancestral offering table on New Year's Day. The main ingredient is the rice cake stick, which is also used in Rice Cake Soup (page 61), but here it is sliced smaller and thinner. This refined appetizer is a very different version from the one found at public eateries in Korea.

Finely mince 1 green onion; slice the other green onion into thin rings and reserve for garnishing. In a bowl, combine 1 tablespoon soy sauce, the ch'ŏngju, minced green onion, 1 clove garlic, and ½ tablespoon sugar. Add the beef and stir to mix well. In a skillet, heat 1 tablespoon vegetable oil over medium-high heat until hot. Add the beef and sauté for 2 minutes, or until the beef is cooked through. Transfer to a stockpot and set aside.

In the same skillet, heat 1 tablespoon vegetable oil over medium-high heat until hot. Add 1 clove garlic and sauté for 2 minutes, or until fragrant. Add the mushrooms and sauté for 4 minutes, or until the mushrooms are wilted. Season with 1 tablespoon soy sauce and a pinch of black pepper. Transfer to the stockpot, next to the beef. In the same skillet, heat the remaining 1 tablespoon vegetable oil over medium-heat until hot. Add the remaining 1 clove garlic and sauté for 2 minutes. Add the cabbage, sweet green onions, and walnuts. Sauté for 3 minutes, or until the cabbage is wilted. Transfer to the stockpot, next to the mushrooms.

In another stockpot, bring 4 cups of water to a boil. Add the rice cake sticks and boil until they are soft and chewy, about 2 minutes for fresh and 3 to 4 minutes for day-old rice cake sticks. Drain and set aside. Add the sesame oil, sesame seeds, the remaining 2 tablespoons soy sauce, 1 tablespoon sugar, and the salt to the first stockpot and toss lightly with a wooden spoon. Add the rice cake sticks and the stock to the first stockpot. Cook over medium heat for 3 minutes, constantly stirring lightly with a wooden spoon so that the flavors mingle well but each stays crisp. Adjust the seasoning with black pepper. Season with additional soy sauce and sugar, if desired.

Divide into individual dishes and garnish with the reserved green onion rings, sil koch'u, and pine nuts. Serve as a main dish with a bowl of rice or as an appetizer.

Note: For ceremonial occasions, this dish must be garnished with the traditional three-color garnish (page 33).

Rice with Vegetables and Meat

Pibimbap

Serves 4 to 6
30 minutes to prepare
and 1 hour to cook

12 ounces lean beef fillet, cut into
thin strips

2 ounces dried p'yogo (shiitake)
mushrooms, rehydrated (page
18), or 8 ounces fresh oyster
mushrooms, slivered

Seasoning for Beef and Mushrooms

4 tablespoons soy sauce

2 tablespoons ch'ŏngju (rice wine)
or vermouth

2 tablespoons sugar

3 green onions, white and pale
green part only, finely chopped

2 cloves garlic, crushed and finely
chopped

2 tablespoons toasted sesame
seeds

2 tablespoons sesame oil

Pinch of salt

Pinch of freshly ground black
pepper

5 tablespoons vegetable oil

12 ounces summer squash, cut
into thin matchsticks

12 ounces cucumber, sliced into
thin disks

1 fresh hot red Korean pepper
or jalapeño pepper, seeded,
deribbed, and sliced diagonally
into ¼-inch strips

Seasoning for Sprouts and Spinach

1 tablespoon soy sauce

3 green onions, sliced into thin
rings

3 cloves garlic

Continued on page 51

Pibimbap is probably the most popular luncheon dish in Korean homes and public eateries. A casual street food or an attractive, elegant dish, depending on the kitchen and how it is served, pibimbap is found in the lunch baskets of the farmers in the field, in the form of a hefty mound of rice with piles of mountain greens and garden salad, and in upper-class households, where exquisitely prepared slices of Fired Beef (page 179), Pan-Fried Fish Fillet (page 174), or Beef Tenderloin Tartare (page 201) perch on a dainty portion of vegetables and a dollop of white rice. Pibimbap is a prime example of a well-balanced meal in one dish. It is a great way to take care of leftovers, too. In my childhood home, an ancestral ceremony or other big event always meant a bounty of leftovers, and we could expect pibimbap for days thereafter, just as Americans enjoy a variety of turkey dishes after a Thanksgiving feast. It is said that pibimbap was fed to an army of fighting soldiers on the battlefield, served in their upturned helmets, as a quick meal on the run.

To make this dish, cook all the major ingredients, except the rice, 2 to 3 hours before serving. These ingredients should be prepared separately and kept apart so that each will retain its individual flavor, texture, and color.

Place the beef and mushrooms in separate bowls. Combine their seasoning ingredients in a small bowl. Pour half the seasoning over the beef, and toss lightly to evenly coat the strips. Pour the rest over the mushrooms, and stir to coat evenly. In a skillet, heat 1 tablespoon of vegetable oil over medium-high heat until hot. Add the beef and sauté, separating each strip, for 2 minutes, or until the meat is cooked to a medium doneness. Transfer to a container, cover, and store in the refrigerator. Using the same skillet (it is not necessary to wash it after sautéing the beef), heat 1 tablespoon of vegetable oil over medium heat until hot. Add the mushrooms and sauté for about 5 minutes, or until they are wilted and moist. Increase the heat to medium-high and sauté for 1 minute more, until the mushrooms absorb all the liquid. (The bits of beef left in the skillet add good flavor to the mushrooms). Transfer the mushrooms to a large tray.

Wipe the bowl that was used for the mushrooms, and place the summer squash in it. Add a pinch of salt and toss to coat. Let sit for 10 minutes, to extract the excess liquid. Wrap the squash in a clean, dry kitchen towel and squeeze out as much liquid as possible. Repeat this process for the cucumber, using another clean, dry kitchen towel. Transfer the squash and cucumbers to a clean work surface. Wipe the bowl for later use.

In a clean skillet, heat 1 tablespoon vegetable oil over medium-high heat until hot, but not smoking. Add the squash and sauté for 2 minutes, or until the color turns light green. Transfer to the tray with the mushrooms. In the same skillet, heat 1 tablespoon of vegetable oil until hot, but not smoking. Add the cucumber and sauté for 2 minutes, or until it turns bright green and transparent. Transfer to the tray. In the same skillet, heat the remaining 1 tablespoon of vegetable oil until hot, but not smoking. Add the red pepper and sauté for 2 minutes, or until it is barely wilted and the color is bright. Transfer to the tray.

In a small bowl, combine the ingredients for seasoning the soybean sprouts and spinach; set aside. Place the soybean sprouts in a large pot with a tight-fitting lid and add 1 cup cold water. Cover, bring to a boil, and cook for 3 minutes, or until fragrant steam seeps out. Do not lift the lid while boiling, or the bean sprouts will have an unpleasant raw bean taste. Drain in a colander and let cool (do not rinse). In the same bowl used for the squash, combine the soybean sprouts and half of the seasoning. Toss lightly to coat, then transfer to the tray, beside the mushrooms, but not touching them.

In the same stockpot, make 4 cups acidulated water (page 10) and bring to a boil. Add the spinach and blanch for no more than 10 seconds, until the leaves are bright green and barely wilted. Plunge it into ice water to stop the cooking, then drain in a colander. Squeeze dry with a paper towel. In the same bowl used for the bean sprouts, combine the spinach and the remaining seasoning. Toss to coat evenly, then transfer the spinach to the tray, keeping it separate from the other vegetables. Loosely cover the vegetable tray with a kitchen towel.

About 1 hour before serving, cook the rice in an electric rice cooker according to the manufacturer's directions. To serve, place 2 scoops of rice in the center of individual large bowls and arrange the meat, mushrooms, and vegetables in a flowery pattern on top. Sprinkle with crumbled deep-fried kelp and egg flakes or a pinch of toasted sesame seeds, if desired. Let each guest toss their own serving. Another presentation is to serve the rice in individual rice bowls and the meat and vegetable in separate bowls. Serve with koch'ujang (red hot pepper paste) and sesame oil on the side. According to Korean tradition, a bowl of hot clear soup plus a few extra side dishes accompany this perfect one-dish meal.

Note: There are no strict rules about color coordination when arranging pibimbap, but customarily this dish displays three to five colors in its ingredients.

Variation: Traditionally, Koreans insist on including fernbracken and bellflower roots in this dish and love to crack a raw egg on top.

3 tablespoons sesame oil

3 tablespoons toasted sesame seeds

Pinch of salt

Pinch of freshly ground black pepper

12 ounces soybean sprouts or mung bean sprouts

1 pound spinach, leafy part only, or ½ recipe Seasoned Spinach (page 125)

2 cups short-grain rice

Deep-Fried Kelp (page 210), crumbled, for garnish (optional)

Egg Flakes (page 34), for garnish (optional)

1 tablespoon toasted sesame seeds, for garnish (optional)

The city of Chŏnju is famous for its pibimbap. The secret may be in the serving dish, a sizzling hot stoneware bowl called a *tolsot*. The heated stone bowl stays hot long after the last kernel of rice has been consumed, leaving a nutty rice crust at the bottom. To season the chiseled granite bowl, it is boiled in salt water and heavily oiled. Repeated seasoning hardens the stone, turning the original gray into shiny jet-black.

Vinegar-Scented Rice Nuggets with Seafood

Saengsŏn Ch'obap

Makes 60 appetizers
1 hour to prepare and 1 hour to cook

---

5 ounces salmon fillet, skin removed

5 ounces squid, cleaned

5 ounces small prawns or shrimp, peeled, deveined, and halved

Salt & freshly ground black pepper

Marinade for Seafood

1/2 tablespoon coarse sea salt

2 tablespoons olive oil

5 tablespoons rice vinegar or distilled white vinegar

3 tablespoons ch'ŏngju (rice wine) or vermouth

2 tablespoons sugar

2 tablespoons freshly squeezed lemon juice

1 medium white onion, sliced into thin rings

1 tablespoon sesame oil

Pinch of salt

Pinch of freshly ground black pepper

2 1/2 cups short-grain rice

8 ounces Korean watercress

Seasoning for Rice

4 tablespoons rice vinegar or distilled white vinegar

1/2 tablespoon sugar

Pinch of salt

1 tablespoon ch'ŏngju (rice wine) or vermouth

1 tablespoon sesame oil

Pinch of freshly ground white pepper

Parsley sprigs, for garnish

Red apple slices, for garnish

1 ounce fresh or pickled ginger, sliced paper-thin, for garnish

Lemon wedges, for garnish

In this dish, bite-size rice morsels (ch'obap) are topped with small slices of seafood. Serve these tidbits on a tray alongside Seaweed Wrapped Rice (page 54)—they make a most attractive display, and they are as tasty as they look. Guests can help themselves with chopsticks or simply use their fingers. Packing the domino-shaped nuggets may take a little practice. All that is needed are skillful hands, luxurious seafood, and soft, chewy cooked rice. To prepare this dish, start your preparations a day in advance. When I was little, my friends and I played at making ch'obap with wet clay. We called it *chilhŭk ch'obap* (clay ch'obap).

❋ ❋ ❋

The day before serving, pat the salmon, squid, and prawns dry with paper towels, and lay them flat on a large bamboo tray. Season lightly with salt and pepper, cover tightly with plastic wrap, and let sit for 2 hours in the refrigerator. Meanwhile, in a small bowl, combine all the ingredients for the seafood marinade and mix well. Set aside. Remove the seafood from the refrigerator and pat dry again. Place the seafood in separate flat, nonreactive dishes. Spoon an equal amount of the marinade over each and, using the back of a spoon, press into the seafood. Cover tightly with plastic wrap and store overnight in the refrigerator.

About 2 hours before serving, make the rice in an electric rice cooker, according to the manufacturer's directions. While the rice is cooking, cut all the seafood into thin strips, about 1 inch by 2 inches long, and return them to their bowls. In a stockpot, make 4 cups acidulated water (page 10) and bring to a boil. Add the watercress and blanch for no more than 10 seconds, until it is barely wilted and turns bright green. Plunge it into ice water to stop the cooking, then drain in a colander. Using a paper towel, squeeze out as much liquid as possible. Season with a pinch of salt and pepper, and set aside.

To make the seasoning for the rice, in a small saucepan, combine the rice vinegar, sugar, and salt. Bring to a boil over low heat and simmer for 1 minute. Let cool. Add the ch'ŏngju, sesame oil, and white pepper, and blend well.

When the rice is done, spread it out in a large, wide bowl. Fluff with a wooden spoon, to cool slightly for handling. Sprinkle the seasoning over the rice. With the wooden spoon, mix the seasoning thoroughly into the rice. Let cool a bit.

To make the rice nuggets, place 1 tablespoon of rice in the palm of one hand, and with the index and middle fingers of the other hand, pack the rice firmly, shaping it into a nugget, about 1 inch by 2 inches by 1 inch thick. Cap each rice nugget with a slice of seafood, and firmly press together. Tie neatly with a string of watercress, like a small package. Repeat with the remaining ingredients.

Arrange attractively on a tray and decorate with parsley, apples, ginger, and lemon wedges. Serve with Vinegar Soy Sauce (page 28) and hot yellow mustard (page 16) on the side.

Vegetable-Wrapped Rice

Ssam

Serves 4
40 minutes to prepare

2 cups short-grain rice

Lettuce, fragrant crown daisies, wild sesame leaves, mint leaves, green and red peppers, peeled fresh garlic cloves, crisp, leafy greens, or other fresh garden vegetables

½ cup of one or more of the following: Fermented Soybean Paste with Garlic and Bean Curd (page 32), Allspice Sauce (page 28), toenjang (fermented soybean paste), or koch'ujang (hot red pepper paste)

Though the Korean kitchen is well known for pickling everything in sight, summer vegetables are often served fresh. My childhood meal table was never without a basketful of cool dew-sprinkled greens and other vegetables from our backyard: leaf lettuce, crown daisies, wild sesame leaves, mint leaves, gleaming hot red and green peppers, nasturtium flower petals, and on and on. It was so much fun creating these delicious ssam. It was always a struggle to gulp it down in one bite. There is nothing tastier on a hot summer day, and it is a visual feast as well!

There is no real recipe for fresh vegetable wrappings (the word *ssam* simply means "to wrap"). Ssam is always eaten in a congenial communal atmosphere, where all the ingredients are spread out on the table, and everyone creates their own wrap. Your guests will love it—if they don't mind the informality, that is. Mingling the hot steaming rice and chilled fresh greens with spicy Korean paste is a gourmand's delight. It is even more incredible when topped with a slice of Fired Beef (page 179). It is so delicious that, to borrow a Korean colloquial expression, *Hado masi issŏsŏ tuli mŏgdaga, hanaga chukŏdo morŭnda!* ("It is so good, you won't even notice if the friend next to you drops dead!").

Cook the rice in an electric rice cooker according to the manufacturer's directions.

Serve each guest a bowl of rice. Arrange the leafy greens and vegetables on a platter in the center of the table, surrounded by bowls of the condiments. Let each guest prepare individual wraps. To assemble the wraps, place a broad lettuce leaf in one hand. Place a piece of crown daisy or other vegetable on top, and add a spoonful of steamed rice. Dab on one of the sauces, and wrap the leaf into a ball. It is ready to eat.

There are many other interesting pastes and sauces to go with ssam. Two of the more assertive sauces are Roasted Hot Peppers in Soy Sauce (page 29) and Hot Red Pepper Sauce (page 30).

Seaweed-Wrapped Rice

Kimbap

Serves 12 to 14
2 hours to prepare

2½ cups short-grain rice

Seasoning for Beef

½ teaspoon soy sauce

½ tablespoon ch'ŏngju (rice wine)
or vermouth

½ tablespoon sugar

1 green onion, white and pale
green part only, finely chopped

1 clove garlic, crushed and finely
chopped

½ tablespoon sesame oil

Pinch of salt

Pinch of freshly ground black
pepper

6 ounces beef tenderloin, cut into
¼ inch by 8-inch strips

1 tablespoon vegetable oil

10 ounces whole spinach leaves

Seasoning for Spinach

1 green onion, white and pale
green part only, finely chopped

½ tablespoon toasted sesame
seeds

½ tablespoon sesame oil

Pinch of salt

Pinch of freshly ground
black pepper

Continued on page 55

This is a favorite dish for Korean children and adults alike. In my childhood, I could hardly wait for lunchtime if our mother had hinted that kimbap was in my lunch box. When our mother made it for us, I knew it would be beautifully presented, not that ordinary kimbap, plain salted rice wrapped into a seaweed ball, descriptively called *chumŏkbap* ("fist rice"). On the contrary, Mother's tasty kimbap always included beef strips, spinach, and pan-fried egg strips with the usual scented rice, all rolled up in a sheet of kim, and neatly sliced. Sometimes, when I was in an especially good mood, I would, with a sense of pride, share one or two pieces with my close friends, barely enough to tantalize them and whet their appetites.

Kimbap is an attractive and convenient finger food and an ideal luncheon dish. It is always included in the family picnic basket and is inevitably a part of the menu offered at community gatherings. As with Vinegar-Scented Rice Nuggets (page 52), making kimbap requires some practice, but in no time anyone can master the skill of rolling the rice up in seaweed, using a special bamboo mat called a *pal*. Kimbap and Japanese sushi are prepared in virtually the same way, and they look alike too, but the ingredients are distinctively different. The traditional Korean recipe calls for seasoned spinach, egg strips, and cooked beef, rather than fish.

✿ ✿ ✿

Cook the rice in an electric rice cooker, according to the manufacturer's directions. Meanwhile, in a small bowl, combine the ingredients for seasoning the beef and mix well. Place the beef in a bowl and pour the seasoning over it. Toss lightly to evenly coat the strips. In a skillet, heat the vegetable oil over medium-high heat until very hot. Add the beef and sauté for 2 minutes. Separate the beef strips and set aside.

In a stockpot, make 6 cups acidulated water (page 10) and bring to a boil. Add the spinach and blanch for no more than 10 seconds, until the spinach is barely wilted and turns bright green. Plunge it into ice water to stop the cooking, then drain in a colander. Using a paper towel, squeeze out as much liquid as possible. Transfer to a bowl. In a small bowl, combine the seasoning ingredients for the spinach. Pour the seasoning over the spinach, toss to coat well, and set aside.

To make the seasoning for the rice, in a small saucepan, combine the rice vinegar, sugar, and salt. Bring to a boil over low heat and simmer for 1 minute. Let cool. Add the ch'ŏngju, sesame oil, and white pepper, and blend well.

When the rice is done, spread it out in a large, wide bowl. Fluff with a wooden spoon, to cool slightly for handling. Sprinkle the seasoning over the rice. With the wooden spoon, mix the seasoning thoroughly into the rice. Let cool a bit.

To assemble the rolls, place the long side of a bamboo mat nearest you so it can be rolled up away from you. Have the following on hand: the rice, egg ribbons, radish, spinach, beef, kim, a bowl of water, a small brush, and a tray on which to place the finished rolls. Align a sheet of kim on the bamboo mat. Place $^1/_2$ cup of rice along the bottom edge of the kim and evenly spread the rice to make a rectangular strip, about $7^1/_2$ inches by 3 inches, using moist fingertips to pack down the rice. Place 1 strip each of beef, spinach, and egg horizontally across the middle of the rice and press them firmly into the rice. Fold the rice strip in half by quickly lifting the edge of the bamboo mat and folding it over. Press and seal the two sides together. Roll up the entire sheet of kim, using the bamboo mat to help keep the roll uniform and tight, but not catching it in the roll. Moisten the edge of the kim with the brush dipped in water and seal tightly by pressing and rolling firmly. The roll should be about $1^1/_4$ inches in diameter. Transfer the finished roll to the tray. Repeat with the remaining ingredients, making 10 rolls. Neatly slice each roll into bite-size disks, each $^3/_4$ inch thick (about 7 to 8 disks per roll). Moisten the knife with water often to prevent the rice from sticking.

On a large serving tray, arrange the pieces like a line of fallen dominoes or in a pinwheel pattern. Decorate with lotus root, pickled ginger, and a few sprigs of parsley. Serve with Vinegar Soy Sauce (page 28) and hot yellow mustard (page 16) on the side.

Note: A wide-mouth wooden tub is ideal for keeping rice warm and moist during preparation. You can alter the size of kimbap according to personal preference.

Seasoning for Rice

4 tablespoons rice vinegar or distilled white vinegar

$^1/_2$ tablespoon sugar

Pinch of salt

1 tablespoon ch'ŏngju (rice wine) or vermouth

1 tablespoon sesame oil

Pinch of freshly ground white pepper

1 recipe Egg Ribbons (page 34), cut into $^1/_4$-inch strips

6 ounces pickled white or yellow radish, cut into $^1/_4$ inch by 8-inch strips

10 sheets of kim (laver), about 8 inches square

Lotus Root Chorim (page 218), for garnish

Pickled Ginger (page 111) or Pickled Whole Garlic (page 111), for garnish

Parsley sprigs, for garnish

✵ Stocks, Soups, and Porridges

The recipes in this chapter are just a sampling of the countless stocks, soups, and porridges that come from the Korean kitchen. Basic Korean stocks (changguk) are made from quality meat and dried seafood. They can then be either enjoyed as simple soups or used as the base for other soups or dishes.

Koreans call themselves *t'angban minjok*, a rice-and-soup-eating people. With rare exceptions, rice and soup are served as a pair at every meal. Rich or poor, in good times and bad, hearty, comforting soups are eaten for every meal. The size of our soup bowls, nearly as big as tureens, indicates the customarily generous portions. Traditionally, soup was the only liquid at meals and tea was served at the end, not during the meal; only men drank rice wine with meals.

The soup (kuk or guk) recipes are selected from the vast array of Korean soups and include light and elegant but easy-to-fix soups as well as more complex soups. Traditionally, the water used to wash the rice was collected and used in soup making. If rice wash is desired, discard the first wash and save the second one.

The extensive list of porridges (chuk or juk) demonstrates the health-conscious Korean psyche. The main ingredients are a great variety of grains, nuts, and vegetables. These nutritious and remarkably tasty porridges are an excellent source of energy. They are considered especially good for elders, babies, the sick, and those who are under the weather or simply have little appetite. The ingredients are usually toasted and sautéed first, then simmered in a large amount of water or stock until very soft and creamy. Use nonreactive utensils and add seasonings sparingly at the last minute. Served in small portions (because of their intense flavors), porridges make superb appetizers, between-meal snacks or, best of all, invigorating breakfasts. They are very simple to prepare.

(above) Pumpkin porridge

(opposite) Ginseng chicken soup and ingredients: ginseng, sweet rice, deer antler shavings, hwanggi (an herb), chestnuts, jujubes, and ginger

Beef Stock

Makes 5 cups
30 minutes to prepare
and 50 minutes to cook

---

1 pound lean beef eye of round or tenderloin, thinly sliced

1 tablespoon vegetable oil

2 cloves garlic, crushed and finely chopped

2 green onions, white part only, finely minced

1 tablespoon ch'ŏngju (rice wine) or vermouth

2 tablespoons soy sauce

1 tablespoon sesame oil

1 kelp strip, 1 inch wide and 6 inches long (optional)

Traditional Korean beef stock is amazingly simple and quick to make. This aromatic, amber-colored stock is made with the choicest cuts of beef and subtle spices. It is the most favored Korean stock.

Soak the meat in ice cold water for 30 minutes. Drain and pat dry with a paper towel. In a heavy stockpot, heat the vegetable oil over medium heat until very hot. Add the garlic and green onions and sauté for 2 minutes. Add the beef and sauté for about 2 minutes, until it is lightly browned on both sides. Add the ch'ŏngju, soy sauce, and sesame oil and sauté together for 1 minute.

Add 6 cups of cold water and the kelp strip. Bring to a boil, skimming off any impurities. Decrease the heat to medium-low and simmer for 45 minutes. Strain through a sieve lined with cheesecloth. Reserve the meat for other uses (it makes a good topping for noodles or salads).

The stock will stay fresh in an airtight container in the refrigerator for a few days and in the freezer for a few months.

Variation: The stock may also be served as a clear soup, called Malgŭnguk. Simply sprinkle green onion rings on top for extra aroma and serve.

Chicken Stock

Tak Changguk

Makes 5 cups
1 hour to prepare
and 4 to 5 hours to cook

---

1 (3-pound) roasting chicken

10 cloves garlic, skinned and halved

5 green onions, white and pale green part only, halved crosswise

½ cup ch'ŏngju (rice wine) or vermouth

Pinch of salt

Pinch of freshly ground black pepper

There are three types of chicken stock in Korean cuisine: clear chicken stock (tak malgun changguk), milky chicken stock (tak chinguk), and heavy chicken stock (tak chinguk). The first is clear and light colored and is used for making consommé-type soups or for stocks. The second chicken stock is thin and milky; it is used for making Spinach and Clam Soup (page 64) and other light soups. The third chicken stock is heavy, milky, and very nutty; it is used in hearty and robust soups such as Kimchi Soup (page 67).

To make a clear chicken stock, cut the chicken into small enough pieces to fit in a stockpot, and soak in ice cold water for 1 hour; drain. In a large stockpot, bring 3 quarts of water to a boil. Add the chicken and boil vigorously, uncovered, for 2 minutes. Pour off all the water and impurities. Rinse the chicken with cold water and drain again.

Return the chicken to the stockpot. Add 3 quarts of fresh cold water, bring to a boil over high heat, and boil for 10 minutes, skimming off the impurities with a slotted spoon. Decrease the heat to medium-low and add the garlic, green onions, ch'ŏngju, salt, and pepper. Cover and boil gently for 45 minutes. With a slotted spoon, transfer the chicken to a bowl to cool. When the chicken is cool enough to handle, remove the meat and reserve it for other uses. Reserve the carcass for the second batch of stock. Strain the stock through a sieve lined with cheesecloth and store in an airtight container in the refrigerator. This first batch is a clear and flavorful broth and is used as a delicate and elegant soup or soup base.

To make milky chicken stock, return the carcass to the stockpot and add another 3 quarts of fresh water. Simmer over low heat for 3 hours. Strain the stock through a sieve lined with cheesecloth. Cool and transfer to another container and store in the refrigerator. This second batch will be opaque and still flavorful, but less so than the first batch.

To make heavy chicken stock, follow the directions for making milky stock, but continue simmering the chicken carcass an additional 4 to 5 hours (for a total of 7 to 8 hours) over very low heat. Strain the stock through a sieve lined with cheesecloth; discard the carcass. Pour the stock in an airtight container and chill overnight in the refrigerator. The next day, remove and discard the solid layer of fat from the top. This stock will have a rich, yogurt-like consistency when chilled.

Anchovy Stock

Myŏlch'i Changguk

Makes 4 cups
15 minutes to prepare and cook

½ ounce dried anchovies (each about 2 inches in length), deveined and heads removed

The Korean cook frequently makes flavorful stocks from preserved seafood, such as salted cod, pollack, shrimp, and mussels. The most commonly used, however, is dried anchovies. The light and flavorful stock made from anchovies is nutritious and economical, and it is very easy to make. The stock is then usually flavored with either fermented soybean paste or red pepper paste.

Place the anchovies in a cheesecloth pouch. Place 4 cups of cold water in a stockpot, and drop in the pouch. Bring to a boil and decrease the heat to medium-low. Boil gently for no more than 10 minutes (overcooked anchovies are somewhat bitter). Discard the anchovies and use the clear broth to make many flavorful soups or stews. The stock will stay fresh in an airtight container in the refrigerator for a few days.

Rice Cake Soup

Ttŏkguk

Serves 4 to 6
30 minutes to prepare
and 25 minutes to cook

6 cups ⅛-inch-thick rice cake stick rounds

1 tablespoon vegetable oil

2 cloves garlic, crushed and finely chopped

8 ounces lean ground beef sirloin

Salt

Freshly ground black pepper

2 large sweet green onions, or 6 green onions, white and pale green part only

8 cups Beef Stock (page 58) or Clear Chicken Stock (page 59)

1 kelp strip, 1 inch wide and 6 inches long (optional)

1 tablespoon sil koch'u (hot red pepper threads), for garnish

New Year's Day *(Sŏl nal)* never fails to remind me of the traditional multicolored *pidan hanbok* silk dress our mother made for me and the *sebae ton* (bowing money) we children received after performing a deep New Year's bow to our grandmother. It has been said that the rice cake was born out of our ancestors' wish for our prosperity and virtue: its round coin shape symbolizes money, and its chalky whiteness signifies purity, chastity, and integrity. In a bygone era, the dexterity in slicing the rice cake sticks into impeccable rounds was regarded as a formidable test of Korean womanhood.

This dish is a must on the ancestral ceremonial table on New Year's Day. On this day only, it replaces the usual bowl of rice and soup in front of each ancestor's tablet. It is not easy to forget that exquisite and chewy rice cake floating in its aromatic beef broth. Koreans enjoy it so much that this once seasonal dish has become year-round fare. This is partially because modern machinery has replaced the ancient and laborious task of making rice cakes by hand, and today they are sold wherever there are Korean markets. In the factory, steamed regular rice is pounded into a mass of dough and forced through an extruder. The result is a long, hotdog-shaped stick about 1 inch in diameter that is usually snipped into 20-inch lengths and packaged for sale. At home, the rice sticks are then cut into desired shapes and lengths before they harden.

In a bowl, soak the rice cake rounds in cold water for 30 minutes to soften the rice cake. Meanwhile, in a skillet, heat the oil over medium heat until hot. Add the garlic and sauté for 2 minutes, until fragrant. Add the ground sirloin and sauté for 5 minutes, until the meat is barely cooked through. Season with salt and pepper and set aside.

Slice a small amount of green onions into thin rings and set aside for garnish. Slice the rest of the onions diagonally into ¼-inch pieces. In a stockpot, bring the stock to a vigorous boil over high heat. Decrease the heat to medium-high, add the green onion pieces and kelp, and boil for 10 minutes. Add the rice cake rounds and cook for 10 minutes, until the rice cakes are soft and chewy, or to desired consistency. Transfer the kelp to the cutting board and cut into diamonds. Set aside.

To serve, ladle the soup into individual serving bowls and top with the meat. Garnish with green onion rings, kelp pieces, and sil koch'u. Serve very hot with a side dish, such as Whole Cabbage Kimchi (page 97) or Cubed Radish Kimchi (page 100).

Note: For ancestral ceremonies, the three-color garnish (page 33) is a must.

Variation: On New Year's Day, a few Steamed Dumplings (page 90) are usually added to this soup, which is then called Rice Cake and Dumpling Soup (Ttŏk Manduguk). Today this delicious combination is popular year-round, but especially during the cold Korean winter months.

In my childhood, *kun ttŏk karae* (toasted rice cake sticks) were a coveted snack for all ages. Secured between a chicken wire mesh, the rice cake sticks were held over a clay brazier's charcoal fire and toasted golden brown. We dipped these yummy cakes into soy sauce with sesame oil and ate them like a white hotdog without a bun.

Ceremonial Soup

T'ang

Serves 4 to 6
30 minutes to prepare
and 1¹/₂ hours to cook

1 pound lean eye of round or
rump roast

¹/₂ pound beef shin (arongsat'ae)

1 pound Korean radishes or
daikon, peeled and cut into
1¹/₂-inch chunks

1 large sweet green onion or
3 green onions, white and pale
green part only

1 kelp strip, 1 inch wide and
6 inches long (optional)

5 cloves garlic, crushed and finely
chopped

8 ounces medium-firm bean curd

Seasoning for Beef

1 tablespoon soy sauce

1 tablespoon ch'ŏngju (rice wine)
or vermouth

1 clove garlic, crushed and finely
chopped

1 green onion, white and pale
green part only, finely minced

1 tablespoon sesame oil

Pinch of salt

Pinch of freshly ground black
pepper

2 green onions, white and pale
green part only, sliced into thin
rings, for garnish

¹/₂ tablespoon koch'u karu (hot
red pepper powder), for garnish

T'ang, which means "soup" in Chinese, is the simplest soup to make
and yet it is the most sophisticated. Made from the choicest beef, this
soup's amber color, flavor, and aroma are so exquisite that it is the only
soup used for ancestral ceremonies.

Soak the meat in ice cold water for 1 hour; drain in a colander. Place
the meat in a stockpot with 10 cups of cold water and bring to a boil.
Boil vigorously for 15 minutes over medium-high heat, skimming off
the impurities with a slotted spoon. Add the radishes, green onion,
kelp, and garlic and bring to a boil. Decrease the heat to low and gently simmer for 1 hour. Add whole bean curd and boil for 30 minutes
more, until the meat and radishes are tender and the bean curd is
cooked but still firm.

With a wide slotted spoon, transfer the meat, radishes, bean curd,
and kelp into a large bowl. When they are cool enough to handle,
slice these ingredients into pieces 1 inch wide by 1¹/₂ inches long and
¹/₂ inch thick. Return everything except the meat to the bowl, cover,
and keep warm on the stovetop.

To make the seasoning for the beef, in a bowl, combine the ingredients. Add the meat and toss well. Return the meat to the bowl with the
radishes, cover, and keep warm on the stovetop.

To serve, reheat the soup to a boil. (For a more refined look, strain
the soup through a sieve lined with cheesecloth before heating.)
Arrange the meat, radishes, bean curd, and kelp in individual serving
bowls. Without disturbing the arrangement, ladle the soup into each
bowl. Garnish each with green onion rings and a pinch of koch'u karu.
Serve very hot, either as a first course or with a bowl of steaming rice.

Note: For a more elaborate garnish, use the three-color garnish (page 33).

Royal Meatball Soup

Wanjat'ang

Serves 4 to 6
20 minutes to prepare and cook

½ tablespoon sesame oil

1 tablespoon ch'ŏngju (rice wine) or vermouth

2 green onions, white part only, finely minced

1 garlic clove, crushed and finely chopped

Pinch of salt

Pinch of freshly ground black pepper

5 ounces lean ground beef tenderloin

4 cups Beef Stock (page 58)

2 tablespoons flour

1 egg, lightly beaten

2 green onions, sliced into thin rings, for garnish

This is an exceptionally elegant and delicious soup that would make a beautiful first course at any dinner table. The marble-size meatballs give the soup a neat and refined appearance. This soup can be made in no time at all.

To make the seasoning for the ground beef, in a small bowl, combine the sesame oil, ch'ŏngju, green onions, garlic, salt, and pepper; mix well. In a bowl, combine the ground beef and the seasoning and mix into a doughy consistency with a wooden spoon or with your fingers. Make 20 hazelnut-size meatballs. (Oil your fingers lightly to prevent the mixture from sticking.)

In a stockpot, bring the stock to a boil. Quickly dredge the meatballs with the flour and coat with the egg. Drop the meatballs one by one into the boiling stock and boil for 5 minutes, until they float to the surface.

To serve, ladle into warmed individual soup bowls. Garnish with green onion rings or with Egg Diamonds (page 34). Serve as a hot appetizer.

Variations: For a different flavor, omit the egg coating, sauté the meatballs in 1 tablespoon of vegetable oil, and add them to the stock just before serving.

To make a chicken version (Tak Wanjat'ang) or a fish version (Ŏalt'ang), substitute an equal amount of ground lean chicken breast or ground white fish for the beef.

To make fragrant Mugwort Soup (Aet'ang), add 1 cup finely chopped mugwort to the meatballs and boil.

Spinach and Clam Soup

Sigŭmch'iguk

Serves 4 to 6
20 minutes to prepare and cook

½ tablespoon vegetable oil

1 clove garlic, crushed and finely chopped

5 cups Milky Chicken Stock (page 59) or rice wash (page 40)

2 tablespoons toenjang (fermented soybean paste)

½ pound spinach, leaves only, washed and cut into 1-inch pieces

6 ounces littleneck clam meat, coarsely chopped

1 green onion, white and pale green part only, sliced into thin rings, for garnish

This sweet, nutty, and nutritious soup is incredibly easy to make. It is a dish that shows up often on the Korean table. This soup can be served without the clams, although they do add a wonderfully clean and refreshingly delicious flavor.

In a saucepan, heat the oil over medium heat, add the garlic, and sauté for 1 minute. Add the stock and stir in the toenjang until it dissolves. Add the spinach, bring to a boil, and cook gently for 2 minutes. Add the clam meat and boil over medium-high heat for 3 minutes.

To serve, ladle into individual serving bowls. Garnish with the green onion rings. Serve hot with a bowl of steamed rice.

Variations: Many other vegetables can be used in this recipe (however, omit the clams) to make Swiss Chard Soup (Kŭndaeguk), Cabbage Soup (Paech'uguk), and Bean Sprout Soup (K'ongnamulguk), to mention but a few. In the springtime, we use the tender leaves and roots of shepherd's purse (naengi) and the young day lily sprouts (wŏnch'uri) and other edible greens to create fragrant springtime soups.

Try Anchovy Stock (page 60) instead of chicken stock for a rustic flavor.

Seaweed Soup

Miyŏkguk

Serves 4 to 6
40 minutes to prepare and cook

1 tablespoon vegetable oil

5 cloves garlic, crushed and finely chopped

3 large sweet green onions, or 9 green onions, white and pale green part only, sliced into ¼-inch rings

4 ounces lean chicken breast, cut into ½-inch cubes

1 ounce dried kelp, rehydrated (page 14) and cut into ½-inch pieces (about 2 cups)

8 ounces medium-firm bean curd, cut into ½-inch cubes

6 cups Clear Chicken Stock (page 59) or Beef Stock (page 58)

1 tablespoon sesame oil

1 tablespoon soy sauce

Salt

Freshly ground black pepper

1 teaspoon toasted sesame seeds, for garnish

In my childhood, this soup had a special place in every Korean child's heart because it was a birthday treat. When our mother made this tasty soup with a generous portion of meat for me, I knew it was my birthday. These days, other exotic extras have been added to a Korean birthday party's steamed rice and seaweed soup: a cake with candles and a happy birthday song sung both in Korean and English.

❁ ❁ ❁

In a nonreactive stockpot, heat the vegetable oil over medium heat until hot. Add the garlic and one-third of the green onions and sauté for 2 minutes, until fragrant. Add the chicken and sauté for 2 minutes. Add the kelp, bean curd, and stock and bring to a boil. Gently boil over medium heat for 5 minutes. Add half of the remaining green onions and the sesame oil and bring to a vigorous boil. Add the soy sauce and season with salt and pepper. Remove from the heat.

To serve, ladle the soup into individual serving bowls. Garnish with the remaining green onion rings and sesame seeds.

Variations: A traditional variation is to add Sweet Rice Balls (page 229) to the hot soup. Float 5 or 6 of them in each soup bowl.

For a cool, thirst-quenching summer soup, chill the soup in the refrigerator. About 30 minutes before serving, add 1 cup shredded cucumber and stir in 4 tablespoons rice vinegar or distilled white vinegar. Garnish with green onion rings and sesame seeds and serve.

While miyŏkguk is a traditional dish for birthday celebrations, it is also an important staple in a pregnant woman's diet. According to our ancestors, this nutritional powerhouse is a bone fortifier and blood cleanser. Today we know that seaweed is an excellent source of iodine, alginic acid, calcium, iron, and vitamins C, B1, B2, and B12. It is Korea's fortune that seaweed is abundant around its peninsula; even in hard times it was within everyone's reach.

Radish and Chive Soup

Muguk

Serves 4 to 6
20 minutes to prepare and cook

---

1 tablespoon vegetable oil

5 cloves garlic, crushed and finely chopped

½ cup ¾-inch chive pieces

12 ounces Korean radishes or daikon, peeled and shaved into paper-thin, bite-size pieces

3 cups Beef Stock (page 58) or Anchovy Stock (page 60) plus 1 cup rice wash (page 40), or 4 cups Beef Stock or Anchovy Stock

1 tablespoon toenjang (fermented soybean paste)

1 tablespoon sesame oil

Salt

Freshly ground black pepper

This soup was almost a daily staple in my childhood, perhaps because it was inexpensive to make. But we never got tired of it. Its sweet and nutty flavor was especially comforting on cold winter evenings. Adding rice wash to the soup enhances the flavor.

In a stockpot, heat the vegetable oil over medium heat until very hot, but not smoking. Add the garlic and chives (reserving some chives for garnish) and sauté for 1 minute. Add the radishes and sauté for 3 minutes, until the radishes become transparent and fragrant. Add the stock and rice wash to the pot. Put a little stock in a small bowl, stir in the toenjang to dissolve it, and add to the pot. Bring to a boil and boil gently for 5 minutes over medium heat.

Just before serving, add the sesame oil and season with salt and pepper. Ladle the soup into individual serving bowls. Garnish with the remaining chives. Serve very hot with rice.

Variations: Instead of the radishes, substitute an equal amount of potatoes to make Kamjaguk or cabbage to make Paech'uguk.

Kimchi Soup

Kimchiguk

Serves 4 to 6
20 minutes to prepare and cook

Seasoning for Pork

¹/₂ tablespoon soy sauce

1 tablespoon ch'ŏngju (rice wine) or vermouth

1 clove garlic, crushed and finely chopped

1 green onion, white and pale green part only, finely minced

1 teaspoon freshly squeezed ginger juice

¹/₂ tablespoon sugar

1 tablespoon sesame oil

4 ounces not-so-lean pork belly, sliced into paper-thin ¹/₂-inch squares

1 tablespoon vegetable oil

5 cloves garlic, crushed and finely chopped

4 small fresh p'yogo (shiitake) mushrooms or other mushrooms, slivered

6 ounces soybean sprouts, cut into ¹/₂-inch pieces (optional)

2 large sweet green onions, or 4 green onions, cut diagonally into ¹/₂-inch pieces

1 cup Whole Cabbage Kimchi (page 97), stem part only and without stuffing, cut into ¹/₂-inch dice

4 cups Heavy Chicken Stock (page 59)

8 ounces medium-firm bean curd, cut into ¹/₂-inch cubes

Salt

Freshly ground black pepper

This all-time favorite is pure home cooking. Our family kitchen always served this spicy and hearty soup to our special guests.

To make the seasoning for the pork, in a bowl, combine the ingredients; mix well. Add the pork and toss to evenly coat with the seasoning.

In a heavy stockpot, heat the vegetable oil over medium-high heat until hot. Sauté the garlic, mushrooms, and pork for 3 minutes, until the pork is no longer pink.

Add the soybean sprouts, half of the green onions, and kimchi. (For a milder soup, rinse the kimchi before adding.) Sauté for 3 minutes. Add the stock and bring to a boil over medium-high heat. Gently boil for 5 minutes. Add the bean curd and boil for 2 minutes. Add the remaining green onions and boil briefly, just until the green onions turn bright green. Season with salt and pepper.

To serve, ladle the soup into individual serving bowls. Serve hot with rice.

Variation: For a lighter version, substitute an equal amount of lean chicken breast or lean beef for the pork belly and 1 tablespoon freshly squeezed lemon juice for the ginger juice.

Ginseng Chicken Soup

(pictured on page 56)

Kyesamt'ang

Serves 1
20 minutes to prepare
and 1¹/₂ hours to cook

---

1 (1¹/₂-pound) young spring chicken (yŏnggye) or Cornish game hen

¹/₃ cup cooked sweet rice

2 fresh chestnuts, shelled, skinned, and halved

5 pitted jujubes, or 10 raisins

3 cloves garlic, peeled and slivered

2 whole 3-year-old fresh ginseng roots (susam)

6 cups Clear Chicken Stock (page 59)

2 green onions, sliced into thin rings, for garnish

Other Korean soups are considered to have even greater tonic benefits. One is black rooster soup (okol kyesamt'ang), made with more than 20 ingredients, including ginseng, chestnuts, jujubes, gingko nuts, ginger, and licorice. Three others in this illustrious group are dragon and phoenix soup (yongbongt'ang), which is brewed with herbs, carp, and chicken, black mountain goat soup (hŭk yŏmsot'ang), and mudfish and beef brisket soup (ch'uŏt'ang). These and others are mostly available at specialty eateries or exclusive restaurants in Korea. On the other hand, Koreans also enjoy a plain chicken soup made with sweet rice and garlic, called white soup (paeksuk).

This is a one-of-a kind traditional Korean soup. It originated in royal and upper-class kitchens. In recent years, as ginseng has become more widely available, many restaurants have begun serving it under the name samgyet'ang. Revered as medicinal soup, there are many specialty houses (samgyet'ang chips), where it is the sole item on the menu. Traditionally, each whole spring chicken is boiled in its own clay pot *(ttugbaegi)* then is served, boiling hot, directly from the hissing flames to the table. Following the traditional rule that this dish be made with utmost care, this recipe calls for making one portion at a time. Increase the recipe according to the number of servings.

Wash the chicken in cold water and pat dry with a paper towel. Form the rice into a ball and stuff it inside the cavity of the chicken. Add the chestnuts, jujubes, garlic, and ginseng roots to the cavity. Sew up the chicken with kitchen thread.

Place the chicken in a stockpot and add the stock. Bring it to a boil, decrease the heat to low, and simmer for 1¹/₂ hours.

Serve immediately with dishes of salt, freshly ground black pepper, koch'u karu (hot red pepper powder), and green onion rings. Allow each guest to adjust the seasoning.

Growing Up in a Korean Kitchen

Fiery Seafood Soup

Saengsŏn Maeunt'ang

Serves 4 to 6
20 minutes to prepare
and 15 minutes to cook

---

¹/₂ pound fresh littleneck clams

1 live blue crab (page 141)

1 pound cod or red snapper fillets

Salt

Freshly ground black pepper

2 tablespoons vegetable oil

5 cloves garlic, crushed and finely chopped

¹/₂ pound napa cabbage, cut into 1-inch by 1¹/₂-inch pieces

¹/₂ pound Korean radish or daikon, peeled and cut into 1-inch sticks

7 cups Clear Chicken Stock (page 59) or Beef Stock (page 58)

1 cup ch'ŏngju (rice wine) or vermouth

2 large sweet green onions, or 5 green onions, white and pale green part only, sliced diagonally into ¹/₄-inch pieces

1 tablespoon koch'ujang (hot red pepper paste)

1 tablespoon koch'u karu (hot red pepper powder)

¹/₂ teaspoon freshly squeezed ginger juice

1 tablespoon sesame oil

8 ounces medium-firm bean curd, cut into 1-inch pieces

1 hot red Korean pepper, or ¹/₂ red bell pepper, seeded, deribbed, and sliced diagonally into ¹/₄-inch pieces

1 hot green Korean pepper or jalapeño pepper, seeded, deribbed, and sliced diagonally into ¹/₄-inch pieces

2 ounces crown daisies, cut into 2-inch pieces

2 ounces spinach leaves, cut into 2-inch pieces

This is one of Korea's most robust and tasty seafood soups. It is infused with a profuse amount of Korean hot red pepper powder and red pepper paste. For this soup, Koreans traditionally favor fresh yellow corvina (chogi), which resembles the croaker, but cod, yellowtail snapper, or red snapper may also be used. Littleneck clams and crabs add sweetness to the soup.

A few hours before cooking, scrub the clams well and soak in salted water for a few hours, to disgorge. Wash the crab and, just before cooking, cut into 4 pieces. Just before serving, cut the cod diagonally into 2-inch cubes, pat dry with a paper towel, and place in a colander in a single layer; season the cod with salt and pepper.

In a 5-quart stockpot, heat the vegetable oil over medium heat until hot. Add the garlic, cabbage, and radish and sauté for 5 minutes. Add the stock and ch'ŏngju and bring to a boil. Add one-half of the green onions, increase the heat to medium-high, cover, and boil for 5 minutes. Add the crab and clams and cover. While the soup is boiling, mix the koch'ujang, koch'u karu, ginger juice, and sesame oil in a bowl and stir into the soup.

Boil over medium-high heat for 2 minutes, add the cod and bean curd, and bring to a boil. Boil vigorously for 2 minutes, until the clams open and the crab's sweet flavor blends into the soup.

Just before serving, add the peppers, remaining green onions, crown daisies, and spinach, pressing them gently into the broth with a spoon. Cover and let cook for 1 minute. Season with salt and pepper.

To serve, divide the seafood and vegetables into individual soup bowls. Without disturbing the arrangement, ladle a few spoonfuls of hot broth into each. Serve with rice, Whole Cabbage Kimchi (page 97), and Cubed Radish Kimchi (page 100).

Beef and Tripe Soup

Komt'ang

Serves 4 to 6
30 minutes to prepare
and 3 hours to cook

1 pound lean beef brisket
(yangjimŏri)

1 pound boneless beef shin
(arongsat'ae)

1/2 pound beef tendons (simjul)

12 ounces beef tripe (yang),
meaty Turkish towel or
honeycomb part

1 pound beef knuckle bones
(sagol or togani)

1/2 pound beef small intestines
(kopch'ang)

1 ounce ginger, peeled and sliced

2 large sweet green onions,
or 4 green onions

5 cloves garlic, peeled and halved

1 pound Korean radish or daikon,
peeled and cut into 1-inch
chunks

Seasoning for Meat

1 tablespoon soy sauce

5 cloves garlic

1 tablespoon ch'ŏngju (rice wine)
or vermouth

2 green onions, white and pale
green part only, finely minced

1 tablespoon sesame oil

Salt

Freshly ground black pepper

1 tablespoon soy sauce

1 green onion, white and pale
green part only, sliced into thin
rings, for garnish

1 tablespoon hot red pepper
flakes, for garnish

This soup and Beef Knuckle Soup (page 71) are the two most popular national soups. They are often called *posint'ang*, or "body-invigorating soups." The cooking method and the list of ingredients are similar for both. Through long hours of simmering, the assortment of beef, innards, and bones becomes flavorful, wholesome, and satisfying soups. If you go to a specialty market for these items, you may need to know their Korean names. The tripe and intestines can be purchased in the market already cleaned and ready to use. Though this soup takes only 3 hours of simmering (the other takes 10!), its name literally translated means "simmered to death soup."

Soak the meat, bones, and innards in ice cold water for 2 to 3 hours; drain in a colander. In a stockpot, bring 3 quarts of cold water to a boil. Add the meat, bones, and innards and boil for 5 minutes. With a slotted spoon, skim off the impurites. Drain and rinse twice in cold water; return to the stockpot. Place 3 quarts of fresh water in the stockpot, add the ginger, green onions, and garlic, and bring to a boil over medium-high heat. Decrease the heat to low, cover, and simmer for 1 1/2 hours. Add the radish and simmer 1 hour more, skimming off the fat.

Transfer all the meat, bones, and radishes to a large bowl, reserving the stock. Let cool, and discard the bones. On a cutting board, cut the meat and radishes into bite-size pieces. (In the traditional kitchen, the brisket is always shredded by hand.)

To make the seasoning for the meat, in a bowl, combine ingredients; mix well. Add the meat and toss well. Just before serving, add the soy sauce to the soup and bring to a boil.

To serve, divide the meat and radishes into individual serving bowls. Ladle in the hot soup. Garnish with green onion rings and sprinkle the red pepper flakes on top. Adjust the seasoning with salt and pepper. Serve hot with a bowl of steaming rice and Cubed Radish Kimchi (page 100).

Beef Knuckle Soup

Sŏllŏngt'ang

Serves 4 to 6
30 minutes to prepare
and 10 hours to cook

- 2 pounds beef knuckle bones (sagol or togani)

- 1 pound beef tripe (yang)

- 1/2 pound beef small intestines (kopch'ang)

- 1 pound beef brisket (yangjimŏri), well trimmed of fat

- 1 pound boneless beef shin (arongsat'ae)

- 1 ounce ginger, peeled and slivered

- 1 pound Korean radish or daikon, peeled and cut into 1-inch cubes

- 5 cloves garlic, crushed and finely chopped

- 2 green onions, white part only, whole pieces

According to Korean medicinal folklore, the extracted juice of long-simmered tripe, the honeycomb part in particular, is one of the most invigorating tonics. It is called *yangjŭp*. In my childhood home, it was our grandmother's favorite and accordingly seemed to be reserved only for her, as I remember. Once when I was in my sickbed and very pale and gaunt, I was served this precious broth and I felt very special.

The ingredients and cooking methods of this soup and Beef and Tripe Soup (page 70) are similar, but the cooking duration of this dish is even more formidable—8 hours or more! One solution is to let the soup simmer overnight. Sŏllŏngtang probably originated from the name of the altar upon which Korean kings made annual offerings to the gods of earth and harvest in the spring. Usually the offering included a delicious soup made from a slaughtered cow.

❀ ❀ ❀

In a large bowl, soak the bones, innards, and meat for 2 to 3 hours in ice cold water; drain and set aside. In a heavy stockpot, bring 3 quarts of cold water to a boil and add the bones, innards, and ginger. Bring to a boil over medium-high heat, skimming off the impurities with a slotted spoon. Decrease the heat to low and simmer for at least 8 hours or overnight.

Remove and discard the bones. Add the meat, radish, garlic, and green onions to the pot and bring to a boil. Decrease the heat to low and simmer for 2 hours. Discard the green onions and ginger. Transfer the meat, innards, and radishes to a work surface and let cool. Cut into bite-size pieces and return to the soup.

To serve, ladle the soup into individual bowls. Serve with bowls of rice, Whole Cabbage Kimchi (page 97), and Cubed Radish Kimchi (page 100). It is customary to serve this milky white soup with a small four-sectioned spice dish containing salt, freshly ground black pepper, koch'u karu (hot red pepper powder), and green onion rings, allowing each guest to adjust the seasoning.

Oxtail Soup

Kkori Komt'ang

Serves 4 to 6
30 minutes to prepare
and 4 hours to cook

---

5 pounds oxtail, trimmed and cut
into 2-inch-thick pieces

3 tablespoons vegetable oil

5 cloves garlic, crushed and finely
chopped

6 green onions, sliced into thin
rings, for garnish

1 tablespoon hot red pepper
flakes or koch'u karu (hot red
pepper powder), for garnish

Korean gourmands find kkori komt'ang to be one of their favorite soups. The long hours of simmering creates a rich stock to savor and a delicious meat, almost nutlike in flavor, to chew on. This soup takes many long hours to cook. A few serious Korean cooks boast that it takes them 38 hours to create the best oxtail soup. I must admit that our family never went that far.

Soak the oxtail in ice cold water for 1 hour; drain. Heat the oil in a stockpot over medium-high heat. Sear the meat on all sides for a total of 5 minutes; pour off the fat. Add the garlic and cook for 1 minute. Add 8 cups of cold water and bring to a boil, skimming off the impurities. Decrease the heat to low and simmer for 3 hours.

With a slotted spoon, transfer the oxtail into a bowl to cool. Set aside 4 to 6 nice-looking pieces of meaty oxtail for the presentation. Remove the meat from the other bones, reserving both meat and bones for other uses (see note). At this stage, you should have about 2 cups of meat and 3 cups of very gelatinous, light brown stock. Refrigerate the stock and oxtail pieces overnight. The next day, remove the solid fat at the top of the stock and discard. Place the stock and oxtail pieces in a stockpot and bring to a full boil. Let boil for 10 minutes, or until the oxtails are heated through.

To serve, place one piece of oxtail in each individual soup bowl and ladle in the hot soup. Garnish with green onion rings and sprinkle red pepper flakes on top.

Note: Most Korean housewives do not throw away the remaining bones, but use them to make beef oxtail stock; use the same method for making Chicken Stock (page 59). This thrifty stock can be used in place of Beef Stock in casual stews. Use the reserved meat in salads or noodles.

Variation: Beef Short Rib Soup (Kalbit'ang) is one of the most popular and tasty Korean soups. In place of the oxtail, substitute 4 pounds beef short ribs, bones in, trimmed and cut into 1-inch pieces. Follow the directions as above, adding a 1-pound chunk of Korean radish as the soup begins to boil, and simmer for 1¹/₂ hours. Transfer the cooked radish to the cutting board and slice into bite-size dominoes. Continue to follow the directions in the base recipe. To serve, divide the meat and radish pieces into individual bowls and ladle in the soup.

Spicy Beef Brisket–Tripe Soup

Yuggaejang

Serves 10

20 minutes to prepare
and 2¹/₂ hours to cook

---

2 pounds beef brisket (yangjimŏri)
or beef flank, trimmed

1 pound beef tripe (yang), meaty
Turkish towel or honeycomb part

¹/₂ pound beef small intestines
(kopch'ang)

2 pounds large sweet green
onions, or 5 pounds green
onions

2 tablespoons koch'ujang
(hot red pepper paste)

2 tablespoons koch'u karu
(hot red pepper powder)

2 tablespoons sesame oil

2 tablespoons soy sauce

12 cloves garlic, crushed and finely
chopped

2 tablespoons toasted sesame
seeds

Pinch of salt

1 teaspoon freshly ground black
pepper

Korean children in my childhood were brought up constantly hearing from grown-ups that good food is like the best medicine. This soup is proof of this firm belief. In Korea, our lives revolve around a year of four distinct seasons: beautiful springs and autumns, and—alas!—yearly bouts of sweltering summer heat (*sam pok nal*, "the three dog days") and teeth-chattering winters (*tong janggun*, "the season of the ferocious winter general"). This dish is our ancestors' thoughtful way of preparing us to combat both heat and cold by *iyŏl ch'iyŏl*, "fighting heat with heat." They believed that we needed this soup for stamina, that it would make us perspire and rid us of all evil sickness. Hence, it became our custom to have yuggaejang every year, especially on the hottest day of summer and on the coldest day in deep winter. But now we don't mind having it year-round, and the hotter and spicier the better!

Soak the meat and innards in ice cold water for 1 hour; drain in a colander and set aside. In a stockpot, bring 8 cups of water to a boil. Add the green onions and blanch for 1 minute. Drain and discard the water, rinse the green onions in ice cold water, and cut into 2-inch pieces; set aside. In the same stockpot, bring 4 quarts of cold water to a boil. Add the meat and innards and bring to a boil over medium-high heat, skimming off the impurities with a slotted spoon. Decrease the heat to low and simmer for 2 hours, until the meat is tender. Transfer the meat and innards to a bowl to cool. When they are cool enough to handle, slice or tear into bite-size pieces. (The meat can be shredded by hand and the innards sliced with a knife.)

In a small bowl, combine the koch'ujang, koch'u karu, and sesame oil and mix well. Stir in the soy sauce, garlic, sesame seeds, salt, and pepper. Add the mixture to the meat and toss well. Return the meat to the stockpot, add the green onions, and cook gently for 25 minutes over medium heat. The soup will become brick red, similar in color to tomato soup.

To serve, ladle the soup into individual soup bowls. Serve with bowls of rice.

Variations: To make Spicy Chicken Soup (Takgaejang), substitute 3 pounds boneless chicken thighs or legs in place of the beef and innards, and follow the directions above. Traditional ingredients for both of these soups are bean sprouts, Korean watercress, sweet potato stems, and fern bracken. Add 1 cup of each to the soup during the last 25 minutes of cooking.

P'yogo Mushroom Porridge

P'yogojuk

Serves 4 to 6
40 minutes to prepare
and 40 minutes to cook

1 cup uncooked short-grain rice

2 tablespoons sesame oil

4 ounces lean beef round

2 cloves garlic, crushed and finely chopped

5 fresh p'yogo (shiitake) mushrooms, thinly slivered

2 tablespoons finely chopped chives

6 cups Clear Chicken Stock (page 59)

Similar to a grainy cream of mushroom soup and a risotto look-alike, this elegant porridge is easy to fix and delicious.

❉ ❉ ❉

In a bowl, soak the rice in hot water for 30 minutes. Drain and set aside. In a large saucepan, heat 1 tablespoon of the sesame oil over medium heat until hot. Add the meat and sauté for 3 minutes, separating it into fine crumbs. Transfer the meat to a bowl, leaving as much oil in the pan as possible. Using the same saucepan without cleaning it, sauté the garlic and mushrooms over medium heat for 5 minutes. Transfer them to the same bowl, next to the meat.

In the same pan, heat the remaining 1 tablespoon sesame oil over medium heat until hot. Add the rice and toast for 15 minutes over medium to medium-low heat, stirring constantly with a wooden spoon. (At this point, the rice will be nutty, fragrant, and chewy.) Add the meat, mushrooms, chives, and stock. Bring to a boil over high heat, and immediately decrease the heat to low. Gently simmer for 15 minutes, until the rice is cooked to the desired consistency, constantly stirring and scraping the bottom with a wooden spoon.

To serve, divide into small individual ceramic bowls. Serve hot with soy sauce, salt, and freshly ground black pepper for guests to adjust the seasoning to their own tastes.

Chive and Clam Porridge

Puch'ujuk

Serves 4 to 6
40 minutes to prepare
and 50 minutes to cook

1 cup uncooked short-grain rice

2 tablespoons sesame oil

1/2 pound chives, snipped into
1/2-inch pieces

4 ounces clam meat, freshly
shucked or canned, finely minced

1 egg, slightly beaten

1/2 tablespoon toasted sesame
seeds, for garnish

In Korea, chives are considered a very valuable herb. In my childhood home, our mother inevitably made this specialty for us when we had bad colds. Though you can use either kind, the Korean chives are much thinner and more tender than the Chinese variety. Some may think puch'ujuk tastes like New England clam chowder.

In a bowl, soak the rice in hot water for 30 minutes; drain and set aside. In a large saucepan, heat the sesame oil over medium to medium-low heat until hot. Add the rice and toast for about 15 minutes, stirring constantly with a wooden spoon. Add 6 cups of water and bring to a boil over high heat. Immediately decrease the heat to low and simmer gently for 15 minutes, until the rice becomes very tender, stirring constantly. Stir in the chives and clam meat and simmer for 10 minutes, stirring constantly. Drizzle the egg onto the boiling porridge, stirring a few times.

To serve, divide into small individual ceramic bowls and sprinkle sesame seeds on top. Serve salt and pepper on the side, allowing guests to adjust the seasoning to their own taste.

Variations: Substitute an equal amount of soybean sprouts, cabbage kimchi, or Swiss chard for the chives. The popular Mussel Porridge (Honghapjuk) and the rare and expensive Abalone Porridge (Chŏnpokjuk) are also made in the same way.

Red Bean Porridge

P'atjuk

Serves 6 to 8
30 minutes to prepare
and 2¹/₂ hours to cook

1 cup small dried red beans

1 cup cooked short-grain rice

48 Sweet Rice Balls (page 229)

1 tablespoon pine nuts, for garnish

I particularly loved the mauve color of p'atjuk, without realizing its hidden meaning. According to Korean thinking, white is auspicious and red is ominous. Red scared away the evil spirits lurking at our compound's gate, particularly on the long night of the last day of the eleventh month, as cited in our poetic phrase *tongji sŏttal kingin pame,* meaning "the long, long night of the winter solstice." So, as is our custom, on this night we sprinkled p'atjuk around our gate and kitchen to shoo away evil spirits. We ate this porridge well into the twelfth month, also sharing with our neighbors, until the bottom of the enormous earthen jar appeared.

It is an age-old Korean custom to eat p'atjuk when, according to the lunar calendar, the nights are longest. This porridge resembles Western rice pudding, except for the sweet rice balls (kyŏngdan). Small as quail's eggs, we nicknamed the rice balls *sae al,* "birds' eggs." By custom, each of us children was supposed to eat the same number of sweet rice balls as our age. It was always such fun eating them, especially when they were sweetened with sugar.

It is also a Korean custom to eat this porridge on house-moving day. Red beans are also said to help cure headaches if they are boiled an extra long time, at least 3 to 6 hours.

Pick over the red beans, wash and drain them, and put them in a saucepan with 5 cups of water. Bring to a boil, then decrease the heat to low. Gently boil for 50 minutes, until the beans are cooked and soft. Reserve 2 tablespoons of the cooked beans for garnish (remove them before they begin to break open). Add 1 cup cold water and gently boil for 1 hour. Force the beans through a strainer into a nonreactive pan and let settle. When the pureed beans have settled to the bottom, carefully pour off the cooking water into a 2-quart measure. Add enough water to make 6 cups of liquid. (Some liquid is lost during the boiling and pureeing process.)

Add the 6 cups liquid and rice to the pot with the pureed beans. Bring to a boil over medium heat. Immediately decrease the heat to low and gently simmer for 15 minutes, constantly stirring and scraping the bottom with a wooden spoon.

To serve, ladle the porridge into individual ceramic or glass bowls, and place 6 to 8 rice balls in each bowl. Garnish with the reserved whole beans and pine nuts. Serve with salt on the side. (Do not add salt during cooking because it makes the porridge separate and turn mushy.)

Variation: To make Sweet Red Bean Porridge (Tan P'atjuk), follow the directions above; just before serving, stir in ¹/₂ cup sugar. Serve as a dessert or a snack.

Pumpkin Porridge

Hobakjuk

Serves 10
1 hour to prepare
and 30 minutes to cook

1 cup dried red beans

1 (5-pound) pumpkin

1½ cups sugar (traditionally, honey
  is used)

4 tablespoons sweet rice flour

48 Sweet Rice Balls (page 229)

1 tablespoon ground cinnamon,
  for garnish

1 tablespoon pine nuts, for garnish

Because of its relatively homely appearance, the flower that blooms on pumpkin plants is the least appreciated of all by most Koreans. Accordingly, the colloquial Korean expression "pumpkin flower" means what "wallflower" does in America.

Native to South America, pumpkins were brought to Korea by the Dutch at the end of the sixteenth century. When I was a little girl, I thought that our country must grow most of the pumpkins in the world because they seemed to be everywhere. In my fond memory, bright orange pumpkins and pale green gourds are still sitting on our thatched roof under the bright autumn moon. We were fed pumpkins more than enough, I thought, but pumpkins do make a very nutritious and tasty porridge or soup. The sweet rice flour and rice balls add a nutty flavor and creamy texture to this recipe.

Cook the red beans following the directions in Rice with Red Beans (page 47); set aside. Meanwhile, wash the pumpkin under running water and dry with a clean kitchen towel. With a long, sharp chef's knife, cut the pumpkin in half and then into quarters for easy peeling. Scrape out the seeds and reserve for later use. Cut off the tough outer skin, and cut the flesh into small chunks. Put the pumpkin in a stockpot, add 3 cups of cold water, and bring to a boil over medium-high heat. Decrease the heat to medium and boil for 15 minutes, until the pumpkin is as soft as mashed potatoes. Stir in the sugar and cooked beans. Boil gently over low heat for 15 minutes, constantly stirring and scraping the bottom with a wooden spoon.

In a small bowl, dissolve the sweet rice flour in ½ cup cold water and add to the pumpkin mixture, stirring lightly. Stir in the sweet rice balls one by one and boil 3 minutes more.

To serve, ladle the porridge into individual glass bowls and sprinkle cinnamon and pine nuts on top. Serve with salt and freshly ground black pepper to allow guests to adjust the seasoning to their taste.

Note: To turn this recipe into a soup, add 1 cup of water or more for the desired consistency.

Variations: To make Corn Porridge (Oksusujuk), substitute 6 cups fresh or frozen corn kernels for the pumpkin, and omit the sweet rice balls. Cook for 15 minutes over medium heat, then decrease the heat to low and simmer for 15 minutes more.

To make another popular variation, Jujube Porridge (Taech'ujuk), substitute 6 cups pitted and finely chopped jujubes for the pumpkin, and omit the sweet rice balls and red beans. This porridge has a chutney-like look and consistency.

Soybean Porridge

K'ongjuk

Serves 4 to 6
30 minutes to prepare and cook

---

¹/₂ cup sweet rice flour

1 cup soybean powder

1 tablespoon pine nuts, for garnish

K'ongjuk is easy to make with the help of a food processor. Easier still, these days grains, beans, and nuts are conveniently sold in powdered form.

In a nonreactive saucepan, dissolve the sweet rice flour in 2 cups of cold water and bring to a boil over medium-high heat. Immediately decrease the heat to medium-low and simmer for 20 minutes, constantly stirring with a wooden spoon.

In a bowl, dissolve the soybean powder in ¹/₂ cup cold water and add it to the porridge. Simmer gently for 10 minutes more, constantly stirring and scraping at the bottom with a wooden spoon.

To serve, ladle the porridge into small individual custard bowls. Garnish with the pine nuts. Serve with salt on the side.

Variations: To make interesting variations, substitute powdered mung beans, millet, or other grains in place of soybeans.

Pine Nut Porridge

Chatjuk

Serves 4 to 6
10 minutes to prepare
and 30 minutes to cook

---

1 cup toasted pine nuts

$^1/_2$ cup rice flour

Chatjuk was once reserved for society's elite, but today every upscale restaurant has it on the menu. Our mother used to make two very fancy porridges—pine nut porridge and sesame seed porridge—and they were only for our grandmother and father's breakfast, always served in tiny portions. Fortunately, today pine nuts and sesame seeds are affordable.

This gracious and invigorating porridge makes a nutritious breakfast. The recipe is simple and easy to make. In our grandmother and mother's time, they used a stone grinder or mortar and pestle to grind the rice and pine nuts, but today we have an electric blender or spice grinder to do the job.

Pick over the pine nuts by uncapping their brown tips. Reserve 8 pine nuts for garnish. Put the pine nuts in a spice grinder and grind them into a paste, adding $^1/_2$ cup of water a little at a time as they are grinding. Scrape out the paste into a strainer lined with cheesecloth. With another $^1/_2$ cup of water, rinse out the grinder, and add this liquid to the paste in the strainer. Squeeze out as much liquid as possible, making 1 cup of milky liquid. Set the liquid aside and discard the residue.

In a nonreactive saucepan, dissolve the rice flour in 3 cups of cold water. (For a thinner version, add another 1 cup of water.) Bring to a boil over medium heat and immediately decrease the heat to low. Simmer for 20 minutes, constantly stirring and scraping the bottom with a wooden spoon. Add the pine nut liquid and simmer for about 1 minute, until the rice and pine nuts are barely blended.

To serve, ladle the porridge into attractive individual custard dishes. Garnish with the reserved pine nuts. Serve with salt and sugar.

Notes: Oil-rich pine nut paste and rice flour should never be cooked together for any length of time. To maintain the porridge's silky texture, do not stir too much and add salt and sugar just before eating, because stirring and salting will cause the porridge to separate.

Variation: To make Sesame Seed Porridge (Kkaejuk), substitute 1 cup toasted sesame seeds for the pine nuts, and grind them up and extract the liquid as directed above. After adding the sesame seed liquid to the rice, increase the simmering time to 5 minutes.

✸ Noodles and Dumplings

Korea is a rice country. In my childhood, we ate rice every day, whereas wheat was regarded as a secondary grain along with barley and millet. When we had noodles a few times a month, it was a special treat. Tasty and easy to prepare, wheat noodles were always served at weddings and whenever there was a large crowd to feed. Until recently, Koreans would greet their unwed friends and acquaintances by saying, "When will you treat me with *chanch'i kuksu* (feast noodles)?"

Whether prepared with extra care for special occasions or as an ordinary meal-on-the-run at home or at a street-hawker's stall, Koreans love noodles. Traditional noodles are purposely cut very long, symbolizing longevity, and they are served in a soupy liquid, not dry as are most Western pasta dishes. Eaters show appreciation for a tasty dish of noodles by loudly slurping and smacking their lips and lifting the bowls to their lips to finish the last drop of soup.

The varieties of interesting noodles sold today are endless: in addition to wheat noodles (mil kuksu), there are sweet potato noodles (tangmyǒn kuksu), barley noodles (bori kuksu), kudzu root starch noodles (ch'ik kuksu), egg noodles (kyeran kuksu), soybean noodles (k'ong kuksu), and many more. The most popular noodles after wheat noodles are buckwheat noodles, which are used to make Chilled Buckwheat Noodles (page 87), a provincial specialty from the north and northeastern mountain regions of North Korea.

Today, although everyone seems satisfied with store-bought noodles, the Korean love of homemade noodles is still present. Handmade noodles are always available at stalls in open-air markets, and recently trendy noodle eateries called *kal kuksu chips* (fresh knife-cut noodle houses) have appeared throughout the country. The best homemade noodles I have ever had are the ones my mother used to make, especially when they were for our fastidious father and grandmother.

(above) Food stall, Kyǒnggi Province

(opposite) Pǒpjusa Temple, North Chungch'ǒng Province

≡ 81 ≡

Homemade Noodles

Kal Kuksu

Makes about 1 pound of noodles
20 minutes to prepare

2½ cups all-purpose flour
(not self-rising)

2 tablespoons soybean powder
(optional)

Pinch of salt

1 cup medium-hot water

1 tablespoon sesame oil

2 cups flour, for dusting

The traditional recipe for homemade flour dough (mil panjuk) serves as the starting point for both homemade noodles and dumpling wrappers.

❀ ❀ ❀

In a large bowl, combine the flour, soybean powder, and salt and mix well. Make a well at the center of the flour, then add the water and sesame oil a little at a time. Mix into a cornmeal-like consistency and, with both hands, knead on a floured work surface for about 15 minutes, or until the dough becomes smooth and elastic. (In this state, we say it is *ik panjuk*, "par-cooked" dough, with a firm and supple texture.) Place the dough in a bowl and cover with a damp kitchen towel. It is ready to use immediately, but letting it settle for about 1 hour will improve the texture.

Divide the dough into two portions. Using one portion at a time, on a floured work surface roll out the dough with a rolling pin into ⅛-inch-thick sheets. Dust the dough with flour often to prevent sticking. Fold the dough into fourths, and using a sharp chef's knife, slice into the desired width, which for most recipes is about the width of a strand of linguini. Don't worry if the strands are irregular; that's the unmistakable sign of homemade noodles!

Fresh noodles take only 3 to 4 minutes to boil. For later use, spread the noodles on a tray to dry, then store in a plastic bag in the refrigerator. The noodles will stay fresh for 1 week in the refrigerator and up to 1 month in the freezer.

Homemade Dumpling Wrappers

Mandu P'i

Makes 64 thin wrappings
1 hour to prepare

2½ cups all-purpose flour
(not self-rising)

2 tablespoons soybean powder
(optional)

Pinch of salt

1 cup medium-hot water

1 tablespoon sesame oil

2 cups flour, for dusting

While store-bought wonton skins are very handy, it is enormously rewarding to make your own. There is nothing like fresh mandu p'i created from scratch.

Prepare the dough as for Homemade Noodles (page 82) and place on a well-floured work surface. With the palms of your hands, roll the dough into a long rope. Divide it into two, then divide each into two again, making 4 ropes; divide each rope into two. Now divide each piece into 4 parts, making 32 pieces. Finally, divide each again, making 64 walnut-size balls. Using a rolling pin, roll each ball into a thin 3½-inch-diameter wrapping. Dust well with flour and stack the wrappings.

To store, tightly wrap the stack in a plastic bag and place in the refrigerator or in the freezer.

Noodles with Chicken and Vegetables

Tak Kuksu

Serves 4 to 6
30 minutes to prepare
and 20 minutes to cook

$^1/_2$ tablespoon soy sauce

1 tablespoon ch'ŏngju
(rice wine) or vermouth

1 green onion, white and pale
green part only, finely chopped

1 clove garlic, crushed and finely
chopped

1 tablespoon freshly squeezed
lemon juice

$3^1/_2$ tablespoons sesame oil

Salt

Freshly ground black pepper

6 ounces chicken breast, sliced
into thin 3-inch strips

1 pound summer squash, sliced
into thin 3-inch strips

3 tablespoons vegetable oil

1 hot green Korean pepper or
jalapeño pepper, seeded,
deribbed, and cut diagonally into
thin 3-inch strips

1 hot red Korean pepper, or
$^1/_2$ red bell pepper, seeded,
deribbed, and cut diagonally into
thin 3-inch strips

$^1/_2$ pound fresh oyster mushrooms
or white mushrooms, shredded

$^1/_2$ pound napa cabbage, stem part
only, cut into thin 3-inch strips

1 cup Whole Cabbage Kimchi
(page 97), stem part only and
without stuffing, or 2 Pickled
Cucumbers (page 109), cut into
thin 3-inch strips

1 pound Homemade Noodles
(page 97), or store-bought Asian
wheat noodles

1 tablespoon toasted sesame
seeds, for garnish

$^1/_2$ tablespoon hot red pepper
flakes, for garnish

Here is our family's favorite noodle recipe, the basic recipe Koreans often enjoy for lunch and supper. It is simple and delicious fare and can be made either with or without soup. Once you have tasted this, you are likely to return to this recipe often.

❀ ❀ ❀

To make the seasoning for the chicken, in a bowl, combine the soy sauce, ch'ŏngju, green onion, garlic, lemon juice, $^1/_2$ tablespoon sesame oil, and a pinch each of salt and pepper. Add the chicken, toss well, and set aside.

Place the summer squash in a bowl and sprinkle with a pinch of salt. Let sit for 15 minutes. Using a kitchen towel, squeeze out as much liquid as possible. In a skillet, heat 1 tablespoon vegetable oil over medium-high heat until hot. Add the squash and sauté for 2 minutes, or until it turns bright green. Season with a pinch of pepper. Transfer to a tray.

In the same skillet, heat 1 tablespoon vegetable oil over medium heat until hot. Add the chicken and sauté for 3 minutes, or until the chicken is cooked through but still moist. Transfer to the tray next to the squash. In the same skillet, heat $^1/_2$ tablespoon vegetable oil over medium-high heat until hot. Add the green pepper strips and sauté for 1 minute, or until they are barely wilted. Season with a pinch each of salt and pepper and transfer to the tray next to the chicken and squash. Repeat with the red pepper strips.

In a stockpot, make 4 cups acidulated water (page 10) and bring to a boil. Blanch the oyster mushrooms for 10 seconds, or until barely wilted. Scoop out the mushrooms and plunge into ice water to stop cooking. Reserve the blanching water. Drain the mushrooms in a colander and, with a clean kitchen towel, squeeze out as much liquid as possible. Set aside on a work surface. Add water to the stockpot and bring to a vigorous boil once again. Add the cabbage, blanch for 3 minutes, and repeat the same process as with the mushrooms.

In a small bowl, combine $^1/_2$ tablespoon sesame oil and a pinch each of salt and pepper. Add the mushrooms, mix well, and transfer to the tray next to the chicken, peppers, and squash. In the same bowl, repeat with the cabbage, and transfer to the tray. With a paper towel, lightly squeeze out the juice from the kimchi strips. In a bowl, combine the kimchi and 1 tablespoon sesame oil, mix well, and transfer to the tray.

In the same stockpot, bring 4 quarts of fresh water to a boil and add the noodles. Cook for 3 to 4 minutes or according to the package directions. Drain in a colander, and transfer back to the same stockpot. Add 1 tablespoon sesame oil and toss well to keep the noodles separate and chewy soft.

To serve, divide the noodles into individual deep bowls. Distribute the cooked ingredients evenly in an attractive arrangement on top. Garnish each with sesame seeds and a pinch of red pepper flakes. Serve with a bowl of Allspice Sauce (page 28) or Roasted Hot Peppers in Soy Sauce (page 29).

Variations: Cooked lean ground round, beef strips, prawn halves, chopped clams, or squid strips or rings may be used instead of chicken. For seafood, use a simple base seasoning: a pinch each of salt and pepper, a drop of sesame oil, and 1 tablespoon ch'ŏngju. For formal occasions, such as weddings, the traditional three-color garnish (page 33) must adorn the noodles.

To make soupy kuksu, cook the noodles for 2 to 3 minutes. Bring 4 cups Clear Chicken Stock (page 59), Beef Stock (page 58), or Anchovy Stock (page 60) to a vigorous boil once, and add the noodles just to heat through. Divide the noodles into individual dishes, and distribute the cooked ingredients on top. Ladle hot broth over the noodles without disturbing the arrangement. Serve as above.

Noodles in Chilled Soybean Milk

K'ong Kuksu

Serves 4 to 6
25 minutes to prepare
and several hours to chill

½ pound fresh Homemade
  Noodles (page 82)
  or store-bought Asian wheat
  noodles

3 tablespoons toasted sesame
  seeds

1 quart soy milk

1 teaspoon salt

½ cucumber, peeled and cut into
  matchsticks

1 cup ice cubes

This is one noodle dish we had frequently in our childhood. Its delightful taste comes from the combination of chewy noodles and nutty soybean milk. This dish should be prepared several hours before serving. It is always served well chilled and with a few ice cubes floating around, like tiny crystal islands in a pale yellow pond; it's a wonderfully refreshing treat, as lunch or as a snack, on a hot summer's day. We children always had fun crunching the ice in our mouths.

❀ ❀ ❀

Bring a pot of water to a boil and cook the homemade noodles for 3 to 4 minutes, or cook the store-bought noodles according to the package directions; drain. Using a mortar and pestle, pound the sesame seeds into a powder. In a bowl, mix together the sesame seed powder and soy milk until well blended. Add the salt to the mixture. Place the noodles, soy milk mixture, and cucumber in three separate containers and chill in the refrigerator for several hours.

To serve, divide the noodles into chilled individual glass bowls, and ladle 1 cup of the soy milk soup into each bowl. Top with the cucumber. Add a few ice cubes to each bowl and serve immediately.

Chilled Buckwheat Noodles

Naengmyŏn

Serves 4
1 hour to prepare
and several hours to chill

---

1 pound buckwheat noodles

2 large sweet green onions,
or 6 green onions

6 ounces lean chicken breast

2 cloves garlic, sliced into thin
slivers

2 to 3 cups Clear Chicken Stock
(page 59)

1/2 Korean or Asian pear, peeled
and cut into long, thin strips

6 ounces cucumber, cut into
long, thin strips

2 hard-boiled eggs, halved

1 tablespoon sesame oil

1 cup Whole Cabbage Kimchi
(page 97), stem part only and
without stuffing, cut into thin,
3-inch-long strips

2 tablespoons sugar

2 tablespoons rice vinegar or
distilled white vinegar

1 teaspoon salt

This North Korean specialty is one of most popular summer dishes in Korean homes, public eateries, and even in upscale restaurants. At lunch hour, office workers, businessmen, and shoppers pack the naengmyŏn houses throughout Korea, slurping away in the summer heat. This dish should be prepared and refrigerated several hours before serving.

❀ ❀ ❀

Cook the noodles according to the package directions; drain. Divide the noodles into 4 bundles and place in a container; chill in the refrigerator. Cut the dark green tops off the onions and put the tops in a stockpot. Cut the white and pale green parts into threads and set aside. Add the chicken, garlic, and 2 cups of cold water to the stockpot and bring to a boil over medium-high heat. Boil for 15 minutes, skimming off the impurities with a slotted spoon. Transfer the chicken to a bowl. When the chicken is cool enough to handle, shred the meat by hand. Strain the stock through a sieve lined with cheesecloth into a 1-quart container. Add enough of the Chicken Stock to make 4 cups total. Chill in the refrigerator.

Place the chicken, pear, cucumber, green onion threads, and eggs in separate containers and chill in the refrigerator. In a bowl, add the sesame oil to the kimchi and mix well. Cover and chill in the refrigerator.

Just before serving, add the sugar and vinegar to the stock. Add the salt, adjusting to taste. Divide the noodles into 4 individual glass bowls, and arrange the chicken and vegetables on top of the noodles. Top with half a hard-boiled egg. Carefully ladle 1 cup of stock over the noodles. Serve with additional salt, vinegar, hot red pepper flakes, and hot yellow mustard (page 16).

Note: Pure buckwheat noodles are quite brittle. Koreans usually mix buckwheat with sweet potato starch to make the noodles more supple and manageable. In the Korean markets in the United States, naengmyŏn noodles are packaged in plastic bags. The labels usually read "Oriental Style Noodles with Buckwheat Vermicelli."

Variation: In the traditional recipe, a rich stock made from beef brisket and shin beef that has boiled for many hours is combined with refreshing Radish Kimchi Soup (page 101) and is used instead of the chicken stock.

Sweet Potato Noodles with Meat and Mixed Vegetables

Chapch'ae

Serves 8 to 10
1 hour to prepare
and 1 hour to cook

4 tablespoons ch'ŏngju (rice wine) or vermouth

3 tablespoons sugar

8 green onions, white and pale green part only, finely chopped

6 cloves garlic, crushed and finely chopped

2 tablespoons freshly squeezed lemon juice

4 walnut halves, finely chopped

2 tablespoons toasted sesame seeds

Salt

Freshly ground black pepper

8 ounces chicken breast, sliced along the grain into ⅛ by 3-inch strips

8 ounces lean beef tenderloin, sliced along the grain into ⅛ by 3-inch strips

3 tablespoons vegetable oil

2 ounces dried p'yogo (shiitake) or other mushrooms, rehydrated (page 18)

3 tablespoons soy sauce

5 tablespoons sesame oil

1 pound napa cabbage hearts, firm stem part only, cut into ¼ by 3-inch strips

1 pound spinach leaves, cut into 3-inch pieces

2 recipes Egg Threads (page 34)

12 ounces sweet potato noodles

2 hot red Korean peppers, or 1 red bell pepper, seeded, deribbed, and cut diagonally into ¼-inch strips

Continued on page 89

This dish is never absent from a Korean feast table. Vegetables, strips of meat, and sweet potato noodles are lightly cooked independently and then blissfully tossed together, making a sumptuous and delightful harmony of colors, textures, and flavors. When prepared as it should be, it is far different from the mangled and oily stir-fried mixture that often passes for it. To make chapch'ae, two points must be stressed. First, each ingredient should be slightly underdone and lightly seasoned before joining the others. Second, to retain individual colors, a crispy texture, and wholesome flavors, the final toss must be executed in a roomy bowl.

The long list of ingredients may appear daunting, but in fact it is a mere assemblage of several dishes presented elsewhere in this book. It may help to have all the seasonings lined up for easy access, as each ingredient will be seasoned separately. There is no need to clean the skillet or the vegetable seasoning bowl between uses. Chapch'ae is particularly suitable as a party dish because it can be prepared in advance and then served at room temperature. It can be made in large quantities, as many Koreans do, and the leftovers eaten later.

To make the seasoning for the chicken and beef, in a bowl combine 2 tablespoons ch'ŏngju, 1 tablespoon sugar, 4 green onions, 2 cloves garlic, lemon juice, walnuts, sesame seeds, and ½ teaspoon each of salt and pepper; mix well. Put the chicken in another bowl and add half the seasoning. Mix well with fingertips or a pair of chopsticks. Put the beef in the bowl with the remaining seasoning and mix well. In a skillet, heat 1 tablespoon vegetable oil over medium heat until hot. Add the chicken and sauté for 10 minutes, separating the strips. Transfer to a large bowl and set aside. (This bowl will be used for storing all cooked ingredients side by side until the final toss together.) Using the same skillet and 1 tablespoon of the vegetable oil, repeat the process with the beef. Transfer to the large bowl, next to the chicken.

Wrap the rehydrated mushrooms in a paper towel and squeeze out as much liquid as possible. Slice into thin slivers. To make the seasoning for the mushrooms, in a small bowl combine 1 tablespoon ch'ŏngju, 1 tablespoon soy sauce, 2 green onions, 2 cloves garlic, 1 tablespoon sesame oil, and a pinch each of salt and pepper; mix well. Add the mushrooms and toss well. Heat 1 tablespoon vegetable oil in the same skillet over medium heat until hot. Add the mushrooms and sauté for 10 minutes, until the flavor is well blended and the mushrooms are soft but not dry. Transfer to the large bowl, next to the chicken and beef.

In a stockpot, make 3 quarts acidulated water (see page 10) and bring to a boil. Blanch the cabbage for 3 minutes, or until barely wilted. Plunge the cabbage into cold water to stop cooking (keep the remaining acidulated water to cook the spinach). Drain in a colander and,

Growing Up in a Korean Kitchen

with a paper towel, squeeze out as much liquid as possible. To make the seasoning for the cabbage, in a bowl, combine 1 tablespoon ch'ŏngju, 1 green onion, 1 clove garlic, 1 tablespoon sesame oil, and a pinch each of salt and pepper; mix well. Add the cabbage and toss well. Transfer to the large bowl, next to the other ingredients.

In the same stockpot, add water to make 3 quarts again and bring to a boil. Blanch the spinach for less than 10 seconds, or until it turns bright green and barely wilted. Plunge the spinach into cold water to stop cooking. Drain in a colander and, with a paper towel, squeeze out as much liquid as possible. To make the seasoning for the spinach, in the same bowl used for the cabbage, combine 1 green onion, 1 clove garlic, 1 tablespoon sesame oil, and a pinch each of salt and pepper; mix well. Add the spinach and toss well. Transfer to the large bowl, next to the other ingredients, along with the egg threads.

To cook the noodles, bring 3 quarts of water to a boil in a small stockpot. Add the noodles and boil for 5 minutes, or until the noodles are slightly underdone. Plunge the noodles into cold water to stop cooking. Drain in a colander, and transfer to a bowl until cool enough to handle. Cut the warm noodles into 5-inch strands. Immediately add 1 tablespoon sesame oil and toss to coat evenly, keeping the noodles chewy and crisp. Add to the large bowl.

Add the peppers to the large bowl and lightly toss everything together with both hands or with a large serving spoon and fork. Add the remaining 2 tablespoons soy sauce, the remaining 2 tablespoons sugar, and the remaining 1 tablespoon sesame oil. Taste and adjust the seasoning with salt and pepper. Toss again briskly and thoroughly.

To serve, transfer to a large serving plate or onto individual dishes. Sprinkle the pine nuts and sil koch'u on top. Serve with rice for a wonderful one-dish meal. Or, this dish is even better accompanied by an array of side dishes, including soup, fish, salad, and a few kinds of kimchi. The leftovers will stay fresh for up to a week in the refrigerator or longer in the freezer. To reheat, cook in a skillet with a few drops of sesame oil until heated through and the noodles become supple.

Note: Traditional ingredients include dry day lilies (wŏnch'uri), strips of broad bellflower roots (toraji), cucumbers, and carrots, all in thin strips.

2 hot green Korean peppers, or jalapeño peppers, seeded, deribbed, and cut diagonally into ¹/₄-inch strips

¹/₂ tablespoon pine nuts, coarsely chopped, for garnish

¹/₂ teaspoon sil koch'u (hot red pepper threads) or hot red pepper flakes, for garnish

In our family kitchen, we prepared chapch'ae in a large wooden bowl, one meter in diameter, serving up to 100 guests. With the dexterous touch of our mother's fingertips, the mound of chapch'ae always turned out as chewy and crispy as can be. I remember dearly those carved wooden bowls and their cracks that had been mended with tin patches by itinerant tinkers.

Stuffed Dumplings

Mandu

Makes 64 dumplings
1 hour to prepare
and 45 minutes to cook

---

1 recipe Homemade Dumpling Wrappers (page 83), store-bought wonton skins, or gyoza skins, defrosted (if frozen)

10 ounces fresh oyster mushrooms or p'yogo (shiitake) mushrooms

1 pound napa cabbage, soft leafy part, finely chopped

1 cup Whole Cabbage Kimchi (page 97), stuffing removed, finely chopped

8 ounces medium-firm bean curd

1 pound coarsely ground chicken breast, or ½ pound coarsely ground chicken and ½ pound coarsely ground lean pork

1 Pickled Hot Green Pepper (page 110), seeded, deribbed, and finely chopped

1 egg, slightly beaten

2 tablespoons ch'ŏngju (rice wine) or vermouth

2 cloves garlic, crushed and finely chopped

2 large green onions, white and pale green part only, finely chopped

1 tablespoon sesame oil

1 teaspoon ginger juice or grated ginger

½ teaspoon salt

Pinch of freshly ground black pepper

2 cups flour, for dusting

Stuffed dumplings will be no stranger to most readers because they are a first cousin to Chinese dim sum dumplings. In the traditional Korean recipe, the stuffing includes ground pork (usually the well-marbled belly meat), cabbage kimchi, and mashed bean curd. This recipe is a lighter and healthier version that uses chicken, lean pork, or seafood.

Typically, one of three different cooking methods is used, to make steamed dumplings (tchin mandu), pan-fried dumplings (kun mandu), or boiled dumplings. Steaming makes the lightest and softest dumplings and also provides the most elegant presentation. Pan-frying (rather than deep-frying, which is how most Asian dumplings are prepared) gives Korean dumplings a light, crusty skin, locking in their moist, rich, nutty flavor. Boiling in water or stock is the quickest method, making light and soft-skinned dumplings for use in other recipes. Directions are given for all three, so you can try them all.

❀ ❀ ❀

Place the wrappers in a bowl covered with a damp towel. Set aside.

In a stockpot, make 4 cups acidulated water (page 10) and bring to a boil. Add the mushrooms and blanch for 10 seconds, or until the mushrooms are barely wilted. Scoop out the mushrooms and plunge them into ice water to stop cooking. Drain in a colander. With a kitchen towel, squeeze out as much liquid as possible and chop fine. Place the mushrooms in a large bowl. Bring the acidulated water back to a boil, add the cabbage, and blanch for 3 minutes, repeating the same process as with the mushrooms. Add the cabbage to the bowl with the mushrooms. Wearing rubber gloves, wrap the kimchi in a paper towel. Squeeze out as much liquid as possible, and add it to the bowl with the mushrooms and cabbage. Wrap the bean curd in a paper towel. Squeeze out as much liquid as possible. Place the bean curd in the bowl, along with all remaining ingredients except the flour. Mix well with a wooden spoon or with your hands until the mixture is smooth and soft.

To assemble the dumplings, have the following on hand: the bowl of wrappers, the bowl of stuffing, a teaspoon, a bowl of cold water, a small brush, and two large baking sheets liberally dusted with flour. Hold a wrapper in the palm of one hand and, using the teaspoon, spoon a walnut-size ball of stuffing in the center of the wrapper. Dip the brush into the water and lightly moisten the wrapper's edge. Fold into a half-moon shape. Seal the edges tightly using your thumb and index finger. Doubly seal the dumpling by pinching the edge with your thumb and middle finger. It will resemble a piecrust edge. (This shape is for steaming or boiling. If pan-frying, shape the dumpling into three sides by flattening the bottom to give it a base.) Line up the finished dumplings on the flour-dusted baking sheets about ½ inch apart to prevent sticking. To store, dust the dumplings well with flour, wrap the baking sheet tightly in plastic wrap, and place in the freezer. After the dumplings are frozen they may be transferred to a plastic bag and kept in the freezer for up to a month.

To steam the dumplings, place as many as will fit in the steamer, leaving space in between to prevent the dumplings from sticking together. Steam for 10 to 12 minutes, until the skin becomes transparent and the stuffing shows through the skin. Transfer to a bamboo tray and set aside. Repeat with the remaining dumplings. Serve as a main course or as an appetizer with Vinegar Soy Sauce (page 28) for dipping.

To pan-fry the dumplings, in a nonstick skillet with a tight-fitting cover heat 1 tablespoon of vegetable oil or olive oil over medium-high heat until very hot. Working quickly, place as many dumplings as will fit in the skillet, setting them on their sides and leaving space in between to prevent the dumplings from sticking together. Cook the 2 sides about 2 minutes each, until golden-brown. Cook the bottom for 1 minute. Decrease the heat to medium. Immediately pour $^{1}/_{3}$ cup ice water into the skillet and quickly cover with the lid. Let steam for about 3 minutes, until all the water is evaporated and the dumplings are juicy inside and crispy outside. Transfer to a bamboo tray and set aside. Repeat with the remaining dumplings. Serve as a main course or as an appetizer with Vinegar Soy Sauce (page 28) for dipping.

To boil the dumplings, in a stockpot bring 8 cups of water to a boil. Drop in one-fourth of the dumplings (about 15 pieces) and bring to a vigorous boil. Decrease the heat to medium and boil gently for 5 to 7 minutes, until the dumplings float to the surface. With a slotted spoon, transfer the dumplings to a large bowl filled with ice water, to stop the cooking and to retain a chewy and soft texture. Remove from the water and drain in a colander. Repeat with the remaining dumplings.

Note: Bean curd and egg are two necessary ingredients in the stuffing. Not only are they flavorful and nutritious, but they also act as crucial binding agents.

Variations: To make Dumpling Soup (Manduguk), follow the directions for boiling the dumplings; drain. Add 4 cups Chicken Stock (page 59) or Beef Stock (page 58) to the stockpot. Bring to a vigorous boil, add the dumplings, and bring to a boil once again. Drizzle 1 egg, slightly beaten, into the stock and stir. Ladle the soup into individual bowls, and garnish with green onion rings. Serve as a main course with rice, as a one-dish meal, or as an appetizer.

In summer, the cooked dumplings are often served cold in ice water and are called Water Dumplings (Mul Mandu).

✸ Kimchi and Changatchi: The Korean Way of Pickling

Each year, as the month of November approaches, the bustling markets in Korea become even busier than usual, thrown into a frenzy of activity by *kimjang ch'ŏl*, the kimchi-making season. This traditional culinary event falls between *Ipdong*, the first day of winter, and *Sosŏl*, the day of the first snowfall. Kimchi is made at other times of the year for immediate use (known as "instant kimchi" or "summer kimchi)," but *kimjang kimchi* will sustain a family through the three long months of the harsh Korean winter. *Kimjang ch'ŏl* is a serious national concern; it is reported on daily, along with current national and international news, supplemented by bulletins on commodity prices, money saving tips, and endless "how to" advice for consumers and suppliers alike. Typically, Korean housewives will exchange daily greetings of "Are you getting ready for *kimjang*?" or "Are you done with your *kimjang*?"

The wholesale produce markets are at their busiest during this period. From a bird's eye view, the Karakdong wholesale market in Seoul is one gigantic mound of green vegetables. In the chilling autumn air, thousands of people mill around, disappearing then reappearing among the piles of greens scattered over the five-block outdoor market square. Beside the square, there are several hangar-size indoor markets, also packed with hundreds of stalls selling fruits, fish, meat, and other important kimchi ingredients. Countless small trucks and private chauffeur-driven cars are there too, trying to load or unload their produce. Here and there, old rickety handcarts, ancient A-frame carriers, and rusty bicycles, summoned into service for the important task, are tangled in a chaotic scramble. People are shouting and bickering, and vehicles are honking, demanding to pass; everything either moves at a snail's pace or is stuck in a total knot.

Cabbages, radishes, mustard greens, green onions of several varieties, garlic tied in long braids, and other ingredients have

(above) Kimchi and sauce pots

(opposite) My mother slicing green onions for kimchi

been lugged by trucks during the night from farms throughout the country. The riotously bursting colors of produce are everywhere, not just in markets like Karakdong, but also in impromptu

Radish vendor, Karak Market, Seoul

mini markets that spring up on the roadsides, in vacant lots, wherever an open space or unclaimed spot can be found. These *pantchak sijang*, "twinkle bazaars," or *bŏngae sijang*, "lightning markets," are so named because small farmers set up their stalls in the wee morning hours, sell their produce, and, when the haggling is over, disappear in the blink of an eye. *Kimjang ch'ŏl* is the time when every street and alley is filled with itinerant vendors hawking knife-sharpening services, kitchen utensils, and all kinds of mixing, grinding, and shredding gadgets related to kimchi making. I love browsing around a *kimjang* market. It is always a lively, messy melange of people, produce, and machinery, among incredible noise and the permeating smell of fresh and decaying vegetables—a feast for the eyes and mind.

In the days of my childhood, kimchi made up virtually half the daily diet. Today, it is a tasty small side dish, but it is still an integral part of everyday life. We Koreans love it so much that, from breakfast to supper, a meal without kimchi is unthinkable. Typically, three or four different kinds of kimchi will be offered at every meal. That is why kimchi holds a very special place in our hearts. Today, Koreans do not eat as much kimchi as in my childhood, but the amount consumed nationwide is still enormous. The average family of five consumes thirty or more large cabbages each winter.

Kimchi making remains a laborious, communal task shared among relatives, neighbors, and friends. Making kimchi accord-

My mother and sister-in-law making kimchi

Growing Up in a Korean Kitchen

ing to a home recipe is a family's pride; there is nothing like homemade kimchi. In America, even though commercially made kimchi is available, Korean markets maintain brisk year-round business selling napa cabbage by two-bushel boxes.

Korean kitchens create more than one hundred kinds of kimchi, using everything from cabbage to watermelon skin and even pumpkin blossoms in summer. Each family's kimchi has its own unique flavor, but the basic process is to salt the vegetable, firming it up by extracting its liquid, locking in the original flavor. A mixture of spices is then introduced and the vegetable is fermented, creating its distinctive character. The most important spices are fresh and powdered hot red peppers, which give the kimchi its biting zest and help seal in its freshness, and crushed garlic and green onions, which enhance its flavor and help to sterilize it. Additional flavor-builders may include ginger, fruits, nuts, and seafood such as salted shrimp and anchovies, fresh oysters, pollack, yellow corvina, skate, and live baby shrimp, or even octopus and squid.

Sauce crock pad, Pongŭn Temple, Seoul

Green seaweed, chŏnggak, may be added to help retain freshness; in the mountainous region of the northern provinces, where seafood is not as available, beef broth is used instead.

Traditionally, kimchi is packed into enormous earthenware crocks to mature. As a price for its extraordinary natural flavor, kimchi has a short shelf life. At a constant cool temperature of 40°F, kimchi will stay crisp and tasty for two to three months. Our ancestors came up with a sagacious method to maximize kimchi's flavor and longevity: in winter they buried the kimchi crocks underground, and in summer, placed them in cold caves or in wells. In my childhood home, besides our backyard cave, we had a two-room storage house near the kitchen. In one room, kimchi jars were cemented in the floor, with only their necks and covers showing. In the countryside, most folks built temporary straw shelters over their buried kimchi jars. Nowadays, most Korean homes have medium-size refrigerators specially designed for kimchi only.

Scientific studies indicate that kimchi is remarkably nutritious—a source of protein and vitamins A and B—and is low in calories. It is also a digestive, due to its fibrous texture and lactic acid content. Most of all, kimchi has a uniquely delightful taste:

sour, yet sweet and spicy, with a nutty flavor. Chilling kimchi enhances its flavor and gives it a sparkling carbonated tang.

The most popular kimchi are Whole Cabbage Kimchi (page 97), Cubed Radish Kimchi (page 100), and Radish Kimchi Soup (page 101). They are available ready-made at Korean and Asian markets year-round but are relatively simple to make. Adding kimchi making to your cooking skill will surely encourage further exploration into Korean cooking. Once the secret is learned, one of the world's most versatile pickling techniques is at one's disposal. Whole Cabbage Kimchi, for example, is not only a wonderful side dish but also a superb relish. As a flavor builder in Korean cookery, the role kimchi plays as a relish can be compared to such Western food condiments as capers and olives.

Note: Use nonreactive materials (glass, stainless steel, and ceramics) for all cooking utensils, measuring spoons, bowls, and containers. Do not use plastic, as it picks up color. Wear rubber gloves when handling peppers. For storage, use sterilized wide-mouth glass or ceramic jars with screw-top lids. Be sure to leave 2 inches of space at the top to provide breathing room for the fermenting kimchi.

Korean Pickles (Changatchi)

Besides the elaborate process of making kimchi, there is a simpler pickling method used in the traditional Korean kitchen. Vegetables are preserved in heavily salted water and without spices (soy sauce, fermented bean paste, or red pepper paste can be used in place of salt water). Almost any vegetable or herb is a good candidate for pickling, including garlic, garlic stems, garlic leaves, cucumbers, hot peppers, hot pepper leaves, sun-dried flowers, ginger, lotus roots, green onions, and herbs. After a couple of months, the fermented vegetables are reconstituted in fresh water and then flavored with vinegar, sweeteners, and additional ingredients such as green onions, hot pepper flakes, sesame seeds, and sesame oil. Pickles bought in Korean markets in America must be reconstituted before they are served.

To fit the modern diet, I have modified the traditional pickling method by drastically reducing the amount of salt used and adding the spices at the beginning of the process, resulting in a shorter maturing time and a longer refrigerator shelf life. Korean pickles are very versatile and can be used as condiments, as relishes, or simply as tasty side dishes. The recipes in this chapter are based on some of the most popular Korean pickles.

Growing Up in a Korean Kitchen

Whole Cabbage Kimchi

T'ong Paech'u Kimchi

Serves 8 to 10

About 2 hours to prepare, 30 minutes to pickle, and 3 days to mature

---

5 pounds napa cabbage

1¼ cups coarse sea salt or kosher salt, plus additional if needed

Stuffing

2 tablespoons sweet rice flour or all-purpose wheat flour

2 tablespoons finely chopped saeu chŏt (salted shrimp) or myŏlch'i chŏt (salted anchovy)

1 cup koch'u karu (hot red pepper powder)

1 pound Korean radishes or daikon, peeled and cut into 3-inch matchsticks

1 hot red Korean pepper, or ½ red bell pepper, seeded, deribbed, and cut diagonally into ¼-inch strips

1 hot green Korean pepper or jalapeño pepper, seeded, deribbed, and cut diagonally into ¼-inch strips

2 large sweet green onions, or 4 green onions, white and pale green part only, cut diagonally into ½-inch pieces

2 green onions, white and pale green part only, cut into 1½-inch pieces

2 cloves garlic, crushed and finely chopped

4 walnut halves, finely chopped

1 tablespoon freshly squeezed ginger juice or grated ginger

½ cup sugar, plus additional if needed

1 tablespoon freshly squeezed lemon juice

½ cup chopped freshly shucked oysters (optional)

Continued on page 98

Napa cabbage kimchi is synonymous with kimchi, and with good reason. After all, over three-quarters of all kimchi is made with this vegetable. Napa cabbage, which is virtually identical to the Korean variety, chosŏn paech'u, is ideal for pickling because of its hardy, firm leaves and long shelf life. When salted, the cabbage sheds over 90 percent of its liquid, firming the texture and leaving it crisp, with its sweet taste intact.

There are two kinds of napa cabbage kimchi: whole cabbage kimchi (t'ong paech'u kimchi) and leaf cabbage kimchi (mak kimchi). The ingredients are exactly the same, but the cabbage is prepared differently. Whole cabbage kimchi is carefully made with whole cabbage heads that are salted, stuffed, and stored intact. (Usually the larger heads are halved or quartered into more manageable pieces.) Leaf cabbage kimchi is made with cabbage that is first cut into bite-size pieces before being salted, spiced, and stored. Whole cabbage kimchi has superior flavor, texture, and shelf life. *Kimjang* kimchi is made only in this way. Leaf cabbage kimchi is more convenient to prepare and almost as tasty, but it does not stay fresh for as long.

🌸 🌸 🌸

Wash the cabbage once and drain. Remove the tough outer leaves and reserve for later use. Trim off the very bottom of the cabbage, leaving enough of the root end intact to hold the cabbage together. Hold the root end up with one hand and, with a sharp knife, slice the cabbage lengthwise halfway down. With both hands, split the cabbage into halves. (In this way, the halves will divide cleanly.) If the cabbage is large, the halves can be sliced lengthwise into quarters. Wash once more, but do not drain.

Place the cabbage pieces and any leaves that have separated from them in a large (at least 6-quart capacity) nonreactive bowl, arranging them in one layer with cut sides up. Sprinkle 1 cup sea salt between the leaves and on top. Dissolve the remaining ¼ cup salt into 1 cup lukewarm water, and sprinkle this evenly over the cabbage. Let sit for 3 hours, shifting the cabbage every hour to evenly salt the pieces. As water is drawn out of the cabbage, the salt solution will eventually cover all the pieces completely. During the last hour, test every 15 minutes: the cabbage should have the consistency of a crunchy dill pickle. Rinse several times and drain on a bamboo tray or in a colander. Set aside. Discard the salt water and reuse the bowl for stuffing the cabbage.

To make the stuffing, in a small saucepan, dissolve the sweet rice flour in 1 cup water. Bring to a boil and decrease the heat to medium-low. Gently cook for 2 minutes, until it becomes a paste, stirring constantly with a wooden spoon. Let cool. In the large bowl, combine the sweet rice paste, saeu chŏt, and koch'u karu. Mix well into a bright, deep red paste. Add all the remaining ingredients for the stuffing and mix into a tomato-sauce-like consistency.

Wearing rubber gloves, place one cabbage piece in the bowl with the stuffing. Starting with the outer leaves and working in, insert the stuffing between the leaves, smearing it generously on each leaf. Tightly press the leaves together to create a bundle, and transfer it into a sterilized 5-quart jar with a screw-top lid. Repeat with the remaining cabbage pieces. Press down firmly on the bundles to pack well and remove trapped air bubbles. Use the reserved outer leaves and loose individual leaves to wipe up the remaining stuffing at the bottom and sides of the bowl; spread these leaves to cover the kimchi. Add a little water to the bowl to mix with the remaining bits and pieces of stuffing, and pour over the kimchi. Pack in well. All must be immersed in liquid (add more water if needed, but be sure to leave at least 2 inches of space at the top of the jar).

Close the jar lid tight and double wrap in plastic bags. Secure the neck of the jar with rubber bands to keep the kimchi fresh and to prevent odors. Set aside at room temperature overnight. The next day, ladle some of the juice out of the jar, taste, and adjust the saltiness if necessary by adding either salt or sugar to the kimchi. Let mature at room temperature for 2 to 3 days more, then transfer to the refrigerator to stop the fermentation. This red-hot and robust kimchi will have hot, sweet, salty, and spicy flavor. For more tang, leave it at room temperature for 1 more day. The kimchi will stay fresh for 1 month or more but will gradually become more sour.

A few hours before serving, wearing rubber gloves, transfer one whole piece to the cutting board and slice it crosswise into $1^1/_2$-inch layered sections. In a glass dish, arrange on a bed of fresh lettuce or cabbage leaves. Garnish with the hot red peppers. Tightly wrap the dish with plastic and return to the refrigerator. Serve well chilled at the center of the table as a side dish or relish.

Note: Traditionally, yuja was used instead of lemon.

Variation: To make Leaf Cabbage Kimchi (Mak Kimchi), cut the whole cabbage head crosswise and then into 1 inch by $1^1/_2$-inch pieces. Follow the directions above for salting the cabbage and for preparing the stuffing, then toss the cabbage and stuffing together in the bowl. The cabbage pieces are fermented and stored as described above. This kimchi can also be eaten right away, before fermenting, as a salad.

1 cup live baby shrimp (optional)

4 ounces Korean watercress, cut into $1^1/_2$-inch pieces (optional)

4 ounces mustard greens, cut into $1^1/_2$-inch pieces (optional)

2 ounces chŏnggak (green seaweed), minced (optional)

2 fresh hot red peppers or Pickled Hot Red Peppers (page 110), for garnish

Leaf cabbage kimchi is referred to as mak kimchi because it is the name used for the roughly mixed kimchi casually served at Korean public eateries and hawkers' stalls. In my childhood, we never served this type of casual kimchi to our grandmother, father, or precious house guests.

White Cabbage Kimchi

Paek Kimchi

Serves 6 to 8

About 1 hour to prepare, 30 minutes to pickle, and 3 days to mature

---

4 pounds napa cabbage

1¼ cups coarse sea salt or kosher salt, plus additional if needed

Stuffing

½ pound Korean radishes or daikon, peeled and cut into 3-inch matchsticks

½ cup sil koch'u (hot red pepper threads)

1 medium Korean or Asian pear, peeled, cored, and cut into thin matchsticks

2 green onions, white and pale green part only, cut into 1½-inch pieces

2 hot red Korean peppers, cut diagonally into ¼-inch pieces

1 clove garlic, thinly sliced

1 ounce mustard greens, washed and cut into 1½-inch pieces

3 chestnuts, shelled, skinned, and slivered

2 tablespoons pine nuts, brown tips removed

2 stone-ear or p'yogo (shiitake) mushrooms, slivered

3 jujubes, pitted and slivered, or 10 raisins

Juice from ½ cup saeu chŏt (salted shrimp)

½ cup sugar, plus additional if needed

1 teaspoon freshly squeezed ginger juice or grated ginger

1 teaspoon freshly squeezed lemon juice

2 stalks Korean watercress, cut into 1½-inch pieces (optional)

2 fresh hot red peppers or Pickled Hot Red Peppers (page 110), for garnish

This kimchi is made by virtually the same process as Whole Cabbage Kimchi (page 97). The result, however, is quite different, as this is one of the few kimchi that does not use hot red pepper powder or sweet rice paste. Instead, only a pinch of hot red pepper threads is used, resulting in a pale pink color (hence the "white cabbage" in the recipe name). The spices are also toned down, providing a more delicate flavor. For the uninitiated, this kimchi may be a good introduction to the world of kimchi. For this recipe, use only the freshest cabbage.

❀ ❀ ❀

Follow the directions for making Whole Cabbage Kimchi (page 97), cutting and salting the cabbage, combining the stuffing ingredients, stuffing the cabbage, and packing it in a jar, as described. It is not necessary to taste after the first day of fermentation, however. Instead, just before serving, taste the kimchi juice and adjust the saltiness if necessary by adding either salt or sugar to the kimchi. It will stay fresh for about 1 month in the refrigerator.

Cubed Radish Kimchi

Kkagdugi

Serves 4 to 6

About 1 hour to prepare, 30 minutes
to pickle, and 3 days to mature

---

1 pound napa cabbage hearts

4 pounds Korean radishes or
daikon, peeled and cut into
1-inch cubes

1 tablespoon salt

4 tablespoons koch'u karu
(hot red pepper powder)

2 tablespoons sweet rice flour or
all-purpose wheat flour

2 tablespoons finely chopped saeu
chŏt (salted shrimp) or myŏlch'i
chŏt (salted anchovy)

1 cup freshly shucked oysters,
chopped

5 green onions, white and pale
green part only, cut into 1-inch
pieces

2 ounces mustard greens, cut into
1-inch pieces

5 cloves garlic, crushed and finely
chopped

2 walnut halves, coarsely chopped

1 teaspoon freshly squeezed ginger
juice or grated ginger

1/2 tablespoon freshly squeezed
lemon juice

1/3 cup sugar

2 ounces Korean watercress, cut
into 1-inch pieces (optional)

The name kkagdugi comes from the sound of radishes being cut into cubes, *"kkagdug, kkagdug."* Koreans especially enjoy eating this kimchi with Beef Short Rib Soup (page 72) and Ginseng Chicken Soup (page 68).

❀ ❀ ❀

Reserve a few whole cabbage leaves, then cut the rest into 1 by 1 1/2-inch pieces. Place the cabbage pieces and radishes in a large bowl, sprinkle with salt, and let sit for about 15 minutes. Toss well with 2 tablespoons of koch'u karu.

In a small saucepan, dissolve the sweet rice flour into 1 cup water. Bring to a boil and decrease the heat to medium-low. Gently cook for 2 minutes, until it becomes a white paste, stirring constantly with a wooden spoon. Let cool. Add the remaining 2 tablespoons koch'u karu and saeu chŏt and stir well. Add to the cabbage mixture and mix well. Add the remaining ingredients and toss well. Transfer into a sterilized 4-quart jar with a screw-top lid. Use the reserved cabbage leaves to wipe up the remaining spices in the bowl; spread these leaves to cover the kimchi. Add a little water to the bowl to mix with the leftover spices and pour over the kimchi. Press down firmly on the kimchi to pack well and remove trapped air bubbles. Make sure that all the kimchi is immersed in liquid (but be sure to have at least 2 inches of space at the top of the jar).

Close the jar lid tight and double wrap in plastic bags. Let mature at room temperature for 2 to 3 days, then transfer to the refrigerator to stop fermentation. The kimchi will stay fresh for 1 month or more.

Variations: Substitute a combination of 3 pounds Korean radish and 1 pound cucumber cubes for the radish and cabbage used above.

Another beloved variation is Bell-shaped Radish Kimchi (Alt'ari Kimchi), which is also called "Bachelor" (Ch'onggak Mu) or "Bell-shaped" (Dallang Mu) Kimchi. One of the hottest and tastiest among the radish kimchi, it will make your hair stand on end. Bell-shaped radishes come in a variety of sizes, ranging from one's pinkie to regular pickling cucumbers. To make this kimchi, substitute 4 pounds whole bell-shaped radishes for the radishes used in the base recipe. Omit the napa cabbage, koch'u karu, salt, and watercress, and instead add 1 1/2 cups Fresh Hot Red Pepper Sauce (page 31) minus the ch'ŏngju and oil. Follow the directions above for making the kimchi. In the countryside, ground wild sesame seed paste (tul kkaejup) is added to this kimchi to give it a richer and nuttier flavor.

Radish Kimchi Soup

Tongch'i Mi

Makes 4 quarts; serves 10 to 12
1 hour to prepare, 30 minutes to pickle, and 2 to 3 weeks to mature

---

2 Korean radishes, about 3 inches in diameter and 6 inches long (about 1½ pounds each)

2 cups coarse sea salt or kosher salt

6 green onions

½ pound whole mustard greens

2 cloves garlic, peeled and thinly sliced

2 ounces fresh ginger, peeled and thinly sliced

1 Korean or Asian pear, unpeeled, cored and quartered

4 stalks chŏnggak (green seaweed) (optional)

2 hot red Korean peppers

5 Pickled Hot Green Peppers (page 110)

Sugar

1 green onion, white and pale green part only, sliced into thin rings, for garnish

Traditionally, Korean housewives placed a heavy sterilized rock on the radishes to keep them immersed in the juices. This may still be the best method.

In the Korean home, three kimchi are typically served at every meal: Whole Cabbage Kimchi (page 97), Cubed Radish Kimchi (page 100), and this tangy, sweet kimchi soup, which is the customary drink at the table. To Koreans, there is no taste combination better than washing down rice cakes with a large bowl of this cool and refreshing soup. It is also an important ingredient in making the stock for Chilled Buckwheat Noodles (page 87). Korean markets in America sell tongch'i mi in tall glass jars revealing white radishes, pickled peppers, and green leaves floating in an opaque salty juice.

Although other recipes in this book allow daikon to be used in place of Korean radish, in this recipe there is no substitute. The radishes must be of the sweet and sturdy thick-skinned Korean variety, because they have to withstand heavily salted water during fermentation.

Wash the radishes in cold water and scrub the skin clean with a vegetable brush. Leave them drenched in water. Sprinkle 1 cup of salt evenly in a large shallow bowl, and roll each wet radish in it until it is thoroughly coated with salt. Transfer the radishes to a sterilized 8-quart jar and cover. Cure for 2 to 3 days.

Place the green onions and mustard greens in a bowl, sprinkle with ½ cup of salt, and let sit for 30 minutes. Meanwhile, remove the salted radishes from the jar and set them aside. Strain the salt water remaining in the jar through a sieve into a 3- or 4-quart saucepan. Dissolve the remaining ½ cup salt into 10 cups of water and add it to the saucepan. Gently boil for 10 minutes and let cool.

Place the garlic and ginger in a cheesecloth pouch and place it at the bottom of the jar. Add the salted radishes. Tie the green onions into a knot and place them on top of the radishes. Do the same with the mustard greens. Add the pear, chŏnggak, fresh red peppers, and pickled green peppers. Pour the salt water into the jar. Be sure the radishes are completely immersed in the juices (but be sure to have at least 2 inches of space at the top of the jar). If they are floating, weigh them down with a heavy object.

Close the jar lid tight. Let mature at room temperature for 2 to 3 weeks, then store in the refrigerator. The kimchi soup will stay fresh for several months.

To serve, slice the desired amount of radishes, with softened skin intact, into 1 by 1½-inch pieces, and arrange them neatly at the center of a ceramic serving bowl. Ladle out some juice from the jar, taste, and dilute the juice with chilled water (a ratio of about 1 cup of the original juice to 3 cups water). Add sugar to taste. Pour the soup carefully over the radishes without disturbing the arrangement. Let sit for 30 minutes to allow the flavor to blend well. Garnish with the green onion rings. Serve as a side dish.

Radish and Cabbage Heart Kimchi

Nabak Kimchi

Serves 8 to 10
1 hour to prepare, 30 minutes to pickle, and 2 days to mature

---

½ pound Korean radishes, peeled and cut into 1 by 1½ by ¼-inch dominoes

½ pound napa cabbage hearts, cut into 1 by 1½-inch pieces

1 tablespoon sea salt or kosher salt

2 green onions, white and pale green part only, cut into 1½-inch pieces

2 cloves garlic, peeled and slivered

¼ ounce ginger, peeled and slivered

1 tablespoon sil koch'u (hot red pepper threads)

1 tablespoon pine nuts

2 stalks Korean watercress, cut into 1½-inch pieces (optional)

2 tablespoons sugar, plus additional if needed

Salt

1 tablespoon koch'u karu (hot red pepper powder), placed in a cheesecloth pouch

In summer, this kimchi is eaten as a refreshing cold soup. One notable use is at the ancestral ceremonial table, and therefore it is no ordinary fare. This delicate pale-pink kimchi is infused with the fragrance of Korean watercress and ginger. It is usually made in small portions because it matures within a day and won't stay fresh for longer than 1 week.

Place the radishes and cabbage in a large nonreactive mixing bowl and sprinkle with the sea salt. Toss and let stand for 30 minutes.

In another nonreactive mixing bowl, combine the green onions, garlic, ginger, sil koch'u, pine nuts, watercress, and sugar; mix well. Add this to the radishes and cabbage in the first bowl and toss well. Transfer the mixture to a sterilized 3-quart jar with a screw-top lid. Add 4 cups water to both mixing bowls, wipe the sides clean with a spatula, and add the water to the jar. Taste and adjust the seasoning with sugar and salt if needed. Add the pouch of koch'u karu to the jar.

Close the jar lid tight and double wrap in plastic bags. Let mature at room temperature for 1 to 2 days, then store in the refrigerator. The kimchi will stay fresh for 1 week at most.

Serve well chilled in a small glass or ceramic dish as a side dish.

Soy Sauce Kimchi

Chang Kimchi

Serves 8 to 10

1 hour to prepare, 30 minutes to pickle, and 2 days to mature

---

$1/2$ pound napa cabbage hearts, cut into 1 inch by $1^1/2$-inch pieces

$1/4$ pound Korean radishes or daikon, peeled and sliced into 1 by $1^1/2$ by $1/4$-inch dominoes

$1/2$ cup soy sauce

$1/2$ Korean or Asian pear, peeled, cored, and sliced into 1 by $1^1/2$ by $1/4$-inch dominoes

$1/2$ apple, peeled, cored, and sliced into 1 by $1^1/2$ by $1/4$-inch dominoes

2 green onions, white and pale green part only, cut into $1^1/2$-inch pieces

2 cloves garlic, peeled and slivered

1 hot red Korean pepper, cut diagonally into $1/4$-inch strips

3 chestnuts or walnuts, shelled, skinned, and slivered

3 jujubes, pitted and slivered, or 6 raisins, halved

2 fresh p'yogo (shiitake) mushrooms, slivered

$1/2$ ounce freshly squeezed ginger juice or grated ginger

$1/2$ tablespoon sil koch'u (hot red pepper threads), cut into $1^1/2$-inch pieces

1 tablespoon sugar or honey

2 stalks Korean watercress, cut into $1/2$-inch lengths (optional)

2 mustard green leaves, cut into $1^1/2$-inch lengths (optional)

4 stone-ear mushrooms, slivered (optional)

$1/2$ tablespoon pine nuts

Like Radish and Cabbage Heart Kimchi (page 102), this is a summer, or "instant," kimchi. Both are served at ancestral ceremonies and formal dinners, but this recipe is prepared with greater care in every detail, from finer ingredients to handsome serving vessels. It has an elegant flavor of fruit, vegetables, and nuts, with a subtle hint of spices. The dark soy sauce is largely responsible for its sweetness and light brown hue.

❀ ❀ ❀

In a nonreactive bowl, place the cabbage, radishes, and soy sauce and toss. Let stand for 1 hour. Drain the liquid into a saucepan, add 4 cups water, and set aside. Meanwhile, in another bowl, combine the remaining ingredients, except the pine nuts, and toss well. Add the cabbage and radishes and toss gently. Transfer into a sterilized 3-quart jar with a screw-top lid. Add the reserved liquid. Sprinkle the pine nuts on top.

Close the jar lid tight and double wrap in plastic bags. Let mature at room temperature for 1 to 2 days, then store in the refrigerator. The kimchi will stay fresh for 1 week at most.

Serve as a refreshing side dish.

Cabbage-Wrapped Kimchi

Possam Kimchi

Serves 5
About 2 hours to prepare, 30 minutes
to pickle, and 3 days to mature

---

5 pounds napa cabbage

1¼ cups coarse sea salt or kosher
salt

Stuffing

2 tablespoons sweet rice flour or
all-purpose wheat flour

Juice from ½ cup saeu chŏt
(salted shrimp)

1 tablespoon koch'u karu (hot red
pepper powder)

½ pound Korean radish or daikon,
peeled and cut into 1 by 1½ by
¼-inch dominoes

1 Korean or Asian pear, peeled,
cored, and cut into 1 by 1½ by
¼-inch dominoes

1 firm apple, peeled, cored, and
cut into 1 by 1½ by ¼-inch
dominoes

½ cup (about 4 ounces) freshly
shucked oysters, finely chopped

10 chestnuts or walnuts, shelled,
skinned, and slivered

2 mustard greens, cut into
1½-inch pieces

2 green onions, white and pale
green part only, cut into 1½-inch
pieces

2 cloves garlic, crushed and finely
chopped

¼ cup sugar

1 teaspoon freshly squeezed ginger
juice or grated ginger

1 teaspoon freshly squeezed lemon
juice

2 stalks Korean watercress, cut
into 1½-inch pieces (optional)

4 tablespoons sil koch'u (hot red
pepper threads)

Continued on page 105

This kimchi is a provincial specialty from Kaesŏng, the ancient capital city of the Koryŏ Dynasty (918–1392). The most attractive and subtly flavored among all kimchi, at first glance it resembles a tightly closed Savoy cabbage. When opened to display the beautifully arranged stuffing inside, it looks like a blooming flower bud. For best results, select tender cabbages with well-formed leaves.

🌸 🌸 🌸

Leaving the cabbage whole, follow the directions in Whole Cabbage Kimchi (page 97) for salting and rinsing the cabbage. Drain in a colander. Cut off the top 5 inches of the cabbage, select 25 good leaves, and set aside. Cut the remaining stem parts into 1 inch by 1½-inch pieces and put them in a large bowl.

To make the stuffing, in a small saucepan, dissolve the sweet rice flour in 1 cup water. Bring to a boil and decrease the heat to medium-low. Gently cook for 2 minutes, until it becomes a paste, stirring constantly with a wooden spoon. Let cool. Add the saeu chŏt juice and koch'u karu, mix well, and add to the bowl with the cabbage pieces. Add the remaining ingredients, reserving 1 tablespoon of sil koch'u, 1 tablespoon of pine nuts, 15 slivers of jujube, 10 slivers of p'yogo mushroom, and 15 slivers of stone-ear mushroom for the garnish. Toss well. Divide the stuffing and garnish into 5 portions.

Using the reserved cabbage leaves, in a bowl about 5 inches in diameter and 2 inches deep, overlap 5 leaves around the bottom of the bowl, leaving the top 2 inches extending over the rim. Fill with one portion of stuffing and add one portion of the garnish in an attractive pattern. Fold the leaves over neatly until the bundle resembles a tightly closed Savoy cabbage. Transfer the tightly wrapped kimchi to a sterilized 4-quart jar with a screw-top lid. Repeat with the remaining ingredients, making a total of 5 kimchi bundles.

Add the juice remaining in the bowls to the jar. Add a little water to the bowl to mix with any remaining bits and pieces of the stuffing, and pour over the kimchi. All must be immersed in liquid (add more water if needed, but be sure to leave at least 2 inches of space at the top of the jar).

Growing Up in a Korean Kitchen

Close the jar lid tight and double wrap in plastic bags. Let mature at room temperature for 2 to 3 days, then transfer to the refrigerator to stop the fermentation. The kimchi will stay fresh for 1 month or more.

Serve in individual glass dishes, allowing each guest to unwrap their own as a surprise package. It is a perfect side dish with a bowl of steamed rice, and it goes well with almost any meat entree.

Note: Traditionally, Kaesŏng folks also used such ingredients as persimmons, octopus, squid, and pollack in their stuffing. Sometimes they garnished this kimchi with beef shin or brisket cold cuts.

2 tablespoons pine nuts, brown tips removed

2 jujubes, pitted and thinly slivered, or 4 raisins

1 fresh p'yogo (shiitake) mushroom, thinly slivered

3 stone-ear mushrooms, thinly slivered (optional)

Stuffed Cucumber Kimchi

Oi Sobaegi Kimchi

Serves 4
1 hour to prepare, 30 minutes to pickle, and 3 days to mature

---

- 1 pound Korean or Japanese cucumbers or other seedless, soft-skinned cucumbers

- 1 tablespoon sea salt or kosher salt, or additional if needed

Stuffing

- 2 ounces Korean radishes or daikon, peeled and shredded into 1½-inch matchsticks

- 6 ounces Korean chives or Chinese chives, snipped into 1½-inch pieces

- 1 clove garlic, crushed and finely chopped

- ½ tablespoon toasted sesame seeds

- 1 walnut, finely chopped

- ½ tablespoon sugar

- ½ tablespoon freshly squeezed lemon juice

- ½ tablespoon freshly squeezed ginger juice or grated ginger

- 1 tablespoon sil koch'u (hot red pepper threads), cut into 1-inch pieces

In days past, this kimchi could only be enjoyed in the summer, when cucumbers were at their prime; today it is available year-round. Like Stuffed Eggplant Kimchi (page 107), this is an "instant" kimchi and is usually made in small portions. Both kimchi are refreshingly flavorful and attractive. Seedless and crunchy cucumbers with soft skins are ideal for this recipe. So-called pickling cucumbers are fine, but avoid the tough-skinned American variety with seeds.

❀ ❀ ❀

Trim the ends off the cucumbers and cut into 2-inch pieces. Carefully slice each piece vertically in half, but do not cut all the way to the bottom. In a large bowl, arrange the cucumbers upright in one layer, sliced side on top. Sprinkle the sea salt evenly over the cucumbers and let stand for about 30 minutes. Pat dry with a clean kitchen towel, being careful not to break apart the pieces. Set aside.

In another bowl, combine all the ingredients for the stuffing, reserving some sil koch'u for garnish, and toss well. Carefully stuff the mixture into each cucumber slit. Layer the cucumbers vertically, stuffed side up, in a sterilized 3-quart jar with a screw-top lid. Add a little water to the bowl to mix with the remaining bits and pieces of the stuffing, and pour over the kimchi.

Close the jar lid tight and double wrap in plastic bags. Let mature at room temperature for 2 to 3 days, then store in the refrigerator. The kimchi will stay fresh for 1 week at most.

Serve in small individual dishes, placing 2 cucumbers in each, stuffed side up. Garnish with reserved sil koch'u. Serve as a side dish.

Variation: This kimchi can also be eaten right away, before fermenting.

Stuffed Eggplant Kimchi

Kaji Sobaegi Kimchi

Serves 4
1 hour to prepare, 30 minutes to pickle, and 2 days to mature

4 Asian eggplants, about 7 inches long and 1½ inches in diameter

1 tablespoon vegetable oil

4 ounces beef ground round, or 1 tablespoon saeu chŏt (salted shrimp)

1 tablespoon soy sauce

½ teaspoon salt

½ teaspoon freshly ground black pepper

1 tablespoon sweet rice flour or all-purpose wheat flour

1 tablespoon Fresh Hot Red Pepper Sauce (page 31) or hot red pepper flakes

½ tablespoon sugar

2 cloves garlic, crushed and finely chopped

½ tablespoon freshly squeezed ginger juice or grated ginger

6 ounces Korean chives or Chinese chives, snipped in 1½-inch pieces

In paintings, eggplants are celebrated for their beautiful shape and purple color. They are also a favorite ingredient in the Korean kitchen, not only for their good looks but also for their flavor. In my childhood memory, eggplants were a sweet and crunchy raw vegetable and when cooked were delightfully chewy and deliciously meaty. Koreans regard this kimchi as a delicacy among all kimchi because of its choice ground beef and spicy ingredients (salted shrimp can be used as a substitute for the beef). Charred and pounded eggplant is used as a remedy for food poisoning in Korean folk medicine.

❀ ❀ ❀

Wash the eggplants well and pat dry with a paper towel. Using a knife, trim off the stem and cut a deep gash lengthwise (be careful not to cut all the way through) to make a pouch. Place in a steamer and steam for 3 minutes, or until the eggplants are barely wilted. Do not overcook. Drain in a colander. Wrap the eggplants in a kitchen towel one at a time and squeeze out as much liquid as possible. Set aside.

In a skillet, heat the oil over medium heat, add the meat, and sauté for 7 minutes. Season with the soy sauce, salt, and pepper. Break the meat into small crumbles with a wooden spoon and let cool. (If saeu chŏt is used, skip this step.) In a saucepan, dissolve the sweet rice flour in ½ cup water. Bring to a boil and decrease the heat to medium-low. Cook for 2 minutes, until it becomes a paste, stirring constantly with a wooden spoon. Let cool. In a bowl, combine the red pepper sauce, sugar, garlic, ginger juice, and sweet rice paste, and mix well. Add the meat (or saeu chŏt, plus the salt and pepper; omit the soy sauce) and chives, and toss gently. Divide into 4 portions.

With a spoon, gently stuff the mixture into each of the 4 eggplants, spreading it evenly. Tightly close up each eggplant, returning it to its original shape. Cut each in half, crosswise, and lay in a sterilized 3-quart jar with a screw-top lid. Add a little water to the bowl to mix with the remaining bits and pieces of stuffing, and pour over the eggplant.

Close the jar lid tight and double wrap in plastic bags. Let mature at room temperature for 2 days, then store in the refrigerator. The kimchi will stay fresh for no longer than a few days.

To serve, slice each eggplant crosswise into 1-inch pieces and place, cut side up, on a bed of fresh greens.

Stonecrops Kimchi

Tol Namul Kimchi

Serves 6 to 8

1 hour to prepare, 30 minutes to pickle, and 1 day to mature

- 1 pound stonecrop greens or Korean radish greens

- 2 tablespoons sea salt or kosher salt

- 1 tablespoon koch'u karu (hot red pepper powder)

- 2 cloves garlic, crushed and finely chopped

- $1/2$ ounce fresh ginger, peeled and grated

- $1/4$ cup all-purpose wheat flour

- 1 fresh hot red Korean pepper, cut diagonally into $1/2$-inch strips

- 1 fresh hot green Korean pepper, cut diagonally into $1/4$-inch strips

- 2 green onions, cut into 1-inch pieces

The word *tol namul* always evokes memories of my childhood. I can see clearly the tiny stonecrop herbs sprouting around our *changdokdae* (sauce crock pad) in the backyard. The tiny leaves would be growing in clusters all summer long, clinging and peeking out from among the pebbles and rocks. The kimchi made from it was so crunchy and tasty that we ate it as fast as our mother was able to make it. Stonecrops may not be available in America, even in Korean markets, but Korean radish leaves are a wonderful substitute. Our mother always made kimchi from radish greens (yŏl mu) when there were no stonecrops. She also made a horde of other kinds, lotus root (yŏngŭn) kimchi and pumpkin blossom (hobak kkot) kimchi among them. These gifts of nature's bounty in the Korean summer are all cool and delicious, but so simple to prepare, especially stonecrops kimchi.

Wash the stonecrop greens and transfer to a mixing bowl. Sprinkle with sea salt, and let stand for 1 hour. Drain and set aside. Meanwhile, in a small bowl, combine 2 cups water, koch'u karu, garlic, and ginger and let sit for 30 minutes. Strain through a cheesecloth-lined sieve, pressing out all the liquid into a small bowl; set aside. Discard the cheesecloth. In a small saucepan, dissolve the flour in 4 cups water. Bring to a boil and decrease the heat to medium-low. Cook for 2 minutes, until it becomes thin and creamy, stirring constantly with a wooden spoon, to prevent scorching. Let cool. Add the spiced liquid and mix well.

In a sterilized 3-quart jar with a screw-top lid, layer the stonecrops with alternate layers of red and green peppers and green onions. Pour the spiced liquid on top of the vegetables.

Close the jar lid tight and double wrap in plastic bags. Let mature at room temperature for 1 day, then store in the refrigerator. The kimchi will stay fresh for about 1 week.

Serve as a side dish.

Growing Up in a Korean Kitchen

Pickled Cucumbers

Oiji

Makes 6 cups

15 minutes to prepare, 10 minutes to pickle, and 3 days to mature

---

- 2 pounds pickling cucumbers, each about 3 inches long
- ¼ cup sea salt or kosher salt
- 2 green onions, white and pale green part only
- 2 cloves garlic, peeled and thinly sliced
- ½ tablespoon sil koch'u (hot red pepper threads)
- ½ cup honey or sugar
- 1½ cups rice vinegar or distilled white vinegar

The pickled cucumbers in this recipe make a chewy, crunchy side dish. They also make a zesty addition to an hors d'oeuvre tray. Be sure to select cucumbers that are uniform in size and without blemishes.

Trim the ends of the cucumbers and wash them, leaving them drenched with water. Sprinkle the salt evenly in a shallow bowl and roll the cucumbers in the salt, coating each well. Sprinkle with some fresh water and let salt for a few hours. Turn the cucumbers a few times for even salting. Drain and discard the salt water.

In a sterilized 2-quart jar with a screw-top lid, stack the cucumbers upright in two tiers, packing them in tightly. Place the green onions, garlic, and sil koch'u on top. Set aside. In a saucepan, combine the honey, rice vinegar, and 1 cup water and bring to a boil over medium-high heat. Decrease the heat to medium and boil, covered, for 5 minutes. Immediately pour the boiling liquid over the cucumbers. (This method makes the cucumbers crunchy and chewy.) Let cool. All the cucumbers must be immersed in liquid (add more vinegar if needed, but be sure to leave at least 1½ inches of space at the top of the jar).

Close the jar lid tight. Let mature at room temperature for 2 to 3 days, then store in the refrigerator. The cucumbers will stay fresh indefinitely.

Pickled Hot Green and Red Peppers

Koch'uji

Makes 6 cups

15 minutes to prepare, 10 minutes to pickle, and 3 days to mature

---

2 pounds whole jalapeño or hot red Korean peppers (about 18), each about 3 inches long

2 cloves garlic, peeled and thinly sliced

1 walnut half, thinly slivered

1 tablespoon coarse sea salt or kosher salt

4 tablespoons honey, or 2 tablespoons sugar

1½ cups rice vinegar or distilled white vinegar

The annual red hot pepper harvest is a very serious national matter, especially as peppers are vital ingredients for winter kimchi making. Naturally sun-dried hot red peppers are reputed to be superior to commercially dried. In autumn, the whole Korean landscape is ablaze with a blanket of red—on thatched roofs, in front yards, on side road pavements, almost anywhere one can find an open sunny space.

These pickles and Pickled Whole Garlic (page 111), are the two most important relishes in the Korean pantry. Pickled peppers can be eaten whole, served on an appetizer or relish tray along with capers and olives. They can also be thinly sliced, finely diced, or roughly chopped and tossed into any noodle or fried rice dish. The exhilarating touch of sweet, sour, and hot flavors will light up any dish. You will be pleasantly surprised to discover how versatile these Korean relishes can be. In America, I use jalapeño peppers for their uniform size, unlike the native Korean variety. Korean peppers, however, have a sturdier texture, and in the authentic recipe for Radish Kimchi Soup (page 101), only pickled Korean peppers will do. For this recipe, be sure to buy unblemished peppers with healthy stems.

Wash the peppers and pat dry well. In a sterilized 2-quart jar with a screw-top lid, stack the peppers in two tiers, stems up, packing them in tightly. Place the garlic and walnut on top.

In a saucepan, combine the salt, honey, rice vinegar, and 1 cup water. Bring to a boil and boil for a few minutes. Immediately pour the boiling liquid over the hot peppers. Let cool. All the peppers must be immersed in liquid (add more vinegar if needed, but be sure to leave at least 1½ inches of space at the top of the jar).

Close the jar lid tight. Let mature at room temperature for 2 to 3 days, then store in the refrigerator. The peppers will stay fresh indefinitely.

Pickled Whole Garlic

Manŭl Changatchi

Makes 6 cups
15 minutes to prepare, 10 minutes to pickle, and 25 days to mature

---

- 1 pound whole spring garlic, each about 2^1/$_2$ inches in diameter
- 2 cups rice vinegar or distilled white vinegar
- 2 cups soy sauce
- 4 tablespoons honey, or 2 tablespoons sugar
- 2 tablespoons ch'ŏngju (rice wine) or vermouth

This dish uses young, tender garlic harvested in springtime. In Korean cuisine, it is as versatile as Pickled Hot Green and Red Peppers (page 110). It makes a great appetizer or side dish, and it is also an interesting garnish for any dish. Mince one or two heads of pickled garlic and add it to any sauce. A tiny bit will heighten the flavor of fried rice, noodles, and many other dishes, including meat dishes. Buy whole, unblemished bulbs of young garlic, about 2^1/$_2$ inches in diameter. The neat, six-sectioned Korean variety, *yuk tchok*, is the best.

Discard the outer skin of the garlic, but leave the inner skin intact. Do not separate the cloves. Wash the garlic and pat dry well. In a sterilized 3-quart jar with a screw-top lid, tightly pack the whole garlic bulbs. Add the rice vinegar. All the garlic must be immersed (add more vinegar if needed, but be sure to leave at least 1^1/$_2$ inches of space at the top of the jar).

Close the jar lid tight. Let mature at room temperature for about 15 days. Pour out and discard the vinegar. In a bowl, combine the soy sauce, honey, and ch'ŏngju and stir until the honey has dissolved. Pour this mixture into the jar, making sure that all the garlic is immersed (add more soy sauce, if needed, but be sure to leave at least 1^1/$_2$ inches of space at the top of the jar).

Close the jar lid tight. Let mature at room temperature for 10 days more. Store in the refrigerator. The garlic will stay fresh indefinitely.

To serve, cut the whole garlic crosswise into thin pieces, revealing its flowery pattern. Serve as a side dish or relish, or use as a garnish.

Pickled Ginger

Saenggang Changatchi

Makes 2 cups
15 minutes to prepare, 15 minutes to pickle, and 1 week to mature

---

- 2 pounds ginger, peeled, washed, and sliced paper-thin
- 1 cup rice vinegar or distilled white vinegar
- 4 tablespoons honey, or 2 tablespoons sugar
- 2 tablespoons ch'ŏngju (rice wine) or vermouth

Pickled ginger makes a good side dish or relish and a delightful appetizer. It's especially good with Seaweed Wrapped Rice (page 54).

In a sterilized 2-quart jar with a screw-top lid, layer the ginger in a pinwheel fashion, stacking one layer on top of another. In a bowl, combine the rice vinegar, honey, and ch'ŏngju, stirring until the honey has dissolved, and pour into the jar.

Close the jar lid tight. Let mature at room temperature for 1 week, by which time the vinegar and ginger pieces will turn pale pink. Store in the refrigerator. The ginger will stay fresh indefinitely.

Side Dishes

✳ Fresh Salad and Vegetable Dishes

The Korean peninsula is blessed with rich soil and an ideal four-season climate. So it is no wonder that Mother Nature's gifts grow abundantly in every nook and cranny of the country. Even the surrounding waters are teeming with sea greens. In my childhood, meat was rare and expensive, so fresh vegetables were always a mainstay at our meal table. We loved our greens, herbs, and flowers—roots, stems, and all.

In Korea, creativity knows no bounds when it comes to preparing vegetables. In addition to being served fresh and with several degrees of spiciness, vegetables are treated to many cooking methods in the Korean kitchen. The most frequently used method is quickly pan-frying or sautéing the vegetable briefly in vegetable oil with a light seasoning, a technique called *pokkŭm*. While this technique may sound similar to stir-frying, it is quite different, as neither a wok nor a large amount of heavy oil is used. Another common cooking technique, called *tetch'im*, involves briefly blanching in acidulated water. When vegetables are blanched, few nutrients are lost and the vegetables retain maximum texture, flavor, and color. Salt curing, *chŏlim*, is another remarkable technique perfected in the Korean kitchen, in which liquid is extracted from vegetables, firming up their texture and locking in their original flavor. After that, a mixture of spices is introduced and the vegetables are fermented, creating a unique and flavorful character. Kimchi is the prime example of this technique.

The recipes in this chapter are easy to prepare and very nutritious, and all make tasty side dishes or, mixed in a bowl of rice, delightful vegetarian one-dish meals.

Note: To revive the freshness of vegetables, immerse them in ice cold water for a few minutes just before cooking.

(above) Bamboo shoots, chive stems, and flowers

(opposite) Watermelon, honey melon, grapes, leaf lettuce, summer squash, hot peppers, eggplant, crown daisies

Leaf Lettuce Salad

Sangch'u Kŏtjŏri

Serves 4
30 minutes to prepare

- 1 pound leaf lettuce
- ½ tablespoon soy sauce
- 1 green onion, white and pale green part only, finely minced
- 1 clove garlic, crushed and finely chopped
- 1 tablespoon ch'ŏngju (rice wine) or vermouth
- 2 tablespoons rice vinegar or distilled white vinegar
- 1 tablespoon saeu chŏt (salted shrimp) or myŏlch'i chŏt (salted anchovy)
- 1 tablespoon freshly squeezed lemon juice
- 1 tablespoon sesame oil
- 1 tablespoon toasted sesame seeds
- 1 teaspoon koch'u karu (hot red pepper powder) or hot red pepper flakes
- Pinch of freshly ground black pepper

This refreshing garden salad, with its distinctive and unique flavor, complements most entrees. Use your favorite lettuce, or try tender napa cabbage leaves, crown daisies, wild sesame leaves (perilla), or combine one or more into a refreshing mixed salad. The dressing for this salad somewhat resembles Italian or French dressing.

❁ ❁ ❁

Prepare the lettuce several hours ahead of time. Wash several times in cold water, and dry with a clean, dry kitchen towel. Wrap in a paper towel and place in a plastic bag. Chill in the refrigerator.

In a large bowl, combine the remaining ingredients and mix well. Add the lettuce and toss lightly. Serve immediately as a salad course. Or, mix with hot rice for a refreshing rice-salad dish.

Green Onion Salad

P'a Kŏtjŏri

Serves 4 to 6
30 minutes to prepare

---

1 tablespoon finely chopped saeu chŏt (salted shrimp) or sea salt

$1/2$ tablespoon sugar

1 tablespoon ch'ŏngju (rice wine) or vermouth

1 clove garlic, crushed and finely chopped

$1/2$ tablespoon koch'u karu (hot red pepper powder) or hot red pepper flakes, plus a pinch for garnish

1 tablespoon sesame oil

1 tablespoon toasted sesame seeds

Pinch of freshly ground black pepper

12 ounces green onions

This salad is a Korean favorite. It is refreshing and very easy to make, but the green onions tend to collapse easily, even before a whiff of spices is added. Thus, the Korean colloquial expression *p'a kimchi ga toeda* ("as tired as green onion kimchi").

In a bowl, combine all the ingredients, except the green onions, and mix well. Snip or cut the green onions into 2-inch pieces, and reserve some for garnish. Add the green onions to the bowl and toss lightly. Transfer to a serving bowl and garnish with the reserved green onions and pinch of koch'u karu. Serve at the center of the table with other side dishes.

Variations: Use chives in place of the green onions to make the tasty Chive Salad (Puch'u Kŏtjŏri). In season, wild rocamboles, a cousin of green onions and chives, also make a flavorful salad.

Cucumber Salad

Oi Saengch'ae

Serves 4 to 6
20 minutes to prepare

3 pounds seedless cucumbers, sliced into paper-thin disks

1½ tablespoons sea salt or kosher salt

½ tablespoon koch'u karu (hot red pepper powder) or hot red pepper flakes

½ cup rice vinegar or distilled white vinegar

1 tablespoon ch'ŏngju (rice wine) or vermouth

2 tablespoons sugar

2 tablespoons freshly squeezed lemon juice

1 clove garlic, crushed and finely chopped

2 green onions, white and pale green part only, finely minced

2 walnut halves, finely chopped, or 1 tablespoon slivered almonds

2 tablespoons sesame oil

1 tablespoon toasted sesame seeds

½ tablespoon freshly ground black pepper

2 tablespoons finely chopped parsley

1 tablespoon sil koch'u (hot red pepper threads) or hot red pepper flakes, for garnish

Oi saengch'ae is a standard Korean side dish and one of the most refreshing. This unique salad goes well with any entree. Prepare it several hours ahead of time or, better yet, prepare it a day ahead and refrigerate. Chilling greatly enhances the flavor.

Place the cucumbers in a large bowl and sprinkle evenly with sea salt. Let sit for 15 minutes, then wrap the cucumbers in a paper towel and squeeze out as much liquid as possible. Set aside. In the same bowl, combine the remaining ingredients, except the sil koch'u and reserving 1 tablespoon of parsley for garnish. Mix well. Add the cucumbers and toss well. Cover and refrigerate.

To serve, transfer the cucumbers to an attractive glass serving dish and garnish with the sil koch'u and reserved parsley.

Chilled Radish Salad

Mu Saengch'ae

Serves 4 to 6
20 minutes to prepare

1 pound Korean radishes or daikon, peeled and cut into long matchsticks

1 Korean or Asian pear, peeled, cored, and cut into matchsticks, or 1 tablespoon freshly squeezed lemon juice

¹/₂ cup shucked oysters (about 8 ounces)

1 tablespoon koch'u karu (hot red pepper powder)

¹/₂ tablespoon saeu chŏt (salted shrimp) or myŏlch'i chŏt (salted anchovy)

¹/₂ tablespoon soy sauce

3 tablespoons rice vinegar or distilled white vinegar

1 tablespoon ch'ŏngju (rice wine) or vermouth

1 tablespoon sugar

1 clove garlic, crushed and finely chopped

2 tablespoons finely chopped walnuts

1 tablespoon freshly squeezed ginger juice

2 tablespoons sesame oil

Pinch of salt

Pinch of freshly ground black pepper

3 green onions, white and pale green part only, finely minced

1 tablespoon toasted sesame seeds

Pinch of sil koch'u (hot red pepper threads) or hot red pepper flakes, for garnish

This salad is a staple side dish in Korean homes and public eateries. Although Japanese daikon can be used, the sweet and peppery Korean radish is preferred—and be sure not to use Western radishes. This energetic and refreshing salad goes well with Fired Beef (page 179).

In a bowl, place the radishes, pear, oysters, koch'u karu, and saeu chŏt and toss well. Set aside. In a small bowl, combine the remaining ingredients, except the sil koch'u and reserving some green onions and sesame seeds for garnish. Mix well. Add to the bowl with the radishes and toss well. Refrigerate for 2 to 3 hours, until well chilled. Transfer the radishes to a chilled glass serving dish. Garnish with the reserved green onions, sesame seeds, and sil koch'u. Serve at the center of the table along with other side dishes.

Fatsia Shoots Salad

Tŭrŭp Saengch'ae

Serves 4
15 minutes to prepare

1 pound fatsia shoots

¹/₂ cup Vinegar and Hot Red Pepper Sauce (page 29)

Cooking with wild herbs (san namul) is an integral part of Korean food culture. They thrive everywhere on Korean soil, but today, because of the demand, most found in the market are grown in hothouses. Popular Korean herbs, often available in Korean markets in America, that may be substituted for herbs in this book's recipes include: amaranth (pirŭm), plantain (chilgaengi), squill (murŭt), prickly ash (sanch'o), wild astor (ch'wi), coltfoot (mŏwi), castor (ajukkari), beachnut (sangsuri), taro (t'oran), wild grapes (mŏru), berries (tarae), and rose hips (porittŏk).

Fatsia shoots are wild, seasonal, silky smooth delicacies, much admired by Korean gourmands. In the spring, these stunning forest green plants, neatly plaited into straw braids, adorn every market in Korea. In my childhood, fortunately, one of our relatives from the countryside regularly supplied us with seasonal fatsia shoots. Fatsia shoots are not common in Korean markets in the United States today, but more than likely they will find their way here in the near future. When they do, you can try this very simple recipe.

In a stockpot, make 4 cups of acidulated water (page 10). Wash fatsia shoots, then add to the water and blanch for no more than 30 seconds, until they turn bright green and are barely wilted. Rinse a couple of times in ice cold water and drain in a colander. Pat dry with a paper towel. Combine with red pepper sauce, tossing lightly. Serve immediately as an appetizer or side dish.

Variations: Fresh fatsia shoots are also delicious raw, simply dipped in the red pepper sauce. They are also good with Vinegar Soy Sauce (page 28).

Bellflower Root Salad

Toraji Saengch'ae

Serves 4
20 minutes to prepare

8 ounces dried bellflower roots

1 tablespoon koch'ujang (hot red pepper paste)

1/2 tablespoon koch'u karu (hot red pepper powder)

1 tablespoon soy sauce

2 tablespoons rice vinegar or distilled white vinegar

1 tablespoon sugar

1 tablespoon ch'ŏngju (rice wine) or vermouth

1/2 tablespoon sesame oil

1 tablespoon toasted sesame seeds

Pinch of salt

Pinch of freshly ground black pepper

Most of the old Korean folk ballads I know are drenched in *han manŭn insaeng,* "life is nothing but regrets and laments." The folk song titled "Toraji" is an exception. Koreans love singing the happy bellflower roots–gathering song. In praise of toraji, the lyrics begin, "Toraji! Toraji! White Toraji! In the deep, deep forest, even after digging only one or two roots, my basket is over-flowing." Youngsters grow up singing and dancing to this plant and eating it too. Seeing a field covered with a blanket of bell-shaped toraji flowers, some snow white, others a shocking purple, is a beautiful sight.

In the Korean kitchen, toraji is considered one of the most important herbal roots. It is served on its own as a tasty side dish, included in simple dishes such as soups or pancakes, or in more complex ones such as pibimbap and chapch'ae. It makes a delicious candied dessert, too, as I remember from my childhood. The following recipe is one of the most popular dishes in the Korean kitchen. Today toraji is sold both fresh and dried. The following recipe is made with the dried version, as it is more readily available. It is simple to cook this crunchy mountain vegetable root.

Soak the bellflower roots overnight in plenty of hot water to soften. Rinse and drain in a colander. Split each root, by hand, as thin as possible. Wrap the bellflower roots in a clean, dry kitchen towel and squeeze out as much liquid as possible. Set aside. In the same bowl, combine the remaining ingredients, reserving 1/2 tablespoon sesame seeds for garnish. Add the bellflower roots and mix well. Cover and refrigerate for 2 to 3 hours, until well chilled. Transfer to a serving bowl and garnish with the reserved sesame seeds. Serve at the center of the table along with other side dishes. It may also be served at room temperature, if desired.

Variations: To make two other well-known chilled herbal root salads, Fresh Ginseng Root Salad (Susam Saengch'ae) and Aralia Root Salad (Tŏdŏk Saengch'ae), reduce the amount of koch'ujang and koch'u karu, so as not to overpower the ginseng or aralia roots. Both may be torn by hand, but aralia roots must first be pounded to soften them. With their exquisite flavor and stunning fragrance, both are more expensive and considered finer than bellflower roots.

Seasoned Soybean Sprouts

K'ong Namul

Serves 4 to 6
20 minutes to prepare

---

1 pound soybean sprouts, tails trimmed

1 tablespoon soy sauce

1 clove garlic, crushed and finely chopped

2 tablespoons sesame oil

Pinch of salt

Pinch of freshly ground black pepper

2 green onions, white and pale green part only, finely minced

1 teaspoon toasted sesame seeds

1 teaspoon sil koch'u (hot red pepper threads) or hot red pepper flakes, for garnish

In my childhood, soybean sprouts were a daily staple. They appeared at every meal, right next to the bowl of kimchi. All the children of my generation used to sing, "Soybean sprouts at breakfast, soybean sprouts at lunch, and more soybean sprouts at suppertime." So accustomed to their look are we that musical notes are called *k'ong namul taegari*, "soybean sprout heads."

Mounds of soybean sprouts can be found in grocery stores, at market stalls, everywhere—a testimonial to how we live among them. Economical and fast growing (faster than Jack's beanstalk), soybean sprouts are added to every dish imaginable. This basic side dish is easy to fix and delicious.

❀ ❀ ❀

Wash the soybean sprouts a few times and drain in a colander. Place the sprouts in a stockpot with $1/2$ cup of cold water and cover tightly. Boil over high heat for 2 minutes, until fragrant steam appears. Do not lift the cover during boiling, or the soybean sprouts will have an unpleasant bean taste. Keep the boiling time to a minimum (this preserves the vitamin C). Drain in a colander.

In a bowl, combine the remaining ingredients, except the sil koch'u and reserving some green onion and sesame seeds for garnish. Mix well. Add the soybean sprouts and toss well. Transfer to a serving bowl. Garnish with the reserved green onions, sesame seeds, and sil koch'u. Serve at room temperature at the center of the table along with other side dishes.

Note: Country folks use toenjang or koch'ujang instead of soy sauce. It's so hot, but so very tasty!

Variations: In the summer, Koreans love to eat this dish chilled instead of at room temperature; the chilled dish is called Chilled Soybean Sprouts (K'ong Namul Naengch'ae). For another summertime variation, make a refreshing Soybean Sprout Soup (K'ong Namul Naengguk) by adding well-chilled clear stock or water to the seasoned soybean sprouts.

Growing Up in a Korean Kitchen

Seasoned Mung Bean Sprouts

Nokdu Namul

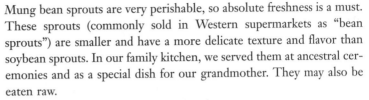

Serves 4 to 6

20 minutes to prepare and cook

---

1 pound mung bean sprouts, tails trimmed

¹/₂ tablespoon soy sauce

1 tablespoon rice vinegar or distilled white vinegar

1 tablespoon sesame oil

1 clove garlic, crushed and finely chopped

Pinch of salt

Pinch of freshly ground black pepper

1 green onion, white and pale green part only, finely minced

1 teaspoon toasted sesame seeds

Mung bean sprouts are very perishable, so absolute freshness is a must. These sprouts (commonly sold in Western supermarkets as "bean sprouts") are smaller and have a more delicate texture and flavor than soybean sprouts. In our family kitchen, we served them at ancestral ceremonies and as a special dish for our grandmother. They may also be eaten raw.

Wash the mung bean sprouts a few times and drain in a colander. Place the sprouts in a stockpot with ¹/₂ cup of cold water and cover tightly. Boil over high heat for no more than 1 minute, until fragrant steam appears. Drain in a colander.

In a bowl, combine the remaining ingredients, reserving some green onion and sesame seeds for garnish. Mix well. Add the mung bean sprouts and toss well. Transfer to a serving bowl. Garnish with the reserved green onions and sesame seeds. Serve at room temperature or well chilled at the center of the table, along with other side dishes.

Variation: Another tasty combination is Mung Bean Spouts and Bamboo Shoots (Chuksun Namul). Use 6 ounces mung bean sprouts and 10 ounces bamboo shoots in place of the mung bean sprouts. Follow the directions as above.

Seasoned Eggplant

Kaji Namul

Serves 4
30 minutes to prepare

4 Asian eggplants, each about
7 inches long and 1½ inches
in diameter

2 tablespoons soy sauce

1 tablespoon ch'ŏngju
(rice wine) or vermouth

1 clove garlic, crushed and finely
chopped

1 green onion, white and pale
green part only, finely minced

1 tablespoon sesame oil

1 tablespoon toasted sesame
seeds

Pinch of salt

Pinch of freshly ground black
pepper

1 teaspoon sil koch'u (hot red
pepper threads) or hot red
pepper flakes, plus a pinch for
garnish

Eggplants are grown in every Korean vegetable patch. The sweet, deep
purple Korean eggplant is similar to other Asian varieties.

✿ ✿ ✿

Slice each eggplant lengthwise into quarters. In a steamer, bring 1 cup
of water to boil, and steam the eggplants for about 7 minutes. Using a
slotted spoon, transfer the eggplant to a colander and cool. Tear or
slice each piece into thin, bite-size strips. Wrap the eggplant in a paper
towel and squeeze out as much liquid as possible. Set aside.

In a bowl large enough to hold the eggplant, combine the remaining
ingredients and mix well. Add the eggplant and toss well. Transfer to
a serving bowl and garnish with a pinch of sil koch'u. Serve at the center of the table along with other side dishes.

Variation: In summer, Chilled Eggplant Soup (Kaji Naengguk) is very
popular. Follow the recipe above, then simply add 2 cups cold water, a
few drops of soy sauce, 3 tablespoons cider vinegar or distilled white
vinegar, and ice cubes. It makes a refreshing instant summer soup.

Seasoned Spinach

Sigŭmch'i Namul

Serves 4 to 6
30 minutes to prepare

- 2 pounds tender leafy spinach, well washed
- 2 tablespoons soy sauce
- 1 clove garlic, crushed and finely chopped
- 1 green onion, white and pale green part only, finely minced
- 1 tablespoon sesame oil
- 1 tablespoon toasted sesame seeds
- Pinch of salt
- Pinch of freshly ground black pepper
- Pinch of sil koch'u (hot red pepper threads) or hot red pepper flakes, for garnish

Spinach is almost as important as soybean sprouts in the Korean kitchen. Although it is not as ubiquitous as soybean sprouts, nutritious and versatile spinach is present at most meals. It is one of the vital ingredients for Rice with Vegetables and Meat (page 50) and Sweet Potato Noodles with Meat and Mixed Vegetables (page 88).

❁ ❁ ❁

In a stockpot, make 4 quarts of acidulated water (page 10). Bring to a boil and add the spinach all at once. Blanch for no more than 10 seconds, or until it turns bright green and is barely wilted. Quickly plunge into ice cold water to stop the cooking, and drain in a colander. Wrap in a paper towel and squeeze out as much liquid as possible. Transfer to a cutting board and cut into bite-size pieces.

In a bowl large enough to hold the spinach, combine the remaining ingredients, except the sil koch'u. Mix well. Add the spinach and toss well. Transfer to a serving bowl and garnish with the sil koch'u. Serve at room temperature at the center of the table with other side dishes.

Seasoned Cabbage Hearts

Paech'usok Namul

Serves 4
20 minutes to prepare and cook

1 large napa cabbage
(about 3 pounds)

4 tablespoons soy sauce

½ tablespoon ch'ŏngju (rice wine)
or vermouth

1 tablespoon rice vinegar or
distilled white vinegar

2 cloves garlic, crushed and finely
chopped

½ tablespoon sesame oil

Pinch of salt

Pinch of freshly ground black
pepper

1 green onion, white and pale
green part only, finely minced

½ tablespoon toasted sesame
seeds

1 cup Clear Chicken Stock (page 59)
or Anchovy Stock (page 60)

Pinch of sil koch'u (hot red pepper
threads) or hot red pepper
flakes, for garnish

Effortless to make, cooked napa cabbage hearts have an exquisite sweet and nutty flavor. They may remind some of braised Belgian endive. This dish goes very well with any entree, Asian or Western.

Wash the cabbage and peel off the outer leaves until the pale yellow heart appears. (A 3-pound cabbage will have about a 1-pound heart.) Reserve the leaves for other uses. With a sharp knife, cut the heart in half lengthwise and set aside. In a bowl, combine the remaining ingredients, except the sil koch'u and reserving some green onion and sesame seeds for garnish. Mix well.

Place the cabbage halves in a skillet, cut side up, and evenly pour the seasoned stock over them. Bring to a boil over medium-high heat, then decrease the heat to medium-low. Cover and simmer for 10 minutes, or until the cabbage is cooked to the desired doneness (it should still be crisp).

Transfer the cabbage to a cutting board and cut each piece in half lengthwise. Place on a serving plate and drizzle the juice left in the skillet over the cabbage. Garnish with the reserved green onion, sesame seeds, and sil koch'u. Serve as a side dish.

Variations: Use shredded cabbage instead of a whole cabbage heart, but reduce the cooking time to 7 minutes. Shredded Korean radishes and fresh and dried radish greens can be braised in the same way, but the cooking time varies depending on the vegetable. Fresh radishes should be cooked for 15 minutes, dry ones for 30 minutes.

Seasoned Summer Squash

Hobak Namul

Serves 4
20 minutes to prepare and cook

2 pounds summer squash, about 1½ inches in diameter, sliced crosswise into ¼-inch disks

2 tablespoons vegetable oil

1 tablespoon soy sauce

½ tablespoon saeu chŏt (salted shrimp) or myŏlch'i chŏt (salted anchovy)

1 tablespoon ch'ŏngju (rice wine) or vermouth

1 green onion, white and pale green part only, finely minced

2 cloves garlic, crushed and finely chopped

1 tablespoon toasted sesame seeds

1 tablespoon sesame oil

½ tablespoon koch'u karu (hot red pepper powder)

In the Korean kitchen, summer squash is presented in a number of ways. This pan-fried version makes a popular dish that goes especially well with seafood.

Place the squash on a bamboo tray to air-dry; set aside. In a large non-stick skillet, heat ½ tablespoon of vegetable oil over medium-high heat until almost smoking. Quickly place about one-fourth of the squash in the skillet and cook for 3 minutes, or until the edges turn bright green and begin to curl. Flip them over and cook for 2 minutes. Turn only once. (The squash will be a pale yellow with light brown specks.) Transfer to a bamboo tray to cool. Repeat three times with the remaining vegetable oil and squash. In a bowl large enough to hold the squash, combine the remaining ingredients and mix well. Add the squash and toss well.

Transfer to a serving bowl or arrange the squash on a platter in a pinwheel or fan pattern. Drizzle any seasoning remaining in the bowl over the squash and serve at room temperature.

Sautéed Cucumbers

Oi Pokkŭm

Serves 4 to 6
30 minutes to prepare and cook

- 3 pounds seedless cucumbers, sliced into near-paper-thin disks
- 1 tablespoon sea salt or kosher salt
- 2 tablespoons vegetable oil
- 3 cloves garlic, crushed and finely chopped
- 2 green onions, white and pale green part only, finely minced
- 1 tablespoon ch'ŏngju (rice wine) or vermouth
- 1 tablespoon sesame oil
- 1/2 tablespoon toasted sesame seeds
- 1 teaspoon sil koch'u (hot red pepper threads) or koch'u karu (hot red pepper powder), plus a pinch for garnish
- 1/2 tablespoon pine nuts, coarsely chopped
- Salt
- Freshly ground black pepper

This very popular and beautiful side dish will complement almost any entree. It is a good example of how Korean cooking can transform a common ingredient into a visually pleasing and uniquely tasty dish.

Place the cucumbers in a bowl and sprinkle with the sea salt. Toss well and let sit for 10 minutes. Wrap the cucumbers in a clean, dry kitchen towel and squeeze out as much liquid as possible. Set aside.

In a skillet, heat the vegetable oil over medium heat until hot. Add the garlic and sauté for 2 minutes. Increase the heat to medium-high, add the cucumbers, green onions, and ch'ŏngju and sauté for 2 minutes, until the cucumbers turn bright green and are very fragrant. Remove from the heat and immediately add the sesame oil, sesame seeds, sil koch'u, and pine nuts, reserving a few pine nuts for garnish. Toss well. Taste and adjust the seasoning with salt and pepper if needed. Let cool.

Transfer the cucumbers to a serving plate or bowl. Garnish with the reserved pine nuts and pinch of sil koch'u. Serve at room temperature at the center of the table along with other side dishes.

Variations: Many vegetables, such as summer squash, gourds, or eggplant, can be prepared in the same way. To add extra flavor to summer squash, add 1 cup chopped scallops or clam meat in the last 2 minutes of cooking. Serve with rice. Scrumptious!

Growing Up in a Korean Kitchen

Sautéed Spring Garlic

Manŭl Ip' Pokkŭm

Serves 4 to 6
20 minutes to prepare and cook

---

1 pound whole spring garlic, leaves and stems included

2 tablespoons vegetable oil

1 green onion, white and pale green part only, finely minced

1 walnut half, finely chopped

1 tablespoon ch'ŏngju (rice wine) or vermouth

2 tablespoons toasted sesame seeds

1 tablespoon soy sauce

2 tablespoons sesame oil

Salt

Freshly ground black pepper

In late spring, Korean gardens are filled with the fragrance of lilac, but in the markets, it is not the scent of lilac but the pungent odor of garlic that permeates the air. The first crop of tender young garlic—bulbs, leaves, stems, and all—are hawked everywhere. What a rich and delicious dish these "stinking roses" turn out to be. Even when sautéed alone with sesame oil or seasoned with just salt and pepper, they are simply delicious. It goes well with any entree.

❀ ❀ ❀

Cut the garlic into bite-size pieces. In a skillet, heat the vegetable oil over medium-high heat until very hot. Add the garlic and sauté for 7 minutes, until it turns bright green and fragrant. Add the green onion, walnut, ch'ŏngju, and sesame seeds, reserving some sesame seeds for garnish. Sauté for 3 minutes. Stir in the soy sauce and sesame oil and immediately remove from the heat. Adjust the seasoning with salt and pepper, if needed, and garnish with the reserved sesame seeds. Serve at room temperature as a side dish.

Variation: Substitute whole chives—leaves, stems, buds, flowers, and all—for the garlic.

To think of our family kitchen is to remember the ever-present sight and smell of pungent garlic. In a dark corner, standing faithfully, would be our heavily garlic-stained granite mortar and its wooden pestle, waiting to pound mounds of garlic. One hundred garlic bulbs, *hanjŏp* by Korean count, were neatly braided on rice straw rope and hung to dry outside the kitchen door or under the eaves or wherever a cool, dry shade could be found—becoming one of a permanent and beautiful part of the Korean landscape. Koreans love to eat raw whole garlic cloves dipped in toenjang (fermented soybean paste).

Sautéed Cabbage Kimchi with Bean Curd and Pork

Kimchi Pokkŭm

Serves 4 to 6
30 minutes to prepare and cook

---

2 tablespoons ch'ŏngju (rice wine) or vermouth

½ tablespoon freshly squeezed ginger juice

Pinch of salt

Pinch of freshly ground black pepper

8 ounces lean pork or chicken fillet, sliced into thin strips

1 tablespoon vegetable oil

5 cloves garlic, crushed and finely chopped

2 large sweet green onions, or 4 green onions, sliced diagonally into thin strips

2 cups Whole Cabbage Kimchi (page 97), stem part only and without stuffing, sliced into ¼-inch strips

½ pound napa cabbage, firm stem part only, sliced into ¼ by 2½-inch strips

1 pound medium-firm bean curd, sliced into thin strips

½ pound summer squash, cut into ¼ by 1½-inch strips

1 fresh hot green Korean pepper or jalapeño pepper, seeded, deribbed, and cut into threads

1 fresh hot red Korean pepper, or ½ red bell pepper, seeded, deribbed, and cut into threads

1 tablespoon soy sauce

½ tablespoon toenjang (fermented soybean paste)

½ tablespoon koch'ujang (hot red pepper paste)

2 tablespoons sesame oil

1 tablespoon toasted sesame seeds, for garnish

In this dish, the flamboyant nature of kimchi is tamed by the addition of other fresh ingredients, making it a good introduction to the world of kimchi. It is a tasty union of cabbage kimchi, pork, and unassuming bean curd, all sautéed with basic Korean spices. The best-quality whole cabbage kimchi is a must for this recipe.

❁ ❁ ❁

In a bowl, combine the ch'ŏngju, ginger juice, salt, and pepper. Add the pork, toss well, and set aside. In a skillet, heat the vegetable oil over medium heat until hot. Add the garlic and sauté for 2 minutes, until fragrant. Increase the heat to medium-high and add the pork and half the green onions. Sauté for 5 minutes, until the pork is cooked through. Add the kimchi and sauté for 5 minutes more. Add the napa cabbage, bean curd, squash, peppers, and remaining green onions, reserving some of the green onions for garnish. Stir lightly, cover, and steam-cook for 5 minutes. (No liquid is needed, as the cabbage and bean curd will release some juice.) Uncover and make a well at the center of the skillet. Add the soy sauce, toenjang, koch'ujang, and 1 tablespoon sesame oil and stir. Sauté for 2 minutes, uncovered. Add the remaining 1 tablespoon sesame oil, stir well, and immediately remove from the heat.

Transfer to a serving dish and garnish with the reserved green onions and sesame seeds. Serve at the center of the table with other side dishes.

Sautéed Fernbracken

Kosari Namul

Serves 4 to 6

30 minutes to prepare (longer if using dried fernbracken) and 15 minutes to cook

1 pound prepared (wet) fernbracken, or 3 ounces dried fernbracken

1 tablespoon vegetable oil

6 cloves garlic, crushed and finely chopped

4 ounces lean beef ground round

1 green onion, white and pale green part only, finely minced

2 tablespoons soy sauce

1 tablespoon sesame oil

1 tablespoon toasted sesame seeds

Salt

Freshly ground black pepper

½ tablespoon sil koch'u (hot red pepper threads), for garnish

Ferns, along with mushrooms, have the most mysterious flavors and tastes of all the mountain vegetables. When we children smelled the earthy scent of kosari boiling, we knew that an ancestor ceremony and good food were coming. The union of the mushroomlike fern and choice beef cooked with garlic, sesame oil, and soy sauce make this dish one of the tastiest the Korean kitchen can offer. Fresh kosari is the best choice, but if it is unavailable, use reconstituted dried kosari.

❀ ❀ ❀

If using prepared fernbracken, rinse once in fresh water, wrap in a kitchen towel, and squeeze out as much water as possible. Trim and discard any tough ends. To reconstitute dried fernbracken, in a heavy 5-quart stockpot, add 3 quarts of cold water and the fernbracken. Bring to a boil over high heat, then decrease the heat to medium-low. Simmer gently for about 45 minutes, until the stems are tender, but still chewy. After 30 minutes, check occasionally for tenderness. (Do not overcook. Overcooked kosari is mushy.) Rinse several times with water until the dark-brown water is clear. Let soak in cold water for at least 3 hours or as long as overnight. The fernbracken will expand to at least three times its original volume and weigh about 1 pound. Drain in a colander and cut each stem in half, trimming and discarding any tough lower stem parts. Wrap it in a paper towel and squeeze dry.

In a skillet, heat the vegetable oil over medium-high heat. Add the garlic and sauté for 2 minutes, until fragrant. Add the beef and sauté for 2 minutes, breaking the meat into small crumbs with a wooden spoon. Add the fernbracken, green onion, and soy sauce and sauté for 7 minutes. Add the sesame oil and sesame seeds, reserving some sesame seeds for garnish. Toss well and immediately remove from the heat. Taste and adjust the seasoning with salt and pepper if needed.

Transfer the fernbracken to a large serving platter. Garnish with the reserved sesame seeds and sil koch'u. Serve at the center of the table along with other side dishes.

Variations: Dried sweet potatoes and taro leaves and stems can be prepared in the same way.

Sautéed P'yogo Mushrooms

P'yogo Pŏsŏt Pokkŭm

Serves 4

25 minutes to prepare and cook

10 ounces fresh p'yogo (shiitake) mushrooms

Marinade for Mushrooms

1 tablespoon ch'ŏngju (rice wine) or vermouth

½ tablespoon soy sauce

1 clove garlic, crushed and finely chopped

1 green onion, white and pale green part only, finely minced

1 tablespoon sesame oil

Pinch of salt

Pinch of freshly ground black pepper

1 tablespoon vegetable oil

5 cloves garlic, crushed and finely chopped

½ tablespoon soy sauce

4 ounces ground beef tenderloin

5 green onions, white and pale green part only, finely minced

1 tablespoon sesame oil

½ tablespoon toasted sesame seeds

Salt

Freshly ground black pepper

½ tablespoon pine nuts, coarsely chopped, for garnish

½ tablespoon sil koch'u (hot red pepper threads), for garnish

Scientific studies indicate that p'yogo mushrooms, or shiitakes as they are commonly known, may be useful in combating several kinds of cancer. But taste alone would be reason enough to serve them. The following recipe is one of the all-time popular dishes made in the Korean kitchen. It is luxuriously rich and quick and easy to prepare.

Pat the mushrooms with a clean, damp kitchen towel. Trim the stems and discard. Slice the caps into ¼-inch slivers. In a bowl, combine the marinade ingredients and mix well. Add the mushrooms and let marinate for 15 minutes.

In a nonreactive skillet, heat the vegetable oil over medium heat until moderately hot. Add the garlic and sauté for 2 minutes, until golden and fragrant. Add the mushrooms and soy sauce. Sauté over medium heat for 5 minutes, or until the flavors mingle well and the mushrooms become soft, but not dry. Add the beef and 2 of the green onions. Sauté for 3 minutes, or until the meat is cooked through, but moist. Add the sesame oil, sesame seeds, and 2 of the green onions. Stir well and immediately remove from the heat. Taste and adjust the seasoning with salt and pepper, if needed.

Transfer to a serving bowl and garnish with the remaining green onion, pine nuts, and sil koch'u. Serve at the center of the table along with other side dishes.

Sautéed Oyster Mushrooms with Scallops

Nŭt'ari Pokkŭm

Serves 4
20 minutes to prepare and cook

1 pound oyster mushrooms

4 ounces sea scallops or clams

1 tablespoon ch'ŏngju (rice wine) or vermouth

Pinch of salt

½ teaspoon freshly ground black pepper

2 tablespoons vegetable oil

5 cloves garlic, crushed and finely chopped

4 ounces chives, snipped into 1½-inch pieces

1 large sweet green onion, or 2 green onions, white and pale green part only, sliced diagonally into ½ by 1½-inch pieces

1 tablespoon sesame oil

½ tablespoon toasted sesame seeds

1 tablespoon freshly squeezed lemon juice

1 tablespoon soy sauce

Pinch of sil koch'u (hot red pepper threads) or hot red pepper flakes, for garnish

Fresh oyster mushrooms resemble real oysters in look and flavor. They have a milky blue tint when young, and gradually grow into a shade of gray as they mature. The stocky, plump stalk variety, without overgrown leafy tops, is best. To handle these fragile and crumbly mushrooms, it is best to blanch them and shred them by hand instead of trying to cut them with a knife. The following recipe is for one of the simplest and most sophisticated mushroom dishes of all. It stands alone as an elegant main dish or as a side dish for any entree, especially with seafood. It is so quick to prepare that it would be wise to have all the ingredients on hand before you begin to sauté.

❋ ❋ ❋

With a clean, damp kitchen towel, wipe the mushrooms clean. Trim the stems and discard. In a stockpot, make 4 cups of acidulated water (page 10) and bring it to a boil. Add the mushrooms and blanch for no more than 10 seconds. Plunge into ice cold water to stop the cooking. Drain and gently squeeze dry by hand. Shred the mushrooms by hand and set aside on a work surface.

Briefly wash the scallops under running water and pat dry with a paper towel. Slice thin and place on a plate in one layer. (If using clams, they should be minced.) Season with ch'ŏngju, salt, and pepper. (Scallops are already somewhat salty, so a minimum of salt will do.)

In a nonreactive skillet, heat the vegetable oil over medium heat until hot. Add the garlic and sauté for 2 minutes, until fragrant. Add the mushrooms and sauté for 5 minutes, until barely wilted. Add the chives and green onion and sauté for 2 minutes, or until they turn bright green and fragrant. Increase the heat to medium-high and make a well at the center of the skillet. Add the scallops and sauté for about 1 minute, until they turn opaque. (Do not overcook.) Add the sesame oil, sesame seeds, lemon juice, and soy sauce and sauté for 1 minute, gently stirring to mix well.

Transfer to a serving bowl and garnish with sil koch'u. Serve at the center of the table along with other side dishes.

Sautéed Kelp

Miyŏk Namul

Serves 4
30 minutes to prepare
and 10 minutes to cook

2 tablespoons sesame oil

2 cloves garlic, crushed and finely chopped

1 green onion, white and pale green part only, finely minced

1 ounce dried kelp, reconstituted (page 14) and cut into bite-size pieces

1 tablespoon soy sauce

1 tablespoon toasted sesame seeds

½ teaspoon freshly ground pepper

This nutritious dish is usually served as a side dish, but it is also wonderful served with a bowl of steamed rice, as an almost instant meal. Kelp may also be cooked together with rice as a one-dish meal in Seaweed with Steamed Rice (page 45).

❀ ❀ ❀

In a nonreactive skillet, heat the sesame oil over medium heat until hot, but not smoking. (Sesame oil burns easily.) Add the garlic and green onion and sauté for 2 minutes, until fragrant. Add the kelp, soy sauce, sesame seeds, and pepper and sauté for 5 minutes. Let cool. Transfer to a serving bowl and serve as a side dish.

Variations: To make Chilled Kelp (Miyŏk Naengch'ae), add 1 tablespoon sugar, 1 tablespoon ch'ŏngju (rice wine), 1 tablespoon distilled white vinegar, and 1 tablespoon lemon juice to the cooked kelp and mix well. Serve well chilled. To make Chilled Cucumber and Seaweed Salad (Oi Miyŏk Much'im or Namul), add 1 cup chilled cucumber slices, 1 tablespoon ch'ŏngju, 2 tablespoons distilled white vinegar, 1 tablespoon sugar, and 1 tablespoon freshly squeezed lemon juice to the cooked kelp. Toss well. Chill before serving.

Toasted Laver

Kim Kui

Serves 4
40 minutes to prepare and cook

---

5 sheets of kim (laver),
about 8 inches square

2 tablespoons sesame oil

½ tablespoon salt

Pine mushrooms (songi pŏsŏt), "the king of mushrooms," are Koreans' pride, as truffles are to Italians and French. They grow wild in pine forests and are hunted by experts when they appear for about 2 weeks in the fall. Their appearance resembles European asparagus. Koreans love to use them in rice and soups, but broiling (songi kui) is the best and simplest way to cook these mysterious mushrooms. Slice the mushrooms lengthwise, skewer with toothpicks, and broil briefly, no more than 1 minute. Serve with sesame oil and salt.

A stack of plain, toasted kim is invariably at every Korean meal. To me, the mere sight of kim whisks me back to my childhood. Whenever I thought our grandmother might take me along on her temple visit, I would be very happy and my mouth would begin to water, anticipating the kim kui I would be able to eat to my heart's content. Kim would always be there, high on the altar among a myriad of other treats, conspicuously shiny with its sesame oil coating. During the Buddhist ceremony, I would always be restless, wishing the eternal chanting would end so we could eat before all the good food got cold and the crispy kim turned soggy. No wonder this was often said: *"Yŏmbul enŭn mam i ŏpko chaetbap e man mam i itta!"* ("Your mind is never on the prayers but only on the altar food!").

Place 1 sheet of kim on a tray. Using a wide pastry brush, lightly coat the kim with sesame oil and sprinkle with a pinch of salt. Repeat with the remaining sheets of kim, and stack them up. Tightly roll up the stack and place it in a plastic bag. Let it rest for 30 minutes, to allow the oil to coat evenly and the flavor to blend well.

Unroll the kim. Turn on the gas or electric stove burner to medium and toast each sheet by waving it ½ inch above the heat for 1 or 2 seconds. (Kim burns easily.) Turn to the other side and repeat the same process. Transfer the kim to a cutting board and stack it up again. With a long, sharp knife, cut in half one way, then in fourths the other. Stack on a serving plate and serve as a side dish with hot steamed rice. Practice picking up kim with chopsticks and wrapping it around a bite-size portion of rice.

✸ Stews, Braised Dishes, and Hot Pots

Korean stew (tchigae) is hearty and casual everyday fare. In fact, almost anything edible can be thrown into a stew pot and be called tchigae. In this chapter we introduce two of the most popular stews. These one-dish meals are delicious and are also easy to prepare.

When a Korean boasts about his country's cuisine, inevitably braised dishes (tchim) is one of the first to be mentioned. In the traditional kitchen, the meat and vegetables had to be simmered for long hours to make the ingredients tender and moist. Because of the higher quality of ingredients today, cooking time is now considerably shorter. This special side dish is usually served in a large serving bowl at the center of the meal table or in individual bowls. The leftovers are reheatable and are just as delicious.

Korean tabletop hot pot cookery (chŏngol) somewhat resembles those of other countries, such as Mongolian hot pot or Japanese shabu shabu, to name a few. Three popular chongol are presented in this chapter, selected from among an endless repertoire. The recipes may look daunting with their parade of ingredients, but the actual cooking technique is relatively simple. Advance preparation is the key: the day before, all ingredients are sliced into thin strips. All that remains is the final act of tabletop cooking, which takes less than 10 minutes. Every detail counts, from a gracious tabletop cooking vessel to attractive working trays and handsome cooking spoons. To accommodate the voluminous amount of fresh vegetables for chŏngol, use a 14-inch, 2½-inch-deep electric skillet with sloping sides and a domed lid. Besides tabletop butane burners, attractive electric skillets specifically for chŏngol are also available.

(above) Braised beef ribs

(opposite) Palace wall with sour plum tree motif, Kyŏngbok Palace, Seoul

Bean Curd and Vegetable Stew with Fermented Soybean Paste

Tubu Toenjang Tchigae

Serves 4 to 6
20 minutes to prepare
and 15 minutes to cook

3 cups Beef Stock (page 58)
or Anchovy Stock (page 60)

4 tablespoons toenjang
(fermented soybean paste),
or to taste

1 kelp strip, about 1 inch by
6 inches long (optional)

5 cloves garlic, crushed and finely
chopped

1 pound medium-firm bean curd,
sliced into 1 by 1^1/$_2$ by ^{1}/$_4$-inch
dominoes

1 pound napa cabbage, cut into
1 by 1^1/$_2$-inch pieces

1 pound Korean radish or daikon,
peeled and sliced into 1 by 1^1/$_2$
by ^{1}/$_4$-inch dominoes

^{1}/$_2$ pound summer squash, sliced
into 1 by 1^1/$_2$ by ^{1}/$_4$-inch
dominoes

5 ounces lean pork, sliced
paper-thin

2 large sweet green onions, or
4 green onions, white and pale
green part only, cut diagonally
into 1^1/$_4$-inch pieces

1 hot green Korean pepper or
jalapeño pepper, seeded,
deribbed, and cut diagonally into
^{1}/$_4$-inch pieces

1 hot red Korean pepper, or ^{1}/$_2$ red
bell pepper, seeded, deribbed,
and cut diagonally into ^{1}/$_4$-inch
pieces

For Koreans young and old, to think of tchigae is to hear *"chigul, chigul, pogul, pogul,"* an onomatopoeia representing the comforting sound of stew as it gurgles and bubbles in a dark brown clay pot and spills over, hissing and spattering, into a mud brazier's flaming red charcoal fire. Tchigae and *ttugbaegi*, the rough unglazed pot in which it is cooked, are inseparable in the Korean mind. Even today, the ugly clay pots sell briskly in the markets, though shiny modern saucepans are available as well. According to a Korean saying, *Ttugbaegi poda changmat!* ("The stew tastes better than its packaging!").

In my childhood, everyone—from all walks of life—had toenjang tchigae several times a week. One may think it is too simple a dish to set before one's honored guests, but it is oh so tasty! And it is a nutritious protein powerhouse—with bean curd, bean paste, bean sprouts, and a variety of other beans, plus meat. It is a breeze to fix and a satisfying meal for family and for friends who drop in unexpectedly. To know and love this unassuming and hearty fare is to understand and appreciate Korean hearts and minds.

❁ ❁ ❁

Pour the stock in a large, deep skillet. Add the toenjang and stir to dissolve. Add the kelp and garlic and bring to a boil over medium-high heat. Place the bean curd, cabbage, radish, and squash in the skillet in a pinwheel pattern, leaving room at the center for the meat. Cover, bring to a boil, and cook gently for 5 minutes.

Place the pork in the center of the skillet, to allow all the flavors to blend evenly. Cover and boil for 2 minutes. Add the green onions and peppers evenly between the other ingredients and cover again. Boil for a few seconds, until the green onions and peppers become fragrant and their colors turn bright. Limit the total cooking time to no more than 15 minutes. Remove and discard the kelp, or save for other use.

Serve the stew immediately with steamed rice and a fresh salad.

Variations: Any combination of meat and vegetables can be thrown into the pot and be called tchigae. In place of bean curd, Korean cooks love to use piji—the dregs remaining after making bean curd. Piji is inexpensive, almost discardable; hence the Korean description *ssange piji ttok* ("cheap as piji"). This dish is then called Piji Tchigae. When kimchi is used in place of bean curd, we have Kimchi Tchigae, another simple dish and an all-time favorite.

Fish Stew

Saengsŏn Tchigae

Serves 4 to 6

20 minutes to prepare
and 20 minutes to cook

1¹/₂ pounds firm white fish fillets

Salt

Freshly ground black pepper

1 tablespoon vegetable oil

5 cloves garlic, crushed and finely chopped

4 cups Clear Chicken Stock (page 59) or Beef Stock (page 58)

4 tablespoons ch'ŏngju (rice wine) or vermouth

1 kelp strip, about 1 inch by 6 inches long (optional)

¹/₂ teaspoon freshly squeezed ginger juice

10 ounces napa cabbage hearts, firm stem part only, cut into 1 by 1¹/₂-inch pieces

10 ounces Korean radishes or daikon, peeled and sliced into 1 by 1 ¹/₂ by ¹/₄-inch dominoes

10 ounces summer squash, sliced into 1 by 1¹/₂ by ¹/₄-inch dominoes

10 ounces oyster or white mushrooms, shredded into bite-size pieces

8 ounces medium-firm bean curd, cut into 1 by 1¹/₂ by ¹/₄-inch dominoes

2 large sweet green onions, or 4 green onions, white and pale green part only, cut diagonally into ¹/₄-inch pieces

2 tablespoons koch'u karu (hot red pepper powder), or to taste

3 tablespoons koch'ujang (hot red pepper paste), or to taste

Continued on page 141

This casual fish stew resembles the French bourride, the prototype of the well-known bouillabaisse, but with a distinctive difference: the Korean version is robust and blisteringly hot.

For this recipe, use firm white fish fillets, such as cod, red snapper, halibut, or gray mullet.

Slice the white fish diagonally into 2¹/₂-inch chunks. Place the fish in a colander in a single layer, season with salt and pepper, and set aside.

In a large, deep skillet, heat the vegetable oil over medium-high heat until very hot. Add the garlic and sauté for 2 minutes, until fragrant. Add the stock, ch'ŏngju, kelp, and ginger juice. Arrange the cabbage, radishes, squash, mushrooms, bean curd, and half of the green onions in the skillet in a pinwheel pattern, leaving room at the center for the fish. Cover and bring to a full boil over medium-high heat. Boil for 7 minutes. Add the koch'u karu and koch'ujang in the center, stirring to dissolve, then add the white fish in the center. Scatter the crab and scallops in the skillet. Evenly spoon the broth over the fish and vegetables, making sure that all are immersed in liquid. Cover and boil vigorously for 3 to 4 minutes, or until the fish are cooked through and opaque. (Do not overcook.) Quickly drop the peppers and the remaining green onion between the vegetables and fish, pressing them lightly into the boiling broth and spooning the broth over all in a basting fashion. Cover and bring to a vigorous boil. Add the crown daisy, cover again, and cook for a few seconds. Turn off the heat. Remove and discard the kelp, or save for other use. Adjust the seasoning with salt and pepper if needed.

Place the skillet in the center of the table or divide the tchigae into individual bowls. Serve with steamed rice. Seasoned Spinach (page 125) and Whole Cabbage Kimchi (page 97) make excellent side dishes.

Note: Be sure to purchase live crabs on the day of cooking. Keep in a plastic bag in the refrigerator until ready to use, then kill the crab before cutting.

1 live blue crab, cut into 4 pieces just before cooking

4 ounces sea scallops, halved

1 hot red Korean pepper, or ½ red bell pepper, seeded, deribbed, and cut diagonally into ¼-inch pieces

1 hot green Korean pepper or jalapeño pepper, seeded, deribbed, and cut diagonally into ¼-inch pieces

6 crown daisy leaves or spinach leaves

Sari fishing village, South Chungch'ŏng Province: shrimp boats returning on the incoming tide to sell saeu chŏt for kimchi making

Braised Chicken

Tak Tchim

Serves 4 to 6
30 minutes to prepare
and 1 hour to cook

---

3 pounds lean chicken legs or thighs, bone in and skin left on

3 tablespoons vegetable oil

5 cloves garlic, crushed and finely chopped

4 walnut halves, coarsely chopped

1 tablespoon hot red pepper flakes

1/2 cup soy sauce

2 tablespoons ch'ŏngju (rice wine) or vermouth

3 tablespoons corn syrup, or 2 tablespoons sugar

4 tablespoons freshly squeezed lemon juice

1 pound napa cabbage, firm stem part only, cut into 1 by 1¹/₂-inch pieces

1 pound Korean radishes or daikon, peeled and cut into 1 by 1¹/₂ by ¹/₄-inch dominoes

1 ounce dried p'yogo (shiitake) mushrooms, rehydrated (page 18) and halved or quartered

4 large sweet green onions, or 8 green onions, white and green part only, cut diagonally into ¹/₄-inch pieces

2 cups Clear Chicken Stock (page 59)

1 hot red Korean pepper, or ¹/₂ red bell pepper, cut diagonally into ¹/₄-inch strips

Continued on page 143

This recipe is a good introduction to the Korean way of braising. Tak tchim, with its casual elegance, is a perennial favorite. Unlike the French coq au vin, which is braised in wine, the exquisite flavor of this dish comes from a soy sauce–based marinade laden with herbs and spices. It is perfumed with a refreshing scent of lemon. Lean and firm thighs or legs are used in this recipe. The bone and lean skin are purposely included to create a moist, gelatinous texture and a depth of flavor.

❀ ❀ ❀

Soak the chicken in ice cold water for 1 hour. Drain and pat dry. In a large cast-iron skillet, heat 2 tablespoons of vegetable oil over high heat until very hot. Add all the chicken in one layer and sear it on all sides until well browned, about 5 minutes per side. Pour out and discard any fat. Decrease the heat to medium and, making room in the center of the skillet, add half of the garlic and all of the walnuts and pepper flakes. Sauté for 1 minute. Stir in the soy sauce, ch'ŏngju, corn syrup, and lemon juice, mix well, and set aside.

In a large stockpot, heat the remaining 1 tablespoon of vegetable oil over medium heat until hot. Add the remaining garlic and sauté for 2 minutes, until fragrant. Add the cabbage, radishes, mushrooms, and green onions, reserving some green onions for garnish. Add 1 cup of the stock, cover, and bring to a boil. Gently boil for 10 minutes, occasionally stirring with a wooden spoon.

Add the chicken and the remaining 1 cup of stock. Bring to a boil, decrease the heat to medium, and cook for 20 minutes, stirring with a wooden spoon. Increase the heat to medium-high and add the peppers. Boil vigorously for 10 minutes, until the stock is reduced to the desired consistency. Adjust the seasoning with salt and pepper if needed.

Arrange the chicken and vegetables on a serving plate. Spoon the juice remaining in the pot on top and garnish with the sil koch'u, pine nuts, and reserved green onion. Serve with steamed rice, Cubed Radish Kimchi (page 100), Seasoned Spinach (page 125), or Leaf Lettuce Salad (page 116).

Notes: Traditionally, juice from yuja (Asian citrus) is used instead of lemon juice in this recipe.

For ceremonial and festive occasions, whole chickens are butterflied and braised, similar to American oven-roasted chickens.

1 hot green Korean pepper or jalapeño pepper, cut diagonally into ¼-inch strips

Salt

Freshly ground black pepper

Pinch of sil koch'u (hot red pepper threads), for garnish

1 tablespoon pine nuts, for garnish

In my family kitchen, we often had pheasant instead of chicken. Our father frequently hunted in the winter countryside, returning with his large hunter's leather mesh sack filled with pheasants and other proud catches. We girls had the chore of plucking feathers before our mother magically transformed them into tasty dishes. We used the abundant feathers as pillow stuffing and as brushes to spread oil on laver before toasting it to make kim kui.

Braised Pork Spareribs

Toeji Kalbi Tchim

Serves 4 to 6
1 hour to prepare and 1 hour to cook

---

3 pounds lean pork spareribs, cut into 2¹/₂-inch pieces

4 tablespoons vegetable oil

Marinade

3 tablespoons koch'ujang (hot red pepper paste)

3 tablespoons koch'u karu (hot red pepper powder)

2 tablespoons soy sauce

5 cloves garlic, crushed and finely chopped

3 green onions, white and pale green parts only, finely minced

3 tablespoons ch'ŏngju (rice wine) or vermouth

1 tablespoon freshly grated ginger

4 tablespoons corn syrup

1 tablespoon sugar

4 walnut halves, finely chopped

1 tablespoon toasted sesame seeds

2 tablespoons sesame oil

1 teaspoon salt

1 teaspoon freshly ground black pepper

Continued on page 145

I cannot help but remember the tantalizing aroma of tchim drifting out from our mother's kitchen and the taste of succulent nuggets of meat, nearly falling off the bone. It was always a visual feast, too, with vegetables and tasty bits of meat showing faintly through the lustrous, translucent, dark brown glaze.

This robust recipe creates a dish with aggressive taste and a vibrant red color, in contrast to the rich, dark-brown Braised Beef Ribs (page 146) and its elegant, subtle taste. The Korean hot red pepper paste, hot pepper powder, spices, and fresh ginger in the marinade are mainly responsible for both its explosive flavor and its color. As with many other Korean dishes, however, the heat of the red pepper paste and powder are pleasantly balanced by the sweetness of sugar, corn syrup, and vegetables. Your palate will go wild with the combination, and your guests will always ask for more.

In a large bowl, soak the pork in ice cold water for 1 hour. Drain and pat dry. In a cast-iron skillet, heat 2 tablespoons of vegetable oil over high heat until very hot. Add the pork and sear it on all sides until it is no longer pink, about 3 minutes per side. Discard any fat, and remove the pan from the heat. In a large bowl, combine the marinade ingredients. Add the pork and toss well. Let marinate for about 30 minutes.

Meanwhile, in a large heavy stockpot, heat the remaining 2 tablespoons of vegetable oil over medium-high heat until hot. Add the cabbage, radishes, mushrooms, and potatoes and sauté for 5 minutes, or until they are barely cooked. Season with salt and pepper. Add the pork and stock and bring to a boil. Decrease the heat to medium, cover, and gently cook for 20 minutes. Increase the heat to medium-high and boil for 20 minutes or until the liquid is reduced to the desired consistency. Add the green onions and gently stir with a wooden spoon.

Ladle out some of the sauce into a small bowl and cool. Dissolve the cornstarch in the sauce and return it to the pot. Boil for 3 minutes, gently stirring a few times. Adjust the seasoning with salt and pepper if needed. Turn off the heat and let settle for a few minutes. Add the sesame seeds and sesame oil and stir well.

Transfer to a large serving dish or divide into individual dishes. Garnish with the sil koch'u and green onion rings. Serve with bowls of steamed rice and other side dishes. Chilled Radish Salad (page 119) goes very well with pork.

1 pound napa cabbage hearts, stem part only, cut into 1 by 1½ -inch pieces

1 pound Korean radishes or daikon, peeled and sliced into 1 by 1½ by ¼-inch dominoes

1 ounce dried p'yogo (shiitake) mushrooms, rehydrated (page 18) and halved or quartered

10 ounces potatoes, peeled and cut into 1-inch cubes

Salt

Freshly ground black pepper

2 cups Heavy Chicken Stock (page 59)

3 large sweet green onions, or 6 green onions, cut diagonally into ¼-inch pieces

2 tablespoons cornstarch or all-purpose wheat flour

1 tablespoon toasted sesame seeds

1 tablespoon sesame oil

Pinch of sil koch'u (hot red pepper threads), for garnish

1 green onion, white and pale green only, sliced into thin rings, for garnish

Braised Beef Ribs

Kalbi Tchim

Serves 4
30 minutes to prepare
and 2 hours to cook

---

3 pounds lean ribs of beef with
bone, or 2¹/₂ pounds boneless
beef, well trimmed

4 tablespoons vegetable oil

1 ounce dried p'yogo (shiitake)
mushrooms, rehydrated (page 18)
and halved

1 pound napa cabbage, firm stem
part only, cut into 1 by 1¹/₂-inch
pieces

10 ounces potatoes, peeled and
cut into 1-inch cubes

3 cups Clear Chicken Stock
(page 59) or water

1 kelp strip, about 1 inch by
6 inches long (optional)

Marinade

1 Korean or Asian pear, peeled
and grated, or 4 tablespoons
freshly squeezed lemon juice
plus 1 tablespoon sugar

4 tablespoons soy sauce

2 tablespoons ch'ŏngju (rice wine)
or vermouth

3 tablespoons corn syrup,
or 2 tablespoons sugar

3 green onions, white and pale
green part only, finely minced

2 cloves garlic, crushed and finely
chopped

1 tablespoon sesame oil

1 tablespoon toasted sesame
seeds

1 teaspoon salt

1 teaspoon freshly ground black
pepper

Continued on page 147

Pork and chicken have their own merits, but they are always over-shadowed by the Korean unrequited passion for beef, particularly the supreme kalbi. *Kalbi* is often translated into English as "short ribs." This is a misnomer, however, as these ribs are actually lean prime cuts of beef, reserved for creating two of Korea's most admired dishes, Fired Beef Ribs (page 180) and this one. In the Korean kitchen, short ribs are only used for making soup. In cooking technique kalbi tchim can be compared to American braised beef or a ragout, but once tasted, comparisons cease.

Preparations for cooking this dish must begin a day in advance. It is reheatable, and in fact, the flavor seems even more extraordinary the following day.

A day in advance, ask the butcher for lean beef ribs, cut into 2-inch chunks. In a large bowl, soak the meat in ice cold water for 1 hour. Drain and pat dry.

In a large heavy stockpot, heat 2 tablespoons of vegetable oil over high heat until very hot. Add the ribs and sear them on all sides until well browned, about 5 minutes per side. With a slotted spoon, transfer the ribs to a bowl. Discard any fat left in the pot. In the same pot, heat 1 tablespoon of vegetable oil over medium heat until hot. Add the mushrooms and cabbage and sauté for 10 minutes. Transfer to another bowl. Heat the remaining 1 tablespoon of vegetable oil over medium-high heat until very hot. Add the potatoes and sauté for 7 minutes. Transfer to the bowl with the mushrooms and cabbage, but do not mix. Return the ribs to the pot and add the stock and kelp. Bring to a boil, decrease the heat to low, and simmer for 30 minutes. Let the meat cool in the liquid, then cover tightly and store in the refrigerator overnight. Tightly wrap the bowl with the cooked vegetables and store in the refrigerator. (Up to this point, the cooking can be done a day ahead.)

A few hours before serving, in a bowl, combine the marinade ingredients and mix well; set aside. Take the ribs out of the refrigerator, and lift off and discard the solidified fat. Remove and discard the kelp, or save for other use. With a slotted spoon, transfer the ribs to another bowl. Transfer the stock to another bowl and set aside. Add the marinade to the ribs and toss well. Let marinate for 15 minutes.

Spread the radish matchsticks on the bottom of the stockpot, then add the marinated ribs, radish dominoes, and reserved stock. Bring to a boil and gently cook over medium heat for 10 minutes. Take the cabbage, potatoes, and mushrooms out of the refrigerator and add them to the stockpot. Gently cook for 10 minutes, occasionally stirring with a wooden spoon. Add the chestnuts and jujubes and cook for 10 minutes over medium heat, stirring a few times. Increase the heat to medium-high and boil, partially covered, for about 25 minutes, or until

Growing Up in a Korean Kitchen

the liquid is reduced to the desired consistency. (To make a thicker sauce, at this point, spoon out some of the liquid into a bowl, allow it to cool, and dissolve 1 to 2 tablespoons cornstarch in it. Return this mixture to the pot, stir in gently, and boil 1 minute more.) Add the gingko nuts and immediately remove from the heat. Cover and let settle for 5 minutes, then taste and adjust the seasoning with salt and pepper.

Transfer to a deep serving bowl, showing off each ingredient. Or, divide into 4 individual serving bowls, 2 to 3 ribs each, on a bed of vegetables. Garnish with egg flakes and sil koch'u. Serve with steamed rice and other side dishes.

Note: Matchstick vegetables, especially radishes or cabbage, placed at the bottom of the pot prevent scorching or burning (and also enhance flavor). This was especially helpful in the traditional kitchen, when braising meant long hours of boiling to tenderize tough meat cuts.

Variations: On the traditional table, the elaborate three-color garnish (page 33) is a must for this dish. This recipe can also be used to prepare Braised Pork (Toaeji Tchim), Braised Oxtail (Kkori Tchim), and Braised Beef Shanks (Sat'ae Tchim). In the case of oxtail or beef shanks, the braising time must be increased three times, in order to tenderize the meat.

1 pound Korean radishes or daikon, peeled, half cut into matchsticks and half cut into 1 by 1¹/₂ by ¹/₄-inch dominoes

5 chestnuts, or 10 walnut halves, shelled, skinned, and halved

5 jujubes, pitted and halved, or 10 raisins

8 gingko nuts, toasted and skinned (page 22) (optional)

Pinch of salt

Pinch of freshly ground black pepper

Egg Flakes (page 34), for garnish

Pinch of sil koch'u (hot red pepper threads), for garnish

Braised Fish

Saengsŏn Tchim

Serves 4 to 6
30 minutes to prepare
and 1 hour to cook

---

2 pounds cod fillets or other firm fish

Pinch of salt

$1/2$ teaspoon freshly ground black pepper

2 tablespoons vegetable oil

10 cloves garlic, crushed and finely chopped

1 pound Korean radishes or daikon, peeled and sliced into 1 by $1^{1}/_{2}$ by $^{1}/_{4}$-inch dominoes

1 pound napa cabbage, stem part only, sliced into 1 by $1^{1}/_{2}$-inch pieces

1 ounce dried p'yogo (shiitake) mushrooms, rehydrated (page 18)

5 large sweet green onions, or 10 green onions, cut diagonally into $^{1}/_{4}$-inch pieces

3 cups Clear Chicken Stock (page 59)

$^{1}/_{2}$ cup soy sauce

2 tablespoons ch'ŏngju (rice wine) or vermouth

1 tablespoon koch'u karu (hot red pepper powder), or to desired hotness

2 tablespoons koch'ujang (hot red pepper paste), koch'ujang, or to desired hotness

3 tablespoons corn syrup or sugar

8 ounces medium-firm bean curd, cut into 1 by $1^{1}/_{2}$ by $^{1}/_{4}$-inch dominoes

1 hot red Korean pepper, or $^{1}/_{2}$ red bell pepper, cut diagonally into $^{1}/_{4}$-inch pieces

1 hot green Korean pepper or jalapeño pepper, cut diagonally into $^{1}/_{4}$-inch pieces

Pinch of sil koch'u (hot red pepper threads), for garnish

In most Korean households, the day begins with this dish. During my childhood, we usually had a hearty breakfast of rice, soup, kimchi, and braised fish or soybean paste stew. The fish was always mackerel, sardine, pollack, and, on rare occasions, herring. Red snapper and sea bream were special treats then. This recipe is our mother's, except she used the entire fish, including the head, tail, and bones. Braised with spicy soy sauce, this dish has a unique sweet and spicy flavor.

❀ ❀ ❀

Just before cooking, wash the fish and pat dry. Slice diagonally into 2-inch pieces and place in a flat basket. Season with a pinch each of salt and pepper.

In a large, deep skillet, heat the vegetable oil over medium heat until hot. Add garlic and sauté for 2 minutes, or until golden and fragrant. Add the radishes, cabbage, mushrooms, and green onions, reserving some green onion for garnish, and sauté for 10 minutes. Season with a pinch of salt and pepper. Add the stock and decrease the heat to medium-low. Cover and simmer for 30 minutes. Meanwhile, in a small bowl, combine the soy sauce, ch'ŏngju, koch'u karu, koch'ujang, $^{1}/_{2}$ teaspoon black pepper, and corn syrup and stir this mixture into the skillet. Cover and simmer for 15 minutes. Increase the heat to medium-high and bring to a vigorous boil. Distribute the fish and bean curd among the boiling vegetables, allowing the flavors to mingle. Boil for 5 minutes, or until the fish and bean curd are cooked through. Scatter the peppers in the skillet, gently pressing them into the stock, cover, and immediately remove from the heat. Let steam for a few seconds.

In a large serving bowl, arrange the vegetables, fish, and bean curd. Garnish with the reserved green onions and sil koch'u. Serve with bowls of steamed rice and other favorite side dishes.

Variations: Traditionally, the fish is cooked whole or cut up, dusted with flour, dipped in egg, and pan-fried before adding to the vegetables and mushrooms. Elaborate preparations are called for when preparing the sea bream version of this dish: mung bean sprouts and cloud ear mushrooms are important ingredients and, instead of chicken broth, sliced beef and tenderloin broth are used; as well, the elaborate three-color garnish or five-color garnish (page 33) decorates the whole fish.

Braised Whole Cabbage Kimchi

Kimchi Tchim

Serves 4 to 6
45 minutes to prepare and cook

1 piece Whole Cabbage Kimchi (page 97)

1 pound fresh napa cabbage heart, firm stem part only, finely chopped

1/2 tablespoon coarse sea salt or kosher salt

1/2 pound lean ground pork

5 fresh p'yogo (shiitake) mushrooms, or 2 ounces dried and rehydrated (page 18), finely chopped

2 cloves garlic, crushed and finely chopped

2 walnut halves, finely chopped

1 egg, slightly beaten

1 tablespoon freshly squeezed lemon juice

2 green onions, white and pale part only, finely minced

1/2 pound Korean radishes or daikon, cut into 2-inch matchsticks

1 cup Beef Stock (page 58)

2 tablespoons sweet rice flour or cornstarch

Pinch of sil koch'u (hot red pepper threads), for garnish

Pinch of freshly ground black pepper

This is an unmistakably Korean dish. In the traditional kitchen, kimchi tchim probably began as a creative way to revitalize aged and sour cabbage kimchi. Today's recipe, especially this one, calls for only fresh and crunchy kimchi, not leftovers. Once you have acquired the taste for it, you are smitten. It is simply addictive.

❀ ❀ ❀

Choose a firm and good-looking piece of kimchi. (One piece is equal to a halved, or in same cases quartered, section of cabbage.) Shake out the stuffing from the kimchi and rinse once in cold water. (Save the stuffing to use in fried rice or noodles.) Drain the kimchi in a colander and wrap in a paper towel. Squeeze out as much liquid as possible, taking care to maintain its original shape. Place the kimchi in a bowl, cut side up, and set aside. (At this point, the color of the rinsed kimchi will be pale pink instead of red.)

Place the fresh cabbage in another bowl, sprinkle with sea salt, and let sit for 15 minutes. Wrap in a paper towel and squeeze out as much liquid as possible, and return it to the bowl. To make the stuffing, combine the cabbage with the ground pork, mushrooms, garlic, walnut, egg, lemon juice, and green onions, reserving some green onions for garnish, and mix well. Stuff the meat mixture into the kimchi, spreading the stuffing between the leaves and packing it tightly. Bundle the kimchi into its original shape and tie with kitchen thread.

Spread the radishes in a layer on the bottom of a stockpot. Transfer the stuffed cabbage kimchi to the stockpot and carefully pour the stock around and over it. Bring to a boil over medium-high heat. Decrease the heat to low, cover, and simmer for about 30 minutes.

When the kimchi is almost done, in a small saucepan, dissolve the rice flour into 3 tablespoons of cold water. Ladle in some cooking liquid from the kimchi and mix. Bring to a boil, and cook until it becomes a thin, milky glaze. Drizzle the glaze over the simmering kimchi, cover, and boil for 1 minute. Transfer the cabbage to a cutting board and carefully slice it crosswise into 1 1/2-inch pieces. Spoon out the radishes from the stockpot and spread them onto a flat serving plate, then arrange the kimchi pieces on top, showing off the tasty layers of stuffing. Spoon the remaining liquid over it. Garnish with the reserved green onions and sil koch'u and add the black pepper. Serve at room temperature. This one-dish meal goes well with a bowl of steamed rice. Or, it will make a delicious side dish for a pork roast or steak.

Vegetable Hot Pot

Ch'aeso Chŏngol

Serves 4 to 6
1 hour to prepare
and 20 minutes to cook

1 pound napa cabbage hearts, stem part only, cut into 2½ by ¼-inch strips

1 pound summer squash, cut into 2½ by ¼-inch strips

1 pound oyster mushrooms or other white mushrooms, torn into thin shreds

½ pound mung bean sprouts, cut into 2½-inch pieces

5 large sweet green onions, or 10 green onions, cut diagonally into ¼-inch pieces

1 hot red Korean pepper, or ½ bell pepper, seeded, deribbed, and cut diagonally into ¼-inch strips

1 hot green Korean pepper or jalapeño pepper, seeded, deribbed, and cut diagonally into ¼-inch strips

1 pound spinach leaves, cut into 2½-inch pieces

4 ounces crown daisy, leaves separated

Seasoning for Beef or Scallops

1 tablespoon soy sauce (for beef only)

1 tablespoon ch'ŏngju (rice wine) or vermouth

Pinch of salt

Pinch of freshly ground black pepper

4 ounces beef tenderloin, sliced into 2½-inch paper-thin strips, or 8 ounces scallops, thinly sliced

Continued on page 151

Although a small amount of fish or beef is usually added to this dish for extra flavor (pork is rarely used), it can be left out to create a light and nutritious vegetarian feast. Scallops, in particular, impart a subtle and delightful flavor to this vegetable dish.

❀ ❀ ❀

Prepare the cabbage, squash, mushrooms, mung bean sprouts, green onions, peppers, spinach, and crown daisy and arrange them on a tray. In a small bowl, combine the seasoning ingredients (if using scallops, omit the soy sauce) and mix well. Add the beef or scallops and toss well. Transfer to a glass dish, and place the dish in the center of the tray with the vegetables. Tightly wrap the tray with plastic wrap and refrigerate. (Up to this point, the preparations can be done a day in advance.)

About 1 hour before serving, begin to prepare the chŏngol. In a bowl, combine the chŏngol sauce ingredients and mix well. Pour the sauce into an attractive bowl and pour the stock into a pitcher, then place both on the table. Place a large, deep electric hot pot near the host's seat, along with a couple of cooking spoons and chopsticks. Heat the vegetable oil in the hot pot over medium heat, add the garlic, and sauté 2 minutes, until golden and fragrant. Add half the stock and half the sauce. Bring to a boil, then turn off the heat. Place the tray with the vegetables and beef or scallops at the center of the table. Place the pitcher of remaining stock and the bowl of sauce near the host's seat.

While your guests are enjoying appetizers, turn on the hot pot. Bring the stock to a boil and add half of the vegetables, except for the spinach and crown daisy, arranging them in a pinwheel pattern and leaving space at the center. Place half of the beef or scallops in the center. With a large spoon, gently stir the boiling stock, helping the flavor of each vegetable mingle well. Boil gently for about 5 minutes. Add half of the spinach and crown daisy, cover, and cook for 30 seconds, or until they turn bright and are barely wilted.

To serve, ladle hot chŏngol into individual bowls, attractively arranging the beef or scallops and vegetables. Spoon in additional broth. Garnish each bowl with the sil koch'u and serve. While the guests are enjoying the first portion, repeat with the remaining ingredients. Keep the hot pot gently boiling and encourage guests to help themselves to a second or third helping directly from the pot. Serve with steamed rice, bowls of Vinegar Soy Sauce (page 28), Allspice Sauce (page 28), or Hot Red Pepper Sauce (page 30), and a generous array of side dishes (see the note following).

Note: Chŏngol and steamed rice make a substantial meal, but I usually add good supporting players: Whole Cabbage Kimchi (page 97), Cubed Radish Kimchi (page 100), and a plate of jewel-like mini-cubed relishes that include olives, Pickled Hot Green and Red Peppers (page 110), Pickled Ginger (page 111), Pickled Whole Garlic (page 111), and sweet cherries.

Chŏngol Sauce

1 tablespoon soy sauce

2 tablespoons ch'ŏngju (rice wine) or vermouth

1/2 tablespoon freshly squeezed lemon juice

1 tablespoon sesame oil

1 tablespoon toasted sesame seeds

Pinch of salt

Pinch of freshly ground black pepper

4 cups Clear Chicken Stock (page 59) or Beef Stock (page 58)

2 tablespoons vegetable oil

5 cloves garlic, crushed and finely chopped

1 teaspoon sil koch'u (hot red pepper threads), cut into 2 1/2-inch pieces, for garnish

Bean Curd and Vegetable Hot Pot

°Tubu Chŏ̊ngol

Serves 4 to 6
1 hour to prepare
and 20 minutes to cook

---

¹/₂ pound napa cabbage hearts, stem part only, cut into 2¹/₂ by ¹/₄-inch strips

¹/₂ pound Korean radishes or daikon, peeled and cut into 2¹/₂ by ¹/₄-inch strips

1 pound summer squash, cut into 2¹/₂ by ¹/₄-inch strips

¹/₂ pound oyster mushrooms or other white mushrooms, torn into thin shreds

¹/₂ pound mung bean sprouts, cut into 2¹/₂-inch pieces

5 large sweet green onions, or 10 green onions, cut diagonally into ¹/₄-inch pieces

1 hot red Korean pepper, or ¹/₂ bell pepper, seeded, deribbed, and cut diagonally into ¹/₄-inch strips

1 hot green Korean pepper or jalapeño pepper, seeded, deribbed, and cut diagonally into ¹/₄-inch strips

¹/₂ pound spinach leaves, cut into 2¹/₂-inch pieces

4 ounces crown daisy, leaves separated

¹/₂ cup all-purpose wheat flour

2 eggs, lightly beaten

1 pound medium-firm bean curd, cut in half lengthwise and cut into ¹/₂-inch-thick dominoes

4 tablespoons vegetable oil

Continued on page 153

Bean curd is the key ingredient in this power package of rich protein. In this modified version of a traditional recipe, the bean curd is fortified with extra flavor and texture by pan-frying it first (pan-fried bean curd is called tubujŏn), then adding it to the other ingredients in the hot pot.

❀ ❀ ❀

Prepare the cabbage, radishes, squash, mushrooms, mung bean sprouts, green onions, peppers, spinach, and crown daisy and arrange them on a tray.

Sprinkle the flour on a plate and place the eggs in a shallow bowl. Dredge the bean curd in flour, then coat it with egg. In a nonreactive skillet, heat 2 tablespoons of vegetable oil over medium heat until hot. Add all the bean curd pieces and cook for 3 minutes per side, until golden brown, turning them only once. Let cool and slice into ¹/₂-inch strips. Add the bean curd to the tray with the vegetables.

In a small bowl, combine the beef seasoning ingredients and mix well. Add the beef and toss well. Transfer to an attractive bowl, and place the bowl in the center of the vegetable tray. Tightly wrap the tray with plastic wrap and refrigerate. (Up to this point, the preparations can be done a day in advance.)

About 1 hour before serving, begin to prepare the chŏngol. In a bowl, combine the chŏngol sauce ingredients and mix well. Pour the sauce into an attractive bowl and pour the stock into a pitcher, then place both on the table. Place a large, deep electric hot pot near the host's seat, along with a couple of cooking spoons and chopsticks. Heat the remaining 2 tablespoons vegetable oil in the hot pot over medium heat, add the garlic, and sauté 2 minutes, until golden and fragrant. Add half the stock and half the sauce. Bring to a boil, then turn off the heat. Place the tray with the vegetables and bean curd at the center of the table. Place the pitcher of remaining stock and the bowl of sauce near the host's seat.

While your guests are enjoying appetizers, turn on the hot pot. Bring the stock to a boil and add half of the vegetables, except for the spinach and crown daisy, arranging them in a pinwheel pattern and leaving space at the center. Place half of the beef and bean curd in the center. With a large spoon, gently stir the boiling stock, helping the flavor of each vegetable mingle well. Boil gently for about 5 minutes. Add half of the spinach and crown daisy, cover, and cook for 30 seconds, or until they turn bright and are barely wilted.

To serve, ladle hot chŏngol into individual bowls, attractively arranging the beef, bean curd, and vegetables. Spoon in additional broth. Garnish each bowl with the sil koch'u and serve. While the guests are enjoying the first portion, repeat with the remaining ingredients. Keep the hot pot gently boiling and encourage guests to help themselves to a second or third helping directly from the pot. Serve with steamed rice, bowls of Vinegar Soy Sauce (page 28), Allspice Sauce (page 28), or Hot Red Pepper Sauce (page 30), and a generous array of side dishes (see the note on page 151).

Variations: In place of the pan-fried bean curd, use the more elaborate Stuffed Pan-Fried Bean Curd (page 167). As simpler alternatives, fresh bean curd (without pan-frying) or store-bought deep-fried bean curd may be used.

Seasoning for Beef

1 tablespoon soy sauce

1 tablespoon ch'ŏngju (rice wine) or vermouth

Pinch of salt

Pinch of freshly ground black pepper

6 ounces beef tenderloin, sliced into 2½-inch paper-thin strips

Chŏngol Sauce

1 tablespoon soy sauce

2 tablespoons ch'ŏngju (rice wine) or vermouth

1 tablespoon sesame oil

1 tablespoon toasted sesame seeds

4 cups Clear Chicken Stock (page 59) or Beef Stock (page 58)

5 cloves garlic, crushed and finely chopped

Pinch of sil koch'u (hot red pepper threads) or hot red pepper flakes, for garnish

Seafood and Vegetable Hot Pot

Haemul Chŏngol

Serves 6 to 8
1 hour to prepare
and 20 minutes to cook

---

1 pound napa cabbage hearts,
firm stem part, cut into 2$\frac{1}{2}$ by
$\frac{1}{4}$-inch strips

1 pound Korean radishes or
daikon, cut into 2$\frac{1}{2}$ by
$\frac{1}{4}$-inch strips

12 ounces summer squash, cut
into 2$\frac{1}{2}$ by $\frac{1}{4}$-inch strips

12 ounces oyster mushrooms or
other white mushrooms, torn
into thin shreds

1 hot red Korean pepper, or
$\frac{1}{2}$ bell pepper, seeded,
deribbed, and cut diagonally
into $\frac{1}{4}$-inch pieces

1 hot green Korean pepper or
jalapeño pepper, seeded,
deribbed, and cut diagonally
into $\frac{1}{4}$-inch pieces

5 large sweet green onions, or 10
green onions, cut diagonally into
$\frac{1}{4}$-inch pieces

1 pound spinach, cut into 2$\frac{1}{2}$-inch
pieces

$\frac{1}{2}$ pound crown daisy, leaves
separated

1 pound medium-firm bean curd,
halved, cut into $\frac{1}{2}$-inch-thick
dominoes, then into $\frac{1}{2}$-inch
strips

1 pound shrimp, shelled, deveined,
and halved

10 ounces baby squid, cleaned
and sliced into $\frac{1}{2}$-inch rings

Continued on page 155

This scrumptious dish will surely please everyone. Its luxurious seafood spread of fresh fish, clams, and crabs along with flavorful vegetables gently boiling in an aromatic broth dares to be compared with Neptune's table. This recipe provides generous and hospitable portions. Any leftovers are reheatable and delicious the following day.

❀ ❀ ❀

Prepare the cabbage, radishes, squash, mushrooms, peppers, green onions, spinach, and crown daisy and arrange them on a tray. Prepare the bean curd and arrange on another tray.

In a stockpot, make 4 cups of acidulated water (page 10). Add the shrimp, squid, and scallops separately, using the same water each time, and blanch each for less than 2 minutes. Rinse once in cold water and drain. Strain the cooking water and save it for other uses; it makes a good stock for the tchigae recipes (pages 138 to 141). Arrange the fish and shellfish, except the crab, on the tray with the bean curd. Tightly wrap both trays with plastic wrap and refrigerate. (Up to this point, the preparations can be done a day in advance.)

About 1 hour before serving, begin to prepare the chŏngol. In a bowl, combine the chŏngol sauce ingredients and mix well. Pour the sauce into an attractive bowl and pour the stock into a pitcher, then place both on the table. Place a large, deep electric hot pot near the host's seat, along with a couple of cooking spoons and chopsticks. Heat the vegetable oil in the hot pot over medium heat, add the garlic, and sauté 2 minutes, until golden and fragrant. Add half the stock and half the sauce. Bring to a boil, then turn off the heat. Place the vegetable tray at the center of the table. Place the pitcher of remaining stock and the bowl of sauce near the host's seat.

While your guests are enjoying appetizers, turn on the hot pot. Bring the stock to a boil and add half of the vegetables, except for the spinach and crown daisy, arranging them in a pinwheel pattern and leaving space at the center. Place half of the bean curd and fish, except the crab, in the center. With a large spoon, gently stir the boiling stock, helping the flavor of each vegetable mingle well. Boil gently for about 3 minutes. Chop up the crab and add it to the pot, gently pressing the pieces into the broth, and cook for 2 minutes. Add half of the spinach and crown daisy, cover, and cook for 30 seconds, or until they turn bright and are barely wilted.

Growing Up in a Korean Kitchen

To serve, ladle hot chŏngol into individual bowls, attractively arranging the seafood, bean curd, and vegetables. Spoon in additional broth. Garnish each bowl with the sil koch'u and serve. While the guests are enjoying the first portion, repeat with the remaining ingredients. Keep the hot pot gently boiling and encourage guests to help themselves to a second or third helping directly from the pot. Serve with steamed rice, bowls of Vinegar Soy Sauce (page 28), Allspice Sauce (page 28), or Hot Red Pepper Sauce (page 30), and a generous array of side dishes (see the note on page 151).

10 ounces scallops, halved

1 pound red snapper fillets, sliced diagonally into 2-inch chunks

1 pound cod fillets, sliced diagonally into 2-inch chunks

1 pound littleneck clams, scrubbed clean

1 live blue crab, cut into pieces just before cooking

Chŏngol Sauce

1 tablespoon soy sauce

1 cup ch'ŏngju (rice wine) or vermouth

1 tablespoon freshly squeezed lemon juice

1 teaspoon freshly squeezed ginger juice

1 tablespoon sesame oil

1 tablespoon toasted sesame seeds

1/2 teaspoon salt

1/2 teaspoon freshly ground black pepper

6 cups Clear Chicken Stock (page 59) or Beef Stock (page 58)

2 tablespoons vegetable oil

10 cloves garlic, crushed and finely chopped

Pinch of sil koch'u (hot red pepper threads) or hot red pepper flakes, for garnish

✹ Pan-Fried Dishes and Pancakes

A variety of flavorful, colorful pan-fried dishes (chŏn or jŏn) are an important part of Korean cuisine. Typically, they are served as appetizers and side dishes, although some are substantial enough to be offered as entrees, and others make fine snack food. Chŏn include flour-based pancakes of all sizes, made with everything from mung beans to kimchi, as well as pan-fried dishes ranging from meat patties to fish fillets to sliced vegetables cooked in egg. A dipping sauce customarily accompanies them, either Vinegar Soy Sauce (page 28) or Allspice Sauce (page 28), sometimes both. The recipes in this chapter are easy to make, and most of them take less than 30 minutes to prepare and cook.

Tips for making and serving pan-fried dishes:

✽ Use a 12- to 14-inch cast-iron or nonstick skillet.

✽ Get organized before you start cooking: have all the necessary utensils and plates on hand, and line up the ingredients by the stovetop in a logical order. The short cooking time requires that ingredients be at the ready.

✽ Chŏn are best served hot out of the pan, but they can be reheated.

✽ Day-old chŏn can go into any stew recipes (pages 138 to 141).

Tips for making and serving pancakes:

✽ For crispy pancakes, always make the batter with ice cold water.

✽ Mix batters sparingly, just until smooth.

✽ Use batters soon after preparing them.

✽ When serving the pancakes, the first side cooked is the one that should be facing up.

(above) A variety of vegetable pancakes

(opposite) Green onion pancake stall, Kyŏnggi Province

Green Onion Pancakes

P'ajŏn

Serves 4
20 minutes to prepare and cook

1 pound small or medium-size thread green onions, white and pale green part only, cut into 7-inch pieces

1 cup all-purpose wheat flour

1 cup ice cold water

Pinch of salt

Pinch of freshly ground black pepper

3 tablespoons vegetable oil

2 cloves garlic, crushed and finely chopped

1 hot red Korean pepper, or 1/4 red bell pepper, seeded, deribbed, and finely diced

Pinch of sil koch'u (hot red pepper threads) or hot red pepper flakes

Vegetable pancakes are a standard offering at the Korean table. This particular favorite is made with lots of whole green onions. It is served as a side dish, an appetizer, or a snack. Tender, small thread green onions (sil p'a) are best for this recipe, but regular green onions are acceptable.

✿ ✿ ✿

Wash the green onions and pat dry with a kitchen towel. Reserve 4 pieces for garnish. To make the batter, in a chilled bowl, combine the flour and ice water and lightly mix with a wooden spoon. Season with the salt and pepper.

In a large cast-iron or nonstick skillet, heat 1 tablespoon vegetable oil over medium-high heat until it begins to smoke. Working quickly, add half of the green onions to the skillet and, using a spatula, form them into a rectangle shape, about 7 inches square. Add half of the garlic, red pepper, and sil koch'u. Quickly pour half of the batter over the green onions, spreading the batter evenly between them and maintaining the rectangular shape as much as possible. With the spatula, lightly flatten the green onions. Cook for 1 1/2 minutes, until the pancake edges turn golden brown and crusty. Shake the pan to loosen the pancake. Flip it over, and add 1/2 tablespoon vegetable oil to the skillet. Using the spatula, flatten and shape the pancake, making it as thin as possible; cook for 2 minutes. Flip again, and cook for 1 minute, to restore crispiness. Slide the finished pancake onto a bamboo tray. Repeat with the remaining ingredients. Transfer both pancakes to a cutting board and cut into bite-size pieces.

To serve, arrange the pancake pieces on 4 individual plates. Garnish each with 1 piece of the reserved green onion. Serve hot as an appetizer or side dish with Vinegar Soy Sauce (page 28) or Allspice Sauce (page 28), or both, in bowls as dipping sauces.

Variations: To make Shellfish and Green Onion Pancakes (Haemul P'a Chŏn), generous amounts of chopped clams, shrimp, prawns, mussels, squid, and other succulent shellfish are sprinkled on the green onions before the flour batter is added, then all is topped with an egg drizzling and cooked for a few minutes. Two southern seaside towns, the hot-spring city of Tongnae and the port of Samch'onp'o, are known for their regional versions of this recipe. It is said that these extraordinarily scrumptious pancakes were favorites of the royal kitchen in Seoul.

Growing Up in a Korean Kitchen

Chive Pancakes

Puch'ujŏn

Serves 4
20 minutes to prepare and cook

1 pound Korean chives or Chinese chives

1 cup all-purpose wheat flour

1 cup ice cold water

2 tablespoons koch'ujang (hot red pepper paste), or a pinch each of salt and freshly ground pepper

3 tablespoons vegetable oil

In the Korean culture, chives are considered to be an especially beneficial herb. Their delicate appearance and exquisite flavor are compatible with shellfish, chicken, mushrooms, and even pork. With this recipe, you can make two different kinds of chive pancakes: a pale-green pancake and a spicy red pancake made with hot red pepper paste.

❀ ❀ ❀

Set aside 8 whole chive stalks for garnish. Using a sharp knife or scissors, snip the rest into $1^1/2$-inch pieces. To make the batter, in a chilled bowl, combine the flour and ice water and lightly mix with a wooden spoon. To make spicy red pancakes, just before cooking, add the koch'ujang and chives to the batter. To make pale-green pancakes, omit the koch'ujang, add the chives, and season with the salt and pepper. Gently mix in a folding motion (chives bruise easily).

In a large cast-iron or nonstick skillet, heat 1 tablespoon vegetable oil over medium-high heat until it begins to smoke. Pour half of the batter into the skillet and spread quickly with a spoon or spatula. Shape into a thin pancake, about 8 inches in diameter. Cook for $1^1/2$ minutes, or until the edges turn golden brown and crispy. Shake the pan to loosen the pancake. Flip it over, and add $^1/2$ tablespoon vegetable oil around the pancake. Cook for 2 minutes, flattening a little more. Flip again and cook for 1 minute, to restore crispiness. Slide the finished pancake onto a tray. Repeat with the remaining batter. Transfer both pancakes to a cutting board and slice into bite-size pieces.

To serve, arrange the pancake pieces on 4 individual plates. Garnish each with 2 of the reserved chive stalks. Serve as an appetizer or side dish with Vinegar Soy Sauce (page 28) or Allspice Sauce (page 28), or both, in bowls as dipping sauces.

Variation: An even simpler pancake recipe is the simple country-style Spicy Pancake called Chang Ttŏk. Follow the recipe above, but omit the chives and add 1 tablespoon of toenjang (fermented bean paste). This down-to-earth and delicious pancake is one of my memory foods.

Summary Squash Pancakes

Hobakjŏn

Serves 4 to 6
25 minutes to prepare and cook

---

1 pound summer squash, cut into
3-inch matchsticks

1 teaspoon sea salt or kosher salt

1 clove garlic, crushed and finely
chopped

1 hot red Korean pepper, or ¼ red
bell pepper, seeded, deribbed,
and finely diced

1 hot green Korean pepper or
jalapeño pepper, seeded,
deribbed, and finely diced

6 ounces sea scallops, shrimp, or
clams, finely chopped

1 egg, lightly beaten

½ cup ice cold water

Pinch of salt

Pinch of freshly ground black
pepper

½ cup all-purpose wheat flour

3 tablespoons vegetable oil

Parsley sprigs or other decorative
greens, for garnish

This recipe mingles light and sweet summer squash, succulent seafood, and finely diced peppers to make a delicate and delicious pancake appetizer. It is my favorite. It is so easy to prepare that I often cook it in front of my guests. They can eat it hot off the griddle as they are enjoying an aperitif.

Place the squash in a bowl and sprinkle with the sea salt. Toss well and let sit for 10 minutes. Wrap the squash in a clean, dry kitchen towel and squeeze out as much liquid as possible. Return the squash to the bowl and add the garlic, peppers, and scallops. Toss well. Add the egg, ice water, salt, and pepper and lightly toss. Sprinkle the flour over the ingredients and lightly toss, just enough to coat the squash.

In a large cast-iron or nonstick skillet, heat 1 tablespoon vegetable oil over medium-high heat until it begins to smoke. Pour half of the squash batter into the skillet and, with the back of a wooden spoon, quickly shape into a thin pancake. Cook for about 2 minutes, or until the edges turn golden brown and crispy. Flip it over, add ½ tablespoon vegetable oil around the pancake, and cook for 2 minutes, flattening and shaping it with a spatula. Flip again and cook for 1 minute, to restore crispiness. Slide the finished pancake to a tray. Repeat with the remaining oil and batter. Transfer both pancakes to a cutting board and slice into wedges or squares.

To serve, arrange the pancake pieces on a platter or on individual dishes. Garnish with the parsley. Serve with Vinegar Soy Sauce (page 28) or Allspice Sauce (page 28), or both, in bowls as dipping sauces.

Potato Pancakes, Kangwŏndo Style

Kangwŏndo Kamjajŏn

Serves 4 to 6
30 minutes to prepare and cook

1 egg

5 tablespoons cornstarch

1 hot red Korean pepper, or ¼ red bell pepper, seeded, deribbed, and finely diced

1 hot green Korean pepper or jalapeño pepper, seeded, deribbed, and finely diced

4 fresh p'yogo (shiitake) mushrooms or other mushrooms, finely diced

2 green onions, white and pale green part only, finely minced

1 clove garlic, crushed and finely chopped

2 pounds potatoes, peeled

Pinch of salt

Pinch of freshly ground black pepper

2 tablespoons vegetable oil

This dish is a spicy local specialty from Kangwon Province, where half of Korea's potatoes are produced. Also called kamja pindae ttŏk, the appearance and cooking method of these pancakes are very similar to Mung Bean Pancakes (page 163).

❁ ❁ ❁

Crack the egg into a large bowl and lightly beat it. Add the cornstarch and mix well. Add the peppers, mushrooms, green onions, and garlic and mix well. With a grater, grate the potatoes into the bowl and lightly mix with the other ingredients (work quickly, to keep the potatoes from turning brown). Do not overmix. Season with salt and pepper.

In a large cast-iron or nonstick skillet, heat 1 tablespoon vegetable oil over medium-high heat until very hot, but not smoking. Using a large spoon, quickly drop the potato batter into the skillet to form 6 small pancakes, each about 3½ inches in diameter. Cook for about 4 minutes per side, or until the edges turn crispy and golden brown. Transfer the finished pancakes to a tray. Repeat with the remaining oil and batter.

To serve, arrange the pancakes on a platter. Serve as an appetizer or side dish with Vinegar Soy Sauce (page 28) or Allspice Sauce (page 28), or both, in bowls as dipping sauces.

Kimchi Pancakes

Kimchijŏn

Serves 4 to 6
25 minutes to prepare and cook

1 cup Whole Cabbage Kimchi
(page 97), firm stem part only
and without stuffing

3 ounces lean ground pork

3 large sweet green onions, or
6 green onions, white and pale
green part only, finely chopped

1 cup all-purpose wheat flour

1 egg, lightly beaten

1 cup ice cold water

4$\frac{1}{2}$ tablespoons vegetable oil

Parsley sprigs, for garnish

We grew up eating kimchi pancakes, and even today my mouth waters just thinking about them. The combination of spicy cabbage kimchi and bits of pork creates a unique taste. They make a very tasty appetizer or snack.

Wearing rubber gloves, wrap the kimchi stems in a paper towel and lightly squeeze out most of the liquid. Chop into fine pieces and place in a bowl. Add the pork, green onions, flour, egg, and ice water. Lightly mix.

In a large cast-iron or nonstick skillet, heat 1 tablespoon vegetable oil over medium-high heat until it begins to smoke. Drop about one-third of the kimchi batter into the skillet to make one large pancake. Cook for about 2 minutes, or until the edges turn brown and crispy. Flip it over, add $\frac{1}{2}$ tablespoon vegetable oil around the pancake, and cook for 2 minutes, flattening and shaping it with a spatula. Flip again and cook for 1 minute, to restore crispiness. Transfer the finished pancake to a tray. Repeat two times with the remaining oil and batter, making 3 pancakes, each about 7$\frac{1}{2}$ inches in diameter. Transfer the pancakes to a cutting board and, with a sharp knife, slice into wedges or squares.

To serve, arrange the pancakes on individual plates. Garnish with the parsley. Serve as an appetizer with Vinegar Soy Sauce (page 28) or Allspice Sauce (page 28), or both, in bowls as dipping sauces.

Note: These fiery pancakes can be easily regulated to create a milder or even hotter tidbit. For a milder version, rinse the kimchi once or let it soak in cold water for 5 minutes before adding it to the batter. To make it hotter, leave the stuffing in and add sweet and hot kimchi juice to your heart's content.

Growing Up in a Korean Kitchen

Mung Bean Pancakes

Pinchajŏn

Serves 6 to 8
30 minutes to prepare and cook

---

1 cup skinned mung beans

1 cup Whole Cabbage Kimchi (page 97), firm stem part only and without stuffing

2 tablespoons all-purpose wheat flour

4 ounces lean ground pork

1 hot red Korean pepper, or ½ red bell pepper, seeded, deribbed, and finely diced

1 hot green Korean pepper or jalapeño pepper, seeded, deribbed, and finely diced

4 tablespoons vegetable oil

½ tablespoon sil koch'u (hot red pepper threads), snipped into 1-inch pieces

Parsley sprigs, for garnish

These delectable pancakes appear on the appetizer menu at most Korean restaurants. As one of the favorites in the royal kitchen, they were sometimes sweetened and served as a dessert. They have a pleasant, grainy texture somewhat resembling cornmeal bread or polenta. Skinned mung beans can be purchased at Korean and Asian markets.

❀ ❀ ❀

The mung beans can be treated in one of two ways: soak the mung beans in 2 cups cold water overnight; or, add 3 cups cold water to the mung beans and boil over medium heat for 30 minutes, or until tender, and let cool. The beans will double in size. Drain, reserving the liquid. In a blender or food processor, puree the beans, gradually adding spoonfuls of the bean liquid, until the consistency becomes slightly thicker than cake batter. Set aside.

Wearing rubber gloves, wrap the kimchi in a paper towel and lightly squeeze out most of the liquid. Chop into fine pieces and place in a large bowl. Add the mung beans, flour, pork, and peppers and lightly mix with a wooden spoon. Adjust with additional bean liquid to make a cake batter–like consistency.

In a large cast-iron or nonstick skillet, heat 1 tablespoon vegetable oil over medium-high heat until it begins to smoke. Using a large spoon, drop the batter onto the skillet to quickly form 4 small pancakes. Do not flatten (this preserves the pancake's soft and fluffy texture). Sprinkle a pinch of sil koch'u on each pancake. Cook for about 2 minutes, or until the edges turn golden brown and crispy. Flip the pancakes and cook for 2 minutes. Flip again and cook for 1 minute, to restore crispiness. Transfer the finished pancakes to a tray. Repeat three times with the remaining oil and batter, making a total of 16 pancakes, each about 3½ inches in diameter.

To serve, arrange 2 to 3 pancakes each on individual plates. Garnish with the parsley. Serve as an appetizer with Vinegar Soy Sauce (page 28) or Allspice Sauce (page 28), or both, in bowls as dipping sauces.

Notes: It is customary to add a host of other ingredients to this basic recipe, including mung bean sprouts, fernbracken, summer squash strips, and slivered p'yogo mushrooms. Mung bean pancakes (and also the soybean pancake variation, below) are crumbly and tend to break apart easily. Adding 1 part all-purpose wheat flour or sweet rice flour to 5 parts beans will help bind the ingredients together. Usually, for easy handling, the pancakes are cooked in a manageable size, about 3 inches in diameter.

Variation: Follow the same recipe, substituting an equal amount of soybeans for mung beans, to make Soybean Pancakes (K'ong Pijijŏn).

Pan-Fried Summer Squash

Hobakjŏn

Serves 4 to 6
5 minutes to prepare
and 40 minutes to cook

1¹⁄₂ cups all-purpose wheat flour

Pinch of salt

Pinch of freshly ground black
  pepper

1 pound fresh summer squash,
  sliced crosswise into ¹⁄₄-inch
  disks

³⁄₄ cup ice cold water

1 egg, lightly beaten

8 tablespoons vegetable oil

This recipe and Summer Squash Pancakes (page 160) are two popular pan-fried dishes in the Korean kitchen. They are delicious and easy to make. Though they are made with identical ingredients (and both are called hobakjŏn), they look quite different. In this one, thin disks of squash are dipped in batter and pan-fried. For best appearance, choose uniformly straight squash, each about 2 inches in diameter.

In a heavy plastic bag, add ¹⁄₂ cup flour, salt, and pepper. Add the squash and shake well to coat each piece. In a bowl, combine the remaining 1 cup of flour, ice water, and egg, stirring lightly to make a smooth batter.

In a large cast-iron or nonstick skillet, heat 1¹⁄₂ tablespoons of vegetable oil over medium-high heat until it begins to smoke. Meanwhile, add one-fourth of the squash to the batter and gently mix, making sure that each piece is well coated. Quickly add the squash to the skillet all at once and cook for about 4 minutes, until the edges turn golden brown and crispy. Flip the squash and add ¹⁄₂ tablespoon vegetable oil, shaking the pan so the oil distributes evenly. Cook for about 3 minutes. Flip again and cook for 1 minute, to restore crispiness. Transfer to a tray. Repeat 3 times with the remaining ingredients, making about 50 squash pieces.

To serve, arrange the squash on a platter in a fan pattern. Serve warm or cold with Vinegar Soy Sauce (page 28) or Allspice Sauce (page 28) drizzled on top.

Growing Up in a Korean Kitchen

Pan-Fried Radishes

Mujŏn

Serves 4 to 6
30 minutes to prepare and cook

---

2 pounds Korean radishes or
  daikon, peeled and sliced
  crosswise into paper-thin pieces

1³/₄ cups all-purpose wheat flour

¹/₂ cup ice cold water

Pinch of salt

Pinch of freshly ground black
  pepper

7¹/₂ tablespoons vegetable oil

Radish greens or parsley sprigs,
  for garnish

An excellent example of Korean country cookery, pan-fried radishes are a mildly sweet appetizer or side dish, and they are very easy to make. It was one of the tasty snacks of my childhood. We all still love their refreshingly clean taste.

In a saucepan, make 1 cup of acidulated water (page 10). Add the radishes and boil for 5 minutes, or until they are almost cooked, but still firm. Drain in a colander, pat dry, and transfer to a plate.

In a shallow bowl, combine 1 cup flour and the ice water and lightly mix to form a batter. Season with the salt and pepper. Spread the remaining ³/₄ cup flour on a plate. Line up the ingredients by the heat source, with the batter closest, followed by the flour, and then the radishes. Place a bamboo tray nearby.

In a large cast-iron or nonstick skillet, heat 1 tablespoon vegetable oil over medium-high heat until it begins to smoke. Meanwhile, working with about 7 radish pieces, dredge in flour, then dip in the batter. Quickly add the radishes to the skillet and cook for about 2 minutes, or until the edges turn golden brown. Flip the radishes and add ¹/₂ tablespoon vegetable oil, shaking the pan so the oil distributes evenly, and cook for 2 minutes. Turn only once. Transfer to the bamboo tray. Repeat with the remaining ingredients, making about 35 radish pieces.

Arrange the radish pieces on a large serving plate in a fan pattern. Garnish with radish greens. Serve as an appetizer or side dish with Vinegar Soy Sauce (page 28) or Allspice Sauce (page 28), or both, in bowls as dipping sauces.

Pan-Fried Potatoes

Kamjajŏn

Serves 4 to 6
10 minutes to prepare
and 30 minutes to cook

2 cups all-purpose wheat flour

2 cups ice cold water

10 Korean chives, snipped into fine specks

Pinch of salt

Pinch of freshly ground black pepper

2 pounds small potatoes, each about 2$^{1}/_{2}$ inches in diameter

7$^{1}/_{2}$ tablespoons vegetable oil

Potato lovers all over the world will rave about this simple way of cooking potatoes. Chives are the source for the special flavor of this dish.

❀ ❀ ❀

To make the batter, in a bowl, combine 1 cup of flour with the ice water and mix until smooth. Add the chives, reserving some for garnish. Season with the salt and pepper. Gently stir and set aside.

Peel the potatoes and cut them into $^{1}/_{4}$-inch-thick rounds. (To prevent the potatoes from turning brown, they can be kept in a bowl of lightly salted water before cooking.) Place the potatoes in a saucepan with about 1$^{1}/_{2}$ cups of cold water. Boil gently over medium-high heat for 4 minutes; drain in a colander and let cool. Thinly spread the remaining 1 cup of flour on a plate and dredge the potato slices on both sides. Set aside.

In a large cast-iron or nonstick skillet, heat 1 tablespoon vegetable oil over medium-high heat until it begins to smoke. Meanwhile, dip about 10 potato slices in the batter to coat well. Add the potatoes to the skillet (use a spatula to evenly separate the chives on each piece). Cook for about 3 minutes, or until the edges are crispy and golden brown. Flip the potatoes and add $^{1}/_{2}$ tablespoon of oil, shaking the pan so the oil distributes evenly. Cook for 3 minutes, adjusting the heat to avoid burning. Turn only once. Transfer to a bamboo tray. Repeat four times with the remaining ingredients, making about 50 potato pieces.

To serve, arrange the potatoes on a large platter or on individual dishes, 6 to 8 slices each. Garnish with the reserved chives. Serve with Vinegar Soy Sauce (page 28) or Allspice Sauce (page 28), or both, in bowls as dipping sauces.

Stuffed Pan-Fried Bean Curd

Tubu Sobaegi

Serves 4 to 6
20 minutes to prepare
and 25 minutes to cook

2 pounds oyster mushrooms or
thinly sliced white button
mushrooms

24 stalks Korean watercress, or
12 green onions

8 ounces finely ground beef sirloin
or ground round

2 green onions, finely chopped

2 cloves garlic, crushed and finely
chopped

1 tablespoon chŏngju (rice wine)
or vermouth

1 tablespoon sesame oil

1 tablespoon toasted sesame
seeds

1 egg yolk, plus 4 whole eggs

½ teaspoon salt

½ teaspoon freshly ground black
pepper

1½ cups all-purpose wheat flour

2 pounds firm bean curd, halved
and cut into 1½-inch dominoes

4 tablespoons vegetable oil

This elaborate bean curd preparation makes an attractive entree, side dish, or appetizer. The meat and mushroom stuffing adds an interesting dimension and flavor to this dish. It is often used in Bean Curd and Vegetable Hot Pot (page 152) in place of the plain pan-fried bean curd.

In a stockpot, make 3 quarts of acidulated water (page 10) and bring to a boil. Add the mushrooms and blanch for 10 seconds, or until well wilted. Plunge into cold water to stop the cooking. Drain in a colander. Wrap the mushrooms in a paper towel and gently squeeze out as much liquid as possible. Chop into fine pieces and transfer to a bowl. Repeat with the watercress and blanch for 1½ minutes, until it turns bright green and is barely wilted. Set aside.

To make the stuffing, add the beef, green onions, garlic, chŏngju, sesame oil, sesame seeds, egg yolk, salt, and pepper to the mushrooms and mix well. Using your hands, roll about a tablespoon of the stuffing into a walnut-size ball. Repeat with the remaining mixture, making 24 balls.

Spread the flour on a plate. Dredge each ball of stuffing well with flour. Slightly flatten 1 ball and place it between 2 pieces of bean curd. Press firmly, making a 1-inch-thick sandwich. Repeat with the remaining bean curd and stuffing. Dredge the stuffed bean curd in flour and transfer to a tray. In a shallow bowl, lightly beat the 4 eggs with a few drops of water and season with a pinch each of salt and pepper. Line up the ingredients by the heat source, with the egg closest, then the stuffed bean curd. Place a bamboo tray nearby.

In a large cast-iron or nonstick skillet, heat 2 tablespoons vegetable oil over medium heat until hot, but not smoking. Meanwhile, divide the bean curd into two batches. Dip the first batch, one at a time, in the egg and evenly coat on both sides. Remove each to a flat, slotted spoon and drain off excess coating. Quickly add the batch to the skillet and cook, without disturbing, for 6 to 8 minutes per side, or until the coating is golden, yet moist. Adjust the heat between medium and medium-high to keep the coating from becoming too brown and dry. Turn only once. Transfer to the bamboo tray. Repeat with the second batch of bean curd. Transfer to a cutting board and tie each piece, crosswise, with a strand of watercress, like a gift package.

To serve, arrange on a serving platter or individual dishes. Serve hot as an entree or side dish with Vinegar Soy Sauce (page 28) or Allspice Sauce (page 28), or both, in bowls as dipping sauces.

Stuffed Pan-Fried P'yogo Mushrooms

P'yogojŏn

Serves 4 to 6
20 minutes to prepare
and 25 minutes to cook

---

30 fresh unblemished p'yogo (shiitake) mushrooms, about 2 inches in diameter, plus 4 small mushrooms for garnish

½ teaspoon salt

½ teaspoon freshly ground black pepper

½ cup all-purpose wheat flour, plus extra for dusting

8 ounces medium-firm bean curd

10 ounces lean ground beef sirloin or ground round

3 eggs

1 tablespoon ch'ŏngju (rice wine) or vermouth

2 green onions, white and pale green part only, finely minced

2 cloves garlic, crushed and finely chopped

1 tablespoon sesame oil

3 tablespoons vegetable oil

4 parsley sprigs, for garnish

Stuffed and pan-fried p'yogo mushrooms are delicious and visually attractive. This dish, along with Stuffed Pan-Fried Peppers (page 169) and Pan-Fried Fish Fillets (page 174), are often served together to form the popular and much-loved *samsaekjŏn* (three-colored pan-fried dishes).

Wipe the mushrooms clean with a damp paper towel and remove the stems (save them for another use). Season with the salt and pepper, and dust the insides of the caps with flour. Set aside.

To make the stuffing, wrap the bean curd in a paper towel and squeeze out as much liquid as possible. In a bowl, add the bean curd, beef, 1 egg, ch'ŏngju, green onions, garlic, and sesame oil and mix well. Using your hands, roll about a tablespoon of the stuffing into a ball. Repeat with the remaining stuffing, making 30 walnut-size balls. Firmly stuff 1 ball into each mushroom cap.

Spread the flour on a plate. In a shallow bowl, lightly beat the remaining 2 eggs with a few drops of water. Line up the ingredients by the heat source, with the egg closest, followed by the flour, then the mushrooms. Place a bamboo tray nearby.

In a large cast-iron or nonstick skillet, heat 1 tablespoon vegetable oil over medium-high heat until very hot, but not smoking. Meanwhile, working with 10 mushrooms, dredge each one in flour on the stuffing side only and coat with the egg. Quickly add the mushrooms to the skillet, stuffed side down, and cook for about 3 minutes, or until the egg coating is golden, yet moist. Flatten each mushroom with a spatula. Adjust the heat between medium and medium-high to keep the coating from becoming too brown and dry. Flip the mushrooms and cook for 5 minutes. Flip only once. Transfer to the bamboo tray. Repeat two times with the remaining ingredients. Transfer to a cutting board and cut each mushroom in half.

To serve, arrange the mushrooms on a large platter in a fan pattern. Garnish with the small mushrooms and parsley sprigs. Serve as an entree or side dish with Vinegar Soy Sauce (page 28) or Allspice Sauce (page 28), or both, in bowls as dipping sauces.

Stuffed Pan-Fried Peppers

Koch'ujŏn

Serves 4 to 6

20 minutes to prepare
and 25 minutes to cook

---

6 hot red Korean peppers or other
hot red peppers, seeded,
deribbed, and halved

6 hot green Korean peppers or
jalapeño peppers, seeded,
deribbed, and halved

1 cup all-purpose wheat flour, plus
extra for dusting

1 pound medium-firm bean curd

1 pound scallops, minced, or
1 pound ground beef sirloin

3 eggs

2 small green onions, white and
pale green part only, finely
minced

2 cloves garlic, crushed and finely
chopped

1 tablespoon ch'ŏngju (rice wine)
or vermouth

1 tablespoon sesame oil

Pinch of salt

Pinch of freshly ground black
pepper

2 tablespoons vegetable oil

Parsley sprigs, for garnish

3 or 4 fresh whole green and red
peppers, for garnish

Fresh peppers taste wonderful when they are cooked. One of the most popular pan-fried dishes, it is often served with Stuffed Pan-Fried P'yogo Mushrooms (page 168) and Pan-Fried Fish Fillets (page 174).

Wash the pepper halves under cold running water and drain in a colander. Pat dry with a paper towel on the skin side only. (Leave the inside moist for easy stuffing.) On a flat tray, place the peppers, cut side up, in 1 layer and dust the insides with flour. To tone down the peppers, if desired, blanch them in 4 cups of acidulated water (page 10) for less than 10 seconds before dusting.

To make the stuffing, wrap the bean curd in a paper towel and squeeze out as much liquid as possible. In a large bowl, add the bean curd, scallops, 1 egg, green onions, garlic, ch'ŏngju, sesame oil, salt, and pepper and mix well. Using your hands, roll about a tablespoon of the stuffing into a ball. Repeat with the remaining stuffing, making 24 walnut-size balls. Firmly stuff 1 ball into each pepper.

Spread the flour on a plate. In a shallow bowl, lightly beat the remaining 2 eggs with a few drops of water. Line up the ingredients by the heat source, with the egg closest, followed by the flour, then the peppers. Place a bamboo tray nearby.

In a nonstick skillet, heat 1 tablespoon vegetable oil over medium-high heat until very hot, but not smoking. Meanwhile, working with 12 peppers, dredge each one in flour on the stuffing side only and coat with the egg. Quickly add the peppers to the skillet, stuffed side down, and cook for 3 minutes, or until the coating is golden, yet moist. Flatten each with a spatula. Adjust the heat between medium and medium-high to keep the coating from becoming too brown and dry. Flip the peppers and cook for 3 minutes. Flip only once. Transfer to the bamboo tray. Repeat with the remaining ingredients.

To serve, arrange the peppers on a platter in a fan pattern. Garnish with the parsley and whole peppers. Serve as an entree or side dish with Vinegar Soy Sauce (page 28) or Allspice Sauce (page 28), or both, in bowls as dipping sauces.

Pan-Fried Crab Cakes

Kyejŏn

Serves 4

25 minutes to prepare and cook

1 pound medium-firm bean curd

1 pound king crab legs, or 1 cup lump or backfin crab meat

3 eggs

1 tablespoon ch'ŏngju (rice wine) or vermouth

1 green onion, white and pale green part only, finely minced

2 cloves garlic, crushed and finely chopped

1 tablespoon sesame oil

Pinch of salt

Pinch of freshly ground black pepper

1 cup all-purpose wheat flour

2 tablespoons vegetable oil

1 lemon, quartered, for garnish

Pinch of sil koch'u (hot red pepper threads), snipped into small pieces, for garnish

Parsley sprigs, for garnish

Korean crab cakes are similar to their American cousins in appearance but have a distinctively different flavor. In this recipe, bean curd is used to moisten and bind the sweet, juicy crab meat, then green onions, garlic, and spices are added. The result is an incredibly succulent and delicious crab cake. This luxurious seafood side dish or entree is a breeze to prepare.

Wrap the bean curd in a paper towel and squeeze out as much liquid as possible. Using a wooden mallet, crack open the crab legs and collect the meat (about 1 cup) in a large mixing bowl (reserve the shells to make stock for future use). Add the bean curd, 1 egg, ch'ŏngju, green onion, garlic, sesame oil, salt, and pepper and lightly mix with a wooden spoon. Do not overmix. Divide the mixture into 8 balls and flatten into small cakes, each about 3 inches in diameter. Set aside.

Spread the flour on a small plate. In a shallow bowl, lightly beat the remaining 2 eggs with a few drops of water. Line up the ingredients by the heat source, with the egg closest, followed by the flour, then the crab cakes. Place a bamboo tray nearby.

In a large nonstick skillet, heat 1 tablespoon vegetable oil over medium-high heat until very hot, but not smoking. Meanwhile, working with 4 crab cakes, dredge each one in flour and coat with the egg. Quickly add the cakes to the skillet and cook for 2 minutes, or until the coating is golden, yet moist. Flip the cakes and cook for 2 minutes. Transfer the finished cakes to a tray. Repeat with the remaining ingredients.

To serve, arrange the crab cakes on a large platter or on 4 individual plates, 2 crab cakes each. Garnish with the lemon, sil koch'u, and parsley. Serve as an entree or side dish with Vinegar Soy Sauce (page 28) in a bowl as a dipping sauce. Steamed rice and Seasoned Spinach (page 125) or other green vegetable side dishes make this sumptuous meal complete.

Pan-Fried Clam Cakes

Chogaejŏn

Serves 4

25 minutes to prepare and cook

---

8 ounces medium-firm bean curd

12 ounces clam meat, drained and finely minced

4 ounces ground beef sirloin

1 tablespoon ch'ŏngju (rice wine) or vermouth

3 eggs

1 green onion, white and pale green part only, finely minced

2 cloves garlic, crushed and finely chopped

1 tablespoon sesame oil

$1/2$ tablespoon toasted sesame seeds

Pinch of salt

Pinch of freshly ground black pepper

$1/2$ cup all-purpose wheat flour

2 tablespoons vegetable oil

1 lemon, quartered or sliced into wheels, for garnish

Pinch of sil koch'u (hot red pepper threads), snipped into small pieces, for garnish

Parsley sprigs, for garnish

Similar to crab cakes, clam cakes are equally succulent and delicious. Adding a mixture of ground sirloin, bean curd, and spices make this Korean version of clam cakes extra flavorful.

❋ ❋ ❋

Wrap the bean curd in a paper towel and squeeze out as much liquid as possible. In a large bowl, combine the bean curd, clam meat, beef, ch'ŏngju, 1 egg, green onion, garlic, sesame oil, sesame seeds, salt, and pepper and mix well. Divide the mixture into 8 balls and flatten into small cakes, each about 3 inches in diameter. Set aside.

Spread the flour on a small plate. In a shallow bowl, lightly beat the remaining 2 eggs with a few drops of water. Line up the ingredients by the heat source, with the egg closest, followed by the flour, then the clam cakes. Place a bamboo tray nearby.

In a nonstick skillet, heat 1 tablespoon vegetable oil over medium-high heat until very hot, but not smoking. Meanwhile, working with 4 clam cakes, dredge each one with flour and coat with the egg. Quickly add the cakes to the skillet and cook for $1^1/2$ minutes, or until the coating is golden, yet moist. Flip the cakes and cook for $1^1/2$ minutes. Flatten each cake with a spatula. Adjust the heat between medium and medium-high to prevent the coating from becoming too brown and dry. Transfer the finished cakes to a tray. Repeat with the remaining ingredients.

To serve, arrange the clam cakes on a platter or on 4 individual plates, 2 cakes each. Garnish with the lemon, sil koch'u, and parsley. Serve as an appetizer or side dish with Vinegar Soy Sauce (page 28) in a bowl as a dipping sauce.

Variations: In place of clams, use minced squid, white fish, or shrimp.

Pan-Fried Beef and Bean Curd Cakes

Kallapjŏn

Serves 4 to 6

30 minutes to prepare and cook

---

1 pound medium-firm bean curd

1 pound ground beef sirloin or ground beef round

2 green onions, white and green part only, finely minced

2 tablespoons freshly squeezed garlic juice

1 hot green Korean pepper or jalapeño pepper, seeded, deribbed, and finely diced

2 tablespoons ch'ŏngju (rice wine) or vermouth

1 tablespoon sesame oil

4 eggs

Pinch of salt

Pinch of freshly ground black pepper

1 cup all-purpose wheat flour

3 tablespoons vegetable oil

Pinch of sil koch'u (hot red pepper threads), snipped into small pieces, for garnish

Parsley sprigs, for garnish

Kallapjŏn look like tiny, yellow hamburger patties. They are made with ground beef round and nutritious bean curd, then are dipped in egg before being pan-fried, which accounts for their color. Traditional kallapjŏn are made the size of half-dollar coins, thus they are also known as *tonjŏn*, "money patties." These are a favorite among Korean children, enjoyed as part of their lunchbox meals or as a snack. Korean children affectionately call them *tonggurang ttaeng*, "yummy circles and dots."

Wrap the bean curd in a paper towel and squeeze out as much liquid as possible. In a large bowl, combine the bean curd, beef, green onions, garlic juice, pepper, ch'ŏngju, sesame oil, 1 egg, salt, and pepper and mix well. Spoon some of the mixture into your hands and make a flat, round patty, about 1/2 inch thick and 3 inches in diameter. Repeat with the remaining mixture, making a total of 12 patties. Set aside.

Spread the flour on a plate. In a shallow bowl, lightly beat the remaining 3 eggs with a few drops of water. Line up the ingredients by the heat source, with the egg closest, followed by the flour, then the patties. Place a bamboo tray nearby.

In a large cast-iron or nonstick skillet, heat 1 tablespoon of vegetable oil over medium-high heat until very hot, but not smoking. Meanwhile, working with 4 patties, dredge each one with flour and coat all sides with the egg. Add the patties to the skillet all at once and cook for 2 1/2 minutes per side, or until the coating is golden, yet moist. Flatten and shape each with a spatula. Adjust the heat between medium and medium-high to keep the coating from becoming brown and dry. Transfer the finished cakes to the bamboo tray. Repeat two times with the remaining ingredients.

To serve, arrange the cakes on a platter. Garnish with the sil koch'u and parsley. Serve as an appetizer or side dish with Vinegar Soy Sauce (page 28) or Allspice Sauce (page 28), or both, in bowls as dipping sauces.

Note: The patties in this recipe are twice the size of the tiny traditional ones. If you like, you can make them coin-sized. If you are in a hurry, you may even make 2 large patties and serve them in hamburger buns. They are delicious at any size!

Pan-Fried Beef Liver

Naejangjŏn

Serves 4
20 minutes to prepare and cook

---

¹/₂ pound beef liver

1 tablespoon distilled white vinegar

1 clove garlic, crushed and finely chopped

1 green onion, white and pale green part only, finely chopped

Pinch of salt

Pinch of freshly ground black pepper

2 tablespoons ch'ŏngju (rice wine) or vermouth

¹/₂ cup all-purpose wheat flour

2 eggs

¹/₂ tablespoon sesame oil

3 tablespoons vegetable oil

Pinch of sil koch'u (hot red pepper threads), snipped into small pieces, for garnish

Parsley sprigs, for garnish

Cooking meat innards remains very much a part of today's Korean kitchen. Beef innards are especially popular among Korean gourmands as an appetizer or side dish. The following is the standard recipe for beef liver.

Remove the membranes from the liver. To make an instant stock for the liver, fill a saucepan with 4 cups of water and add the vinegar, garlic, and green onion; bring to a boil. Add the liver and gently boil for 2 minutes, to season and firm the liver for easy slicing. Cool and cut into ¹/₄-inch pieces. On a large plate, arrange the liver in 1 layer, season with salt and pepper, and evenly sprinkle with ch'ŏngju. Set aside.

Spread the flour on a small plate. In a shallow bowl, lightly beat the eggs with the sesame oil and a few drops of water. Line up the ingredients by the heat source, with the egg closest, followed by the flour, then the liver. Place a bamboo tray nearby.

In a large nonstick skillet, heat 1 tablespoon of vegetable oil over medium heat until hot. Meanwhile, divide the liver into 2 batches. Working with the first batch, dredge each piece with flour and coat with the egg. Quickly add the liver to the skillet. Cook for 2 minutes, or until the edges begin to curl. Flip the liver, add ¹/₂ tablespoon vegetable oil, tipping the skillet to evenly distribute the oil, and cook for 2 minutes. Flip only once. Transfer to the bamboo tray. Repeat with the remaining ingredients.

To serve, arrange the liver slices on a large serving plate in a fan pattern. Garnish with the sil koch'u and parsley. Serve as an appetizer or side dish with Vinegar Soy Sauce (page 28) in a bowl as a dipping sauce.

Variations: Beef lung and tripe can both be pan-fried in the same manner. Beef lung must be boiled for at least 30 minutes first, because the meat is too wobbly to slice. Tripe does not need to be boiled—just give it light crisscross slashes, to prevent curling during cooking.

Pan-Fried Fish Fillets

Saengsŏnjŏn

Serves 4

35 minutes to prepare and cook

---

1 pound fish fillets, such as sole, red snapper, flounder, or cod, cut diagonally into ¹/₂-inch slices

1 teaspoon salt

1 teaspoon freshly ground black pepper

1 tablespoon ch'ŏngju (rice wine) or vermouth

¹/₂ cup all-purpose wheat flour

2 eggs

2 tablespoons vegetable oil

1 lemon, quartered or sliced into lemon wheels, for garnish

Pinch of sil koch'u (hot red pepper threads), snipped into small pieces, for garnish

Parsley sprigs, for garnish

Pan-frying fish the Korean way produces a wonderfully light and tasty dish. Any succulent and delicate white-fleshed fish is a good candidate: sole, red snapper, cod, mullet, halibut, sea perch, croaker, and flounder are all excellent. This dish is often included as one of the *samsaekjŏn* (three-colored pan-fried dishes), along with Stuffed Pan-Fried P'yogo Mushrooms (page 168) and Stuffed Pan-Fried Peppers (page 169).

❀ ❀ ❀

Rinse the fish and pat dry with a paper towel. Place it in a colander in a single layer. Add the salt and pepper, and sprinkle the ch'ŏngju on top. Set aside for 5 minutes.

Spread the flour on a small plate. In a shallow bowl, lightly beat the eggs with a few drops of water. Line up the ingredients by the heat source, with the egg closest, followed by the flour, then the fish. Place a bamboo tray nearby.

In a large nonstick skillet, heat ¹/₂ tablespoon vegetable oil over medium-high heat until very hot, but not smoking. Meanwhile, divide the fish into four batches. Working with the first batch, dredge each piece with flour and coat with the egg. Quickly add the fish to the skillet and cook for 2 minutes per side, or until the coating is golden, yet moist. Adjust the heat between medium and medium-high to keep the coating from becoming too brown and dry. Transfer to the bamboo tray. Repeat three times with the remaining ingredients. Transfer to a cutting board and cut each fish into bite-size pieces.

To serve, arrange the fish on a platter in a fan pattern. Garnish with the lemon, sil koch'u, and parsley. Serve as an entree or side dish with Vinegar Soy Sauce (page 28) in a bowl as a dipping sauce. Seasoned Spinach (page 125) or any fresh Korean salad goes very well with this dish.

Note: Traditionally, a few drops of gardenia seed extract (ch'ija) were added as a food dye to heighten the yellow color of the egg coating.

Variation: To make Pan-Fried Prawn Butterflies (Saeujŏn), substitute 12 large prawns or large tiger shrimp for the fish. Peel, devein, and butterfly the prawns, make a few crisscross slashes on the back of each prawn, and flatten them with the flat side of a knife to prevent curling while cooking. Follow the directions in the base recipe, but pan-fry for only 1¹/₂ minutes per side. Serve as an appetizer, entree, or side dish.

Pan-Fried Oysters

Kuljŏn

Serves 4
20 minutes to prepare and cook

---

1 pound freshly shucked oysters
(about 12 medium-sized)

Pinch of salt

Pinch of freshly ground black
pepper

1 tablespoon ch'ŏngju (rice wine)
or vermouth

1 cup all-purpose wheat flour

2 eggs

2 tablespoons vegetable oil

1 lemon, quartered or sliced into
wheels, for garnish

Pinch of sil koch'u (hot red pepper
threads), snipped into small
pieces, for garnish

Parsley sprigs, for garnish

American Pacific oysters are the ideal choice for this recipe. Pan-fried with a light film of vegetable oil, the oysters turn out light, crispy, and delicious. The recipe is easy to follow and quick to make.

❀ ❀ ❀

Place the oysters on a flat bamboo tray and pat them dry with a paper towel. Season with the salt and pepper (oysters are naturally salty, so use a minimum of salt). Sprinkle with ch'ŏngju and set aside for 5 minutes.

Place the oysters in a plastic bag, add $^1/_2$ cup flour, and shake to evenly coat all. Spread the remaining $^1/_2$ cup of flour on a small plate. In a shallow bowl, lightly beat the eggs with a few drops of water. Line up the ingredients by the heat source, with the egg closest, followed by the flour, then the oysters. Place a bamboo tray nearby.

In a large nonstick skillet, heat 1 tablespoon of vegetable oil over medium-high heat until very hot. Meanwhile, working with 6 oysters, dredge each piece with flour and coat with the egg. Add the oysters to the skillet all at once and cook for 2 minutes, or until the coating is golden, yet moist. Flip the oysters and cook for 1 minute. Adjust the heat between medium and medium-high to keep the coating from becoming too brown and dry. Transfer to the bamboo tray. Repeat with the remaining ingredients.

To serve, arrange the oysters on a serving plate or individual plates. Garnish with the lemon, sil koch'u, and parsley. Serve as an appetizer or side dish with Vinegar Soy Sauce (page 28) in a bowl as a dipping sauce. Chilled Radish Salad (page 119) and Cucumber Salad (page 118) make excellent side dishes.

✿ The Art of Korean Barbecue

Korea's ancient way of cooking, open-fire grilling, is as popular and exciting today as it was before the introduction of the modern stove. Traditional Korean grilling was usually done over natural oak charcoal, and until recently every family owned one or two clay charcoal braziers (p'ungno) and a couple of grilling racks. Today, most urban apartment-dwellers and restaurants have replaced their charcoal braziers with the more convenient, but otherwise less desirable, propane gas grills. Still, wisps of white-gray smoke rising in the remote countryside sky give a hint that the fading art of charcoal making is still practiced, and that somewhere, oak stumps are still being stacked inside mud kilns and baked for days. In the markets we can still see the occasional charcoal vendors. Whenever I catch sight of wood-burning braziers in street food stalls anywhere in Asia, I think of the p'ungno in our old family kitchen.

Koreans love to grill. Grilled dishes (kui) include meat, fish, seafood, vegetables, hot peppers, garlic, mushrooms, fruits, and herbal roots. Depending on their particular character, they are dressed with either a rich marinade or a subtle seasoning. The meat is sliced very thin, marinated, and then quickly grilled, making it flavorful, moist, and tender on the inside and delightfully crusty on the outside. When a combination of meat and vegetables are skewered into a colorful and attractive presentation, the dishes are called sanjŏk.

There is no substitute for open-fire grilling over either a charcoal or gas flame, especially for meat. A recent innovation, a dome-shaped charcoal pulgogi grill with a ridge at its base for collecting the delicious juices, is popular for home and restaurant use. The alternative methods of broiling or pan-grilling will do the job, but the results will not be quite as good. Pan-grilling is the least favorable method, but even this has its merits. It is an easy way to cook, and it also can create rich, naturally deglazed brown juices that collect at the bottom of the pan.

(above) Aralia roots

(opposite) Grilling fired beef, pork, beef ribs, and rice cake sticks

Here are some grilling tips to remember:

❀ If possible, have your butcher cut the meat for you. If you must do it yourself, wash the meat and pat dry with a paper towel, place it in a plastic bag, and freeze for 3 to 4 hours, until the meat is firm. Slice the meat using a sharp meat cleaver or chef's knife. Pat dry with a paper towel before marinating.

❀ Most of the marinades in this chapter are subtle variations on two basic Korean sauces: the milder Allspice Sauce (page 28) and the more robust Hot Red Pepper Sauce (page 30). These sauces may be used instead, if desired. Leftover marinade will stay fresh in the refrigerator for 3 to 4 days.

❀ Cook the food in two or more batches. As you and your guests are enjoying an aperitif, cook the first batch and serve immediately, sizzling hot off the grill. Repeat with the next batch. If this is not possible, cook all at once and keep hot in a covered pan until ready to serve.

❀ When charcoal grilling, use a grilling basket lightly brushed with vegetable oil. Or, cover a barbecue grill with aluminum foil and brush lightly with oil. With a fork or chopstick, puncture the foil to make many holes.

❀ When broiling, use a broiling pan that allows fats and juices to drip down, or use a rack set in a roasting pan. If possible, prepare two pans and put in the next batch as soon as the first is done.

❀ When pan-grilling, use a 12-inch cast-iron or 14-inch nonstick skillet.

❀ Use bamboo skewers that have been soaked in cold water for 1 hour (this will keep them from burning). Thread the skewers starting 1 inch from the top and leaving 2 inches at the bottom. During cooking, the end pieces will shrink and secure the other ingredients on the skewer.

Fired Beef

Pulgogi

Serves 4 to 6
20 minutes to prepare
and 15 minutes to cook

2 pounds lean beef tenderloin
   roast, eye of round, or sirloin

Marinade for Fired Beef

3 tablespoons soy sauce

½ cup ch'ŏngju (rice wine) or
   vermouth

1 Korean or Asian pear, peeled
   and grated, or 4 tablespoons
   freshly squeezed lemon juice

2 green onions, white and pale
   green part, finely minced

3 cloves garlic, crushed and finely
   chopped

4 walnut halves, finely chopped

2 tablespoons corn syrup

1 tablespoon sugar

1 tablespoon sesame oil

1 tablespoon toasted sesame
   seeds

½ tablespoon freshly ground black
   pepper

Pinch of salt

1 to 5 tablespoons vegetable oil

Cabbage hearts or lettuce leaves

1 tablespoon coarsely chopped
   pine nuts, for garnish

½ tablespoon sil koch'u (hot red
   pepper threads) or hot red
   pepper flakes, for garnish

Thoughtful Korean hosts insist that pulgogi be a part of the menu when they entertain special guests. Pulgogi simply means "fired meat," but it has become synonymous with grilled beef because of the Korean passion for it, particularly the meat from the native, grass-fed, free-grazing cattle called *hanu kogi*. Although it costs more and is admittedly less tender than imported beef, Koreans believe it has an exceptionally exquisite flavor. The following recipe is our family's. It is similar to Nŏbiani, the original royal kitchen recipe, but in the royal recipe the meat is lightly tenderized with a knife and each piece of beef is secured with bamboo skewers on both ends during cooking for a formal presentation.

Slice the beef across the grain into large ⅛-inch-thick pieces. In a large bowl, combine the marinade ingredients and mix well with a spoon. Add the beef and, with your fingers, massage the marinade into the meat. Wrap the bowl tightly with plastic wrap and marinate in the refrigerator for 1 hour.

To grill the beef, start the coals 30 minutes before cooking; or, preheat a gas grill. Lightly brush the grilling rack with the vegetable oil and set it 4 inches from the heat source. Add the beef, in batches or all at once, and grill 5 to 6 minutes per side, or until caramel brown and crusty and to the desired doneness. Repeat if necessary with the remaining beef.

To broil the beef, preheat the broiler. Lightly brush the broiler pan with the vegetable oil and set it 6 inches from the heat source. Add the beef, in batches or all at once, and broil for 2 minutes per side, or to the desired doneness. Repeat if necessary with the remaining beef.

To pan-grill the beef, in a 12-inch cast-iron or 14-inch nonstick skillet, heat 1 tablespoon vegetable oil over medium-high heat until it begins to smoke. Add the beef, in batches or all at once, and cook for 2 minutes per side, or to the desired doneness, flattening with a spatula to prevent curling. Turn only once. Repeat if necessary with the remaining beef. Save the pan juices to spoon over the beef before serving.

On a cutting board, slice the beef into bite-size pieces. Make a bed of cabbage on individual plates and place the beef on top of each. Garnish with the pine nuts and sil koch'u. Serve with hot steamed rice. Chilled Radish Salad (page 119), Cucumber Salad (page 118), and Leaf Lettuce Salad (page 116) are customary side dishes.

Fired Beef Ribs

Kalbi Kui

Serves 4
20 minutes to prepare
nd 15 minutes to cook

---

3 pounds lean prime ribs of beef, cut crosswise into 12 bone-in strips, each about 1 inch long

Marinade for Fired Beef Ribs

½ cup soy sauce

1 Korean or Asian pear, peeled and grated, or 4 tablespoons freshly squeezed lemon juice

½ cup ch'ŏngju (rice wine) or vermouth

5 cloves garlic, crushed and finely chopped

3 large sweet green onions, or green onions, white and pale green part only, finely minced

½ cup corn syrup, or 3 tablespoons sugar

1 tablespoon sugar

2 tablespoons sesame oil

2 tablespoons toasted sesame seeds

4 walnut halves, finely chopped

Pinch of salt

1 tablespoon freshly ground pepper

1 to 2 tablespoons vegetable oil

2 tablespoons pine nuts, finely chopped, for garnish

1 tablespoon sil koch'u (hot red pepper threads) or hot red pepper flakes, for garnish

Kalbi's exquisite flavor is sometimes compared to that of grilled ricebirds *(ch'amsae kui),* another Korean delicacy. These tiny sparrows are eaten in one or two crunchy bites, bones and all, with just sesame oil and salt.

To Koreans, this is the ultimate choice among beef dishes. Inviting friends out for kalbi is a special treat. It appears on nearly every restaurant menu, and kalbi restaurants and kalbi houses *(kalbi chip)* prosper in every region of Korea. During Korean holidays, all butcher shops, supermarket food departments, and gourmet shops do a brisk business selling gift-packaged kalbi.

In Korean markets in America, meat counters usually display three cuts of ribs: lean prime ribs for grilling, well-marbled cuts for stew, and less expensive short ribs (American short ribs) for soup. For this dish, only the lean prime ribs will do; pan-grilling is not recommended.

❁ ❁ ❁

In a large pan, soak the ribs in ice cold water for 1 hour. Drain and pat dry. Using a sharp knife, make crisscross slashes across each strip toward the bone, but without cutting through. In a wide, shallow baking pan, place the ribs in one layer, slashed side up. In a bowl, combine the marinade ingredients and mix well. Spoon the marinade over the ribs and, with your fingers, massage the marinade into the ribs. Wrap the pan tightly with plastic wrap and marinate in the refrigerator for a few hours or as long as overnight.

To grill the ribs, start the coals 30 minutes before cooking; or, preheat a gas grill. Lightly brush the grilling rack with the vegetable oil and set it 4 inches from the heat source. Add the ribs, in batches or all at once, and grill for 6 to 8 minutes per side, or until caramel brown and crusty and to the desired doneness. Repeat if necessary with the remaining ribs.

To broil the ribs, preheat the broiler. Lightly brush the broiler pan with the vegetable oil and set it 6 inches from the heat source. Add the ribs, in batches or all at once, and broil for 5 to 6 minutes; turn, and broil the second side for 2 minutes, or to the desired doneness. Repeat if necessary with the remaining ribs.

Garnish with the pine nuts and sil koch'u. Serve the ribs immediately with hot steamed rice (if desired, the ribs may be cut into smaller pieces before serving). Have plenty of napkins ready, because everyone will be eating these with their hands! White Cabbage Kimchi (page 99) and Cubed Radish Kimchi (page 100) are good side dishes.

Beef and Vegetable Skewers

Sogogi Sanjŏk

Serves 4
30 minutes to prepare
and 20 minutes to cook

2 pounds tenderloin of beef

12 large sweet green onions,
halved lengthwise, or 24 green
onions, white and pale green
part only

12 oyster mushrooms or p'yogo
(shiitake) mushrooms, halved

8 ounces napa cabbage, firm stem
part only, cut into 24 pieces,
each 1 inch by 3 inches

12 hot green Korean peppers or
jalapeño peppers, seeded,
deribbed, and halved

Marinade for Fired Beef (page 179)

1 to 5 tablespoons vegetable oil

A more stylized version of this dish is prepared for ancestral ceremonies. The strips are painstakingly skewered through the middle, dusted in sweet rice flour, dipped in egg, pan-grilled, and then trimmed into perfect squares. One of the joys of my childhood was anticipating the incredibly delicious scraps that would fall as my mother performed a solemn trimming ritual at ceremonial times.

This dish is a nutritious and tasty assemblage of colorful vegetables and marinated beef. The meat has a wonderful flavor because of its contact with the sweet, juicy vegetables.

Slice the beef across the grain into 36 strips, each $^1/_8$ inch thick. Cut the green onions into 3-inch pieces. On a 7-inch skewer, thread in the following order: 1 beef strip, 1 piece of each vegetable, beef, vegetables, and beef. Repeat, making a total of 12 skewers. Place half of the skewers in an oblong pan, spoon over half of the marinade, lay the other skewers on top, and spoon over the remaining marinade. Wrap the pan tightly with plastic wrap and marinate in the refrigerator for 15 minutes.

To grill the skewers, start the coals 30 minutes before cooking; or, preheat a gas grill. Lightly brush the grilling rack with the vegetable oil and set it 4 inches from the heat source. Add the skewers, in batches or all at once, and grill for 5 to 6 minutes per side, or until the beef is caramel brown and crusty and to the desired doneness. Repeat if necessary with the remaining skewers.

To broil the skewers, preheat the broiler. Lightly brush the broiler pan with the vegetable oil and set it 6 inches from the heat source. Add the skewers, in batches or all at once, and broil for 4 minutes per side, or to the desired doneness. Turn only once. Repeat if necessary with the remaining skewers.

To pan-grill the skewers, in a 12-inch cast-iron or 14-inch nonstick skillet, heat 1 tablespoon vegetable oil over medium-high heat until it begins to smoke. Add the skewers, in batches or all at once, and cook for 3 minutes per side, or to the desired doneness. Turn only once. Repeat if necessary with the remaining skewers. Save the pan juices to spoon over the beef before serving.

Serve on individual plates with hot steamed rice. Chilled Radish Salad (page 119), Cucumber Salad (page 118), and Leaf Lettuce Salad (page 116) make nice side dishes.

Fired Chicken

Tak Kui

Serves 4
30 minutes to prepare
and 15 minutes to cook

4 lean chicken breast halves,
   6 to 8 ounces each, boned and
   skinned

Marinade for Fired Chicken

3 tablespoons soy sauce

1/3 cup ch'ŏngju (rice wine) or
   vermouth

3 green onions, white and some
   green part only, finely minced

8 cloves garlic, crushed and finely
   chopped

2 tablespoons syrup, or
   1 tablespoon sugar

1 tablespoon sesame oil

1 tablespoon toasted sesame
   seeds

4 walnut halves, finely chopped

3 tablespoons freshly squeezed
   lemon juice

1 tablespoon hot red pepper
   flakes

1½ teaspoons freshly ground black
   pepper

Pinch of salt

1 to 4 tablespoons vegetable oil

Pinch of sil koch'u (hot red pepper
   threads), snipped into short
   pieces, for garnish

1 teaspoon toasted sesame seeds,
   for garnish

For ancestral ceremonies, our family makes fired whole chicken (t'ong tak kui), which is given a prominent place at the altar, elaborately blanketed with a traditional three-color garnish.

Tender chicken breasts, marinated and grilled over a charcoal fire, make one of the juiciest and tastiest chicken dishes of all. It is easy to prepare, even for the busiest cook.

Place each chicken breast between two sheets of waxed paper. Flatten with a wooden mallet, until each piece is about one and a half times its original size, keeping the original shape. In a small bowl, combine the marinade ingredients and mix well. Place the chicken breasts in a large bowl, and spoon the marinade over each piece. Wrap the bowl tightly with plastic wrap and marinate in the refrigerator for 30 minutes.

To grill the chicken, start the coals 30 minutes before cooking; or, preheat a gas grill. Lightly brush the grilling rack with the vegetable oil and set it 4 inches from the heat source. Add the chicken, in batches or all at once, and grill for 6 minutes per side, or to the desired doneness. Repeat if necessary with the remaining chicken.

To broil the chicken, preheat the broiler. Lightly brush the broiler pan with the vegetable oil and set it 6 inches from the heat source. Add the chicken, in batches or all at once, and broil for 4 minutes per side, or to the desired doneness. Repeat if necessary with the remaining chicken.

To pan-grill the chicken, in a 12-inch cast-iron or 14-inch nonstick skillet, heat 1 tablespoon vegetable oil over medium-high heat until it begins to smoke. Add the chicken, in batches or all at once, and cook for 3 minutes per side, or to the desired doneness, flattening with a spatula to prevent curling. Turn only once. Repeat if necessary with the remaining chicken. Save the pan juices to spoon over the chicken before serving.

On a cutting board, cut the chicken diagonally into thin slices. Divide on individual plates, in a fan pattern. Garnish with the sil koch'u and sesame seeds. Serve with hot steamed rice, if desired. As side dishes, serve Chilled Radish Salad (page 119), Cucumber Salad (page 118), and Leaf Lettuce Salad (page 116).

Variations: To make an exuberant fired chicken, marinate the chicken with Hot Red Pepper Sauce (page 30).

Another variation uses Cornish game hens. Make double the amount of marinade. Split open 4 (24-ounce) game hen breasts and flatten. Thread each with 10-inch skewers at the top and bottom, to keep flat. Place in a large roasting pan, cut side up. Spoon half of the marinade, turn over, and spoon the remaining marinade. To grill, set the rack 4 inches from the coals and grill for 6 minutes per side. To broil, set the pan 6 inches from the heat source and broil for 7 minutes per side.

Chicken and Vegetable Skewers

Tak Sanjŏk

Serves 4
20 minutes to prepare
and 15 minutes to cook

4 chicken breast halves, about 6
to 8 ounces each, boned and
skinned

12 large sweet green onions,
halved lengthwise, or 24 green
onions, white and pale green
part only

12 medium oyster mushrooms or
other mushrooms such as porto-
bello or p'yogo (shiitake) mushrooms, cut into 24 pieces

8 ounces napa cabbage, firm stem
part only, cut into 24 pieces,
each 1 inch by 3 inches

6 hot red Korean peppers,
or 1 red bell pepper, seeded,
deribbed, and cut into 24 strips,
each 3 inches long

6 hot green Korean peppers or
jalapeño peppers, seeded,
deribbed, and cut into 24 strips,
each 3 inches long

Marinade for Fired Chicken
(page 182)

1 to 5 tablespoons vegetable oil

There is no more gracious way to grill chicken than this skewered dish.
The combination of colors is a visual feast, and the sweet and zesty vegetables and subtle marinade doubly enhance the flavor of the sweet
chicken breast. This easy-to-prepare recipe makes a perfect side dish
for a Korean meal or a delicious entree for any dinner setting.

❀ ❀ ❀

Cut the chicken into 36 strips, each $1/8$ inch thick. Cut the green
onions into 3-inch pieces. On a 7-inch skewer, thread in the following
order: 1 chicken strip, 1 piece of each vegetable, chicken, vegetables,
and chicken. Repeat, making a total of 12 skewers. Place half of the
skewers in an oblong pan, spoon over half of the marinade, lay the
other skewers on top, and spoon over the remaining marinade. Wrap
the pan tightly with plastic wrap and marinate in the refrigerator for
15 minutes.

To grill the skewers, start the coals 30 minutes before cooking; or,
preheat a gas grill. Lightly brush the grilling rack with the vegetable
oil and set it 4 inches from the heat source. Add the skewers, in batches
or all at once, and grill for 6 minutes per side, or to the desired doneness. Repeat if necessary with the remaining skewers.

To broil the skewers, preheat the broiler. Lightly brush the broiler
pan with the vegetable oil and set it 6 inches from the heat source. Add
the skewers, in batches or all at once, and broil for 5 minutes per side,
or to the desired doneness. Repeat if necessary with the remaining
skewers.

To pan-grill the skewers, in a 12-inch cast-iron or 14-inch nonstick
skillet, heat 1 tablespoon vegetable oil over medium-high heat until it
begins to smoke. Add the skewers, in batches or all at once, and cook
for 4 minutes per side, or to the desired doneness. Turn only once.
Repeat if necessary with the remaining skewers. Save the pan juices to
spoon over the chicken before serving.

Serve on individual plates with hot steamed rice, if desired. As side
dishes, serve Chilled Radish Salad (page 119), Cucumber Salad (page
118), and Leaf Lettuce Salad (page 116).

Variations: For a special menu, make Pheasant Skewers (Kkuŏng
Sanjŏk) or Shrimp Skewers (Saeu Sanjŏk). Follow the directions above.

Fired Pork

Toejigogi Kui

Serves 4
20 minutes to prepare
and 15 minutes to cook

2 pounds pork loin roast or loin
chops

Marinade for Fired Pork

4 tablespoons soy sauce

¼ cup koch'ujang (hot red pepper
paste), or to desired hotness

1 tablespoon koch'u karu (hot red
pepper powder), or to desired
hotness

¼ cup ch'ŏngju (rice wine) or
vermouth

3 tablespoons corn syrup

1 tablespoon sugar

2 ounces ginger, peeled and
grated

6 cloves garlic, crushed and finely
chopped

3 green onions, white and pale
green part only, finely minced

4 walnut halves, finely chopped

2 tablespoons sesame oil

1 tablespoon toasted sesame
seeds

½ tablespoon freshly ground black
pepper

1 to 5 tablespoons vegetable oil

1 hot red Korean pepper, seeded,
deribbed, and slivered, for
garnish

1 hot green Korean pepper,
seeded, deribbed, and slivered,
for garnish

The fingertip massage applied
to the meat is affectionately
called *chomul chomul,* an onomatopoeia for the sound it
makes.

This is one of the richest and most robust of the grilled dishes. The cut of meat used in the traditional version is samgyŏbsal, a Korean version of bacon slices with three layers of meat and fat. It is a favorite among gourmands. However, I prefer to use a leaner cut of pork, such as loin roast or loin chops. The marinade of hot red pepper paste and additional assertive spices perfectly matches the pork's rich flavor (it also gives a passionate character to shrimp and chicken). This recipe is a vigorous bonding of irresistible flavors.

🏵 🏵 🏵

Trim the fat from the pork and slice into long, thin bacon-like slices. In a large bowl, combine the marinade ingredients and mix well with a spoon. Add the pork, and with your fingers, massage the marinade into the meat. Wrap the bowl tightly with plastic wrap and marinate in the refrigerator for 1 hour.

To grill the pork, start the coals 30 minutes before cooking; or, preheat a gas grill. Lightly brush the grilling rack with the vegetable oil and set it 4 inches from the heat source. Add the pork, in batches or all at once, and spread flat, to grill evenly and quickly. Grill for 6 to 8 minutes per side. Let unwanted fat drip into the fire, but be careful not to let flare-ups char the meat. Repeat if necessary with the remaining pork.

To broil the pork, preheat the broiler. Lightly brush the broiler pan with the vegetable oil and set it 6 inches from the heat source. Add the pork, in batches or all at once, and broil for 4 minutes per side, or to the desired doneness. Repeat if necessary with the remaining pork.

To pan-grill the pork, in a 12-inch cast-iron or 14-inch nonstick skillet, heat 1 tablespoon vegetable oil over medium-high heat until it begins to smoke. Add the pork, in batches or all at once, and cook for 3 to 4 minutes per side, or to the desired doneness, flattening with a spatula to prevent curling. Turn only once. Repeat if necessary with the remaining pork. Save the pan juices to spoon over the pork before serving.

Transfer the pork to a cutting board and slice into bite-size pieces. Divide the pork on individual plates and garnish with the peppers. Serve with hot steamed rice, if desired. As side dishes, serve Chilled Radish Salad (page 119), Cucumber Salad (page 118), and Leaf Lettuce Salad (page 116).

Variation: Grilled Pork Ribs (Toeji Kalbi) is another favorite. Substitute 4 pounds of pork ribs and grill a few minutes longer.

Growing Up in a Korean Kitchen

Pork and Vegetable Skewers

Toejigogi Sanjŏk

Serves 4 to 6

30 minutes to prepare
and 30 minutes to cook

---

2 pounds lean pork

12 large sweet green onions,
halved lengthwise, or 24 green
onions, white and pale green
part only

6 hot red Korean peppers, or
1 red bell pepper, seeded,
deribbed, and cut into 24 strips,
each 3 inches long

1 piece Whole Cabbage Kimchi
(page 97), stem part only and
without stuffing, or napa
cabbage leaves, stem part only,
cut into 24 strips, each 3 inches
long

6 hot green Korean peppers or
jalapeño peppers, seeded,
deribbed, and cut into 24 strips,
each 3 inches long

Marinade for Fired Pork (page 184)

1 to 4 tablespoons vegetable oil

In this recipe, tender strips of pork are combined with a spicy marinade, sweet vegetables, and fresh peppers to produce a distinctive Korean flavor (with added zest from cabbage kimchi). It is a wonderful melange of colors, tastes, and textures. Uncomplicated to prepare, yet thoughtful in presentation, it creates a superb and sophisticated dish.

❀ ❀ ❀

Cut the pork into 36 strips, each $1/8$ inch thick. Cut the green onions into 3-inch pieces. On a 7-inch skewer, thread in the following order: 1 pork strip, 1 piece of each vegetable, pork, vegetables, and pork. Repeat, making a total of 12 skewers. Place half of the skewers in an oblong pan, spoon over half of the marinade, lay the other skewers on top, and spoon over the remaining marinade. Wrap the pan tightly with plastic wrap and marinate in the refrigerator for 15 minutes.

To grill the skewers, start the coals 30 minutes before cooking; or, preheat a gas grill. Lightly brush the grilling rack with the vegetable oil and set it 4 inches from the heat source. Add the skewers, in batches or all at once, and grill for 6 to 8 minutes per side, or to the desired doneness. Repeat if necessary with the remaining skewers.

To broil the skewers, preheat the broiler. Lightly brush the broiler pan with the vegetable oil and set it 6 inches from the heat source. Add the skewers, in batches or all at once, and broil for 4 minutes per side, or to the desired doneness. Repeat if necessary with the remaining skewers.

To pan-grill the skewers, in a 12-inch cast-iron or 14-inch nonstick skillet, heat 1 tablespoon vegetable oil over medium-high heat until it begins to smoke. Add the skewers, in batches or all at once, and cook for 4 minutes per side, or to the desired doneness. Turn only once. Repeat if necessary with the remaining skewers. Save the pan juices to spoon over the pork before serving.

Serve on individual plates with hot steamed rice, if desired. As side dishes, serve Chilled Radish Salad (page 119), Cucumber Salad (page 118), and Leaf Lettuce Salad (page 116).

Grilled Red Snapper

Tomi Kui

Serves 4

15 minutes to prepare
and 15 minutes to cook

4 whole red snappers, or any delicate sweet fish (about 10 ounces
each), scaled and washed, with
heads and tails intact

1 recipe Allspice Sauce (page 28)

2 tablespoons vegetable oil

Cabbage hearts or lettuce leaves

Sil koch'u (red pepper threads), for
garnish

Lemon slices, for garnish

Parsley sprigs, for garnish

In the Korean kitchen, two kinds of sauces are used to marinate fish. A milder marinade goes well with sole, cod, red snapper, and other delicate, sweet white fish. A more robust marinade complements strong, rich-flavored fish such as mackerel, mackerel pike, sardine, and herring. With quick grilling, the sauce glazes the surface of the fish skin, leaving a crusty shell and imparting the interior with subtle flavors. This recipe uses red snapper, but other fish or seafood in combination with the marinade of your choice make delightful alternatives.

❀ ❀ ❀

To prepare the fish for grilling, carefully pat it dry and make a few diagonal slashes on both sides. Place the fish in 1 layer in a large oblong pan, and spoon over half the sauce. Turn the fish over and spoon over the remaining sauce. Wrap the pan tightly with plastic wrap and marinate in the refrigerator for 15 minutes.

To grill the fish, start the coals 30 minutes before cooking; or, preheat a gas grill. Lightly brush the grilling rack with the vegetable oil and set it 4 inches from the heat source. Add the fish and grill for 4 to 5 minutes per side, occasionally basting with sauce.

To broil the fish, preheat the broiler. Lightly brush the broiler pan with the vegetable oil and set it 6 inches from the heat source. Add the fish and broil for 4 minutes per side.

To pan-grill the fish, in a 12-inch cast-iron or 14-inch nonstick skillet, heat the vegetable oil over very high heat until it begins to smoke. Add the fish and cook for 3 to 4 minutes per side, turning each fish carefully with a wide spatula to retain its shape.

Make a bed of cabbage on individual plates and place a fish on top of each. Garnish with the sil koch'u, lemon, and parsley sprigs. Serve immediately with hot steamed rice, if desired. Seasoned Spinach (page 125) and Cucumber Salad (page 118) go very well with fish.

Variation: For an unusually exuberant and different flavor, marinade the red snapper in Hot Red Pepper Sauce (page 30).

Growing Up in a Korean Kitchen

Grilled Whole Squid

Ojingŏ Kui

Serves 4
15 minutes to prepare
and 10 minutes to cook

4 squid, about 10 ounces each

1 recipe Hot Red Pepper Sauce (page 30)

2 tablespoons vegetable oil

Cabbage hearts or lettuce leaves

Lemon wedges, for garnish

Parsley sprigs, for garnish

Koreans love to tell this folk-tale: At one time, the rubbery and tasteless squid had lots of bones. One day, the herring, boneless at the time, complained to the squid that it was always sought after for its tasty meat. The neglected, unwanted squid kindly offered to give its bones to the herring. The scheme didn't work, however. Not only did Koreans continue to covet the succulent herring, no matter how many bones it had, but to its dismay, the once scoffed squid, too, became popular.

This dish is a good example of how hot red pepper sauce can transform a rather bland food into a dynamic and colorful dish. The similar marinade for Fired Pork (page 184) is also suitable. Whichever cooking method you use, take care not to overcook the squid, or it will become tough.

❀ ❀ ❀

To prepare the squid, remove the head and tentacles (either cut or gently pull them off); reserve for other uses. Peel off the purplish-brown skin from the body, and remove the ink sac. Rinse the squid body. Using a sharp knife, cut each squid lengthwise so it opens to a flat piece. Make crisscross slashes, without cutting through, on the outer side. Thread each end of a squid piece through a 7-inch skewer (this will prevent curling during cooking). Repeat with remaining squid pieces, making a total of 8 skewers. Place half of the skewers in an oblong pan, spoon over half of the sauce, lay the other skewers on top, and spoon over the remaining sauce. Wrap the pan tightly with plastic wrap and marinate in the refrigerator for 15 minutes.

To grill the skewers, start the coals 30 minutes before cooking; or, preheat a gas grill. Lightly brush the grilling rack with the vegetable oil and set it 4 inches from the heat source. Add the skewers and grill for 2 minutes per side.

To broil the skewers, preheat the broiler. Lightly brush the broiler pan with the vegetable oil and set it 4 inches from the heat source. Add the skewers and broil for 2 minutes per side.

To pan-grill the skewers, in a 12-inch cast-iron or 14-inch nonstick skillet, heat the vegetable oil over medium-high heat until hot, but not smoking. Add the skewers and cook for 1 1/2 minutes per side.

On a cutting board, remove the squid from the skewers and cut into bite-size pieces. Make a bed of cabbage on individual plates and place the squid on top of each. Garnish with the lemon and parsley sprigs. Serve immediately with hot steamed rice, if desired.

Grilled Beef Heart

Yŏmt'ong Kui

Serves 6 to 8
10 minutes to cook

1 pound beef heart

6 ounces beef tenderloin

Marinade for Fired Beef (page 179)

2 tablespoons vegetable oil

Innards are a part of Korean cookery, although not as important today as in the past. Undoubtedly, innards were one of the prized delicacies in traditional Korean cuisine. They were among our grandmother's favorite dishes. Usually the recipes called for a rich marinade as well as flavorful cuts of meat, such as beef tenderloin, to tone down the strong flavor of the innards. This recipe for grilled beef heart is a good example. As with Fired Beef (page 179), there is no better way to cook beef hearts than to grill them outdoors over an oak charcoal fire, although they can be broiled; pan-grilling is not suitable.

Trim the sinew, membrane, and outer skin from the beef heart and thinly slice. Slice the tenderloin across the grain into near paper-thin slices. In a large bowl, add the meat and marinade and, with your fingers, massage the marinade into the meat. Wrap the bowl tightly with plastic wrap and marinate in the refrigerator for several hours or as long as overnight.

To grill the skewers, start the coals 30 minutes before cooking; or, preheat a gas grill. Lightly brush the grilling rack with the vegetable oil and set it 4 inches from the heat source. Add the meat, laying each piece flat, and grill for 4 minutes per side, or to the desired doneness.

To broil the skewers, preheat the broiler. Lightly brush the broiler pan with the vegetable oil and set it 6 inches from the heat source. Add the meat and broil for 4 minutes per side, or to the desired doneness.

On a cutting board, slice the meat into bite-size pieces. Serve with hot steamed rice and Leaf Lettuce Salad (page 116).

Variations: Kidneys, lungs, small intestines, and tripe can also be used in this recipe.

Growing Up in a Korean Kitchen

Grilled Aralia Roots

Tŏdŏk Kui

Serves 4 to 6
10 minutes to cook

½ pound aralia roots, each about 4 to 5 inches long

2 tablespoons sweet rice flour, for dredging

Marinade

1 tablespoon soy sauce

1 tablespoon corn syrup or sugar

1 teaspoon garlic juice, freshly squeezed from 1 clove garlic (use a garlic press)

1 thread green onion or green onion, white and pale green part only, finely minced

1 tablespoon sesame oil

1 tablespoon toasted sesame seeds

1 tablespoon koch'ujang (hot red pepper paste)

1 tablespoon koch'u karu (hot red pepper powder)

1 tablespoon vegetable oil

Parsley sprigs, for garnish

Grilled aralia roots make a wonderfully fragrant and crunchy vegetable dish. Fresh aralia roots are significantly better than dried ones, but the dried roots are still very tasty. If using fresh, be sure to select plump, straight roots. Before cooking, the roots need to soak in water, to soften and tone down their bitterness. Spices must be used sparingly, so as not to overpower the exceptional fragrance of the roots. Pan-grilling is not recommended for this dish.

❁ ❁ ❁

Wash and peel the aralia roots with a sharp paring knife. Soak in cold water for 1 hour. On a cutting board, flatten each root with a mallet or the back of a cleaver, and split into strips. Pat dry and dust with the sweet rice flour. In a bowl, combine the marinade ingredients and mix well. Add the aralia roots and, with your fingers, massage the marinade into the roots. Marinate for 15 minutes.

To grill the roots, start the coals 30 minutes before cooking; or, preheat a gas grill. Lightly brush the grilling rack with the vegetable oil and set it 4 inches from the heat source. Add the roots and grill for 3 minutes per side.

To broil the skewers, preheat the broiler. Lightly brush the broiler pan with the vegetable oil and set it 6 inches from the heat source. Add the roots and broil for 2 minutes per side.

On a cutting board, cut each root into bite-size pieces. Place on individual plates and garnish with parsley sprigs. Serve with hot steamed rice and Stuffed Cucumber Kimchi (page 106).

Variation: Use the same recipe and amounts to make Grilled Fresh Ginseng (Susam Kui).

✳ Dishes for Special Occasions

he special dishes *(t'ŭkpyŏl ŭmsik)* in this chapter derive mostly from Korea's classical and royal cuisine tradition. This dramatic repertoire of beautiful and exquisitely flavorful dishes once belonged almost exclusively to the royal family and a few upper-class kitchens, where they were used for entertaining, ancestral ceremonies, and other special occasions. These elite families were the only ones who could afford the expensive ingredients required or who had the resources, time, and kitchen help necessary for the preparation of the dishes. But today, with the easy availability of ingredients and the time and labor-saving equipment of the modern kitchen (and with some adjustments made to the original recipes), these elegant, extraordinary dishes can be prepared by everyone.

(above) Lunch counter, Namdaemun Market, Seoul

(opposite) Koryŏ celadon incense burner, 12th or 13th century, replica

Scallops Wrapped in Green Onion

P'a Kanghoe

Serves 6
30 minutes to prepare and cook

---

8 ounces sea scallops, halved or quartered

1 tablespoon ch'ŏngju (rice wine) or vermouth

½ tablespoon freshly squeezed lemon juice

Pinch of salt

Pinch of freshly ground black pepper

1 tablespoon vegetable oil

1 clove garlic, crushed and finely chopped

10 ounces thread green onions, or 18 tender green onions, each about 14 inches long

2 hot red Korean peppers, or ½ red bell pepper, seeded, deribbed, and sliced into ¼ by 1-inch strips

36 pine nuts

4 lemon wedges, for garnish

This delightful tidbit also makes an attractive and edible garnish. Thread green onions (sil p'a) are best suited for this recipe. Usually, 2 to 6 stalks grow from one root, and they can be easily separated. Their tender texture, delicate flavor, and extra long stem (some longer than 16 inches) make them ideal for making this elegant appetizer. When in season, they can be found at Korean markets.

Wash the scallops briefly in cold running water. Drain in a colander and pat dry with a paper towel. In a bowl, combine the ch'ŏngju, lemon juice, salt, and pepper and mix well. Add the scallops and lightly toss.

In a skillet, heat the vegetable oil over medium heat until very hot. Add the garlic and sauté for 2 minutes. Add the scallops all at once and sear for 2 to 3 minutes, or until they turn opaque. Transfer to a bowl and set aside.

In a saucepan, make 2 quarts of acidulated water (page 10) and bring to a boil. Add the green onions and blanch for 1½ minutes, or until they turn bright green and are barely wilted. Plunge into ice water to stop the cooking. Drain in a colander and pat dry.

To assemble the pieces, with the thumb and index finger, hold 1 green onion 1 inch from the end, and put 1 scallop and 1 red pepper strip on the end. Bring the long end up and over the scallop and red pepper, wind it one or two times around, and securely tuck in the end. Carefully push 2 pine nuts into the bundle. Repeat with the remaining ingredients, making about 18 pieces resembling tiny sisal ropes.

Arrange the pieces in a small dish and garnish with the lemon wedges. Serve as an appetizer or side dish with a small bowl of Vinegar Soy Sauce (page 28).

Variations: The traditional recipe calls for strips of boiled beef brisket or Beef Tenderloin Tartare (page 201) in place of the scallops. To make the brisket, place 8 ounces beef brisket in a saucepan, add 2 cups water, a pinch each of salt and pepper, and 1 crushed garlic clove. Bring to a boil over medium-high heat. Decrease the heat to low and simmer for 1 hour; let cool. Slice into thin, bite-size strips. Then follow the recipe above. Blanched shrimp may also be used in place of the scallops.

If Korean watercress strings are used in place of the thread green onions, this dish is called Watercress Appetizer (Minari Kanghoe).

Cold Meat Platter

P'yŏnyuk and Cheyuk

Serves 5 to 10
10 minutes to prepare
and 1 to 1½ hours to cook

---

2 pounds beef shin (arongsat'ae)

2 pounds lean pork loin roast
(toeji tŏngsim)

Seasoning for Beef

2 tablespoons ch'ŏngju (rice wine)
or vermouth

2 large sweet green onions, or
5 green onions, white and pale
green part only

5 cloves garlic, slivered

1 tablespoon soy sauce

Seasoning for Pork

2 tablespoons ch'ŏngju (rice wine)
or vermouth

2 large sweet green onions, or
5 green onions, white and pale
green part only

5 cloves garlic, slivered

¼ cup soy sauce

2 ounces fresh ginger, sliced

Salted Shrimp Sauce

1 cup saeu chŏt (salted shrimp)

1 clove garlic, crushed

1 tablespoon minced green onion

1 tablespoon toasted sesame
seeds

1 tablespoon sesame oil

½ tablespoon hot red pepper
flakes

Lettuce leaves or cabbage hearts

Parsley sprigs, for garnish

Cold boiled beef (p'yŏnyuk) and cold boiled pork (cheyuk) are popular side dishes and appetizers. Though each can be served alone, they are usually paired, especially when offered as *anju* (drink companions). Typically, a less expensive cut of meat is used for the p'yŏnyuk. Boneless beef shin is best, as it has a good flavor with a chewy and attractive gelatin-marbled texture and look. According to the traditional recipe, cheyuk is made with pork belly (samgyŏbsal), the same cut used for bacon, but I prefer to use lean pork loin. The beef and pork, which are similarly prepared, can be cooked simultaneously, in separate pots. Both are delicious with vinegar soy sauce; cheyuk is also accompanied by a salty shrimp sauce (yaknyŏm saeu chŏt), in contrast to the Western custom of serving a sweet fruit sauce with pork.

Soak the beef shin and pork separately in ice cold water for 1 hour. Drain and pat dry. In a large pot, bring 4 cups of water to a boil over medium-high heat, add the beef, and boil for 15 minutes, skimming the impurities with a slotted spoon. Decrease the heat to medium and add the seasoning ingredients. Boil the beef, rotating it several times to evenly distribute the flavor, for 1 hour and 15 minutes, or until a chopstick goes easily through the meat.

Meanwhile, in another large pot, bring 4 cups of water to a boil over medium-high heat, add the pork, and boil for 15 minutes, skimming off the impurities. Decrease the heat to medium and add the seasoning ingredients. Boil the pork, rotating it several times to evenly distribute the flavor, for 1 hour, or until a chopstick goes easily through the meat.

Turn off the heat and let both the beef and pork cool in their stocks. Transfer each to separate plastic containers, cover, and refrigerate overnight. Reserve the stocks for other uses. In a small bowl, combine the salted shrimp sauce ingredients and mix well. Set aside.

Just before serving, thinly slice both meats. On a large platter, arrange the slices on a bed of lettuce and garnish with a few parsley sprigs. Serve with Vinegar Soy Sauce (page 28) and the salted shrimp sauce in bowls on the side.

The meats will stay fresh in the refrigerator for 1 week. Leftovers make great sandwiches. Diced or shredded, they perk up fried rice and noodle dishes.

Note: Many other cold cuts are popular in private homes and in markets. These delicacies include beef tongue, beef brisket, and beef headcheese. As for pork, every part is made into cold cuts: pig's trotter, ear, innards, sausage, and pork headcheese. All take hours to boil, until the meat falls off the bone.

Nine Variety Royal Appetizer

Kujŏlban

Serves 6 to 8
1 hour to prepare and cook

---

6 ounces mung bean sprouts

6 ounces napa cabbage hearts, stem part only, cut into 2-inch matchsticks

6 ounces summer squash, sliced into thin 2-inch matchsticks

6 ounces spinach, soft leafy part only, cut into 2-inch pieces

6 ounces beef tenderloin

$1/2$ tablespoon ch'ŏngju (rice wine) or vermouth

$5^1/2$ tablespoons sesame oil

Salt

Freshly ground black pepper

1 tablespoon vegetable oil

1 ounce dried p'yogo (shiitake) mushrooms, rehydrated (page 18) and thinly slivered

1 recipe Egg Threads (page 34), cut into $1/8$-inch threads

1 cup all-purpose wheat flour

Kujŏlban is available at the finest Korean restaurants in Korea and America. The name of this most elegant appetizer derives from the elaborate nine-sectioned lacquer tray in which it is served. Each of the outer sections of the tray holds a different subtly spiced ingredient, and the center section contains a stack of thin mini pancakes resembling crepes. Guests create their own wrap from among the assorted delicacies, then dip it into a sauce before eating. The portions are small, intended only to whet one's appetite for the coming feast. Most of this dish can be prepared unhurriedly a few hours ahead of time. The extra preparation time and care you take will be rewarded, as the colorful appearance and subtle tastes of this dish will make a lasting impression on your guests.

Begin preparations about $1^1/2$ hours before serving time. In a saucepan, make 2 cups of acidulated water (page 10) and bring to a boil. Add the mung beans and blanch for 10 seconds, then plunge into ice water to stop the cooking. Add the cabbage to the same acidulated water and blanch for 1 minute, then plunge into ice water (be sure to use fresh ice water each time). Repeat with the squash and spinach. Drain each vegetable in a colander, then wrap in a paper towel and squeeze out as much liquid as possible. Set aside on a work surface.

Slice the beef with the grain into thin threads. (Do not slice it across the grain, or it will crumble into small pieces.) In a bowl, combine the ch'ŏngju, $1/2$ tablespoon sesame oil, and a pinch each of salt and pepper, and mix well. Add the beef and toss well. In a skillet, heat the vegetable oil over medium-high heat until hot. Add the beef and sauté for 1 minute, or until cooked through but not browned. Return the beef to the bowl to cool. In the same skillet, heat 1 tablespoon of sesame oil and sauté the mushrooms for 2 minutes, or until supple and fragrant. Season with a pinch each of salt and pepper. Transfer to the same bowl, next to the meat, to cool.

On a kujŏlban tray or a large serving plate, place the meat and mushrooms in separate sections of the tray or in separate mounds on the plate. Place the yellow and white egg threads in two separate sections. (Prepare the egg threads no more than 1 hour ahead of time, to ensure its freshness.) In a bowl, add the mung bean sprouts, $1/2$ tablespoon sesame oil, and a pinch each of salt and pepper, and toss well. Transfer the sprouts to the tray. Repeat with the other vegetables, making a total of 8 sections, leaving room in the center for the pancakes.

In a bowl, combine the flour and 1¹/₂ cups water and mix well with a pair of chopsticks. The batter will be thin. Heat a nonstick skillet over medium-low heat until hot, and lightly coat the bottom of the pan with ¹/₂ tablespoon sesame oil. Quickly add 1 tablespoon batter for each pancake to form 5 thin pancakes, each about 3 inches in diameter. Cook for 1 minute per side, or until the pancakes are set, but not crusty. Transfer to a basket or tray to cool. Repeat with the remaining batter, making a total of 18 to 20 pancakes. Place the pancakes in the center section of the tray, surrounded by the other 8 ingredients.

Place the tray at the center of the table. Serve at room temperature along with bowls of Vinegar Soy Sauce (page 28) and hot yellow mustard (page 16) on the side.

Note: Traditionally, thin slices of boiled radish are used in place of flour pancakes; also, rice flour is used instead of wheat flour. For a subtler flavor, use chicken breasts, prawns, or crabmeat instead of the beef.

Peace and Harmony Salad

T'angpyŏng Ch'ae

Serves 4 to 6

30 minutes to prepare
and 30 minutes to cook

---

1 clove garlic, sliced

1 green onion, white and pale
green part only

1 tablespoon ch'ŏngju (rice wine)
or vermouth

Salt

Freshly ground black pepper

6 large prawns, unshelled

8 ounces nokdumuk (mung bean
curd) or tot'orimuk (acorn curd)

3 tablespoons sesame oil

8 ounces mung bean sprouts

8 ounces Korean watercress or
spinach

1 tablespoon vegetable oil

1 ounce fresh oyster mushrooms,
torn into thin shreds

Spicy Hot Yellow Mustard Sauce
(Kyŏja Chip)

2 tablespoons hot yellow mustard
powder

1 tablespoon ch'ŏngju (rice wine)
or vermouth

1 tablespoon distilled white
vinegar

1/2 tablespoon sugar

1/2 tablespoon soy sauce

1/2 tablespoon sesame oil

1 sheet of kim (laver)

1 sweet Korean or Asian pear

1/2 recipe Egg Threads (page 34),
cut into 1/8-inch threads

Parsley sprigs, for garnish

This recipe is modified from the original version once enjoyed by the royal family in spring and summer. Mung bean curd (nokdumuk), acorn curd (tot'orimuk), mung bean sprouts, beef cold cuts, crumbled laver, and Korean watercress in a subtle vinegar soy sauce are its standard ingredients. But my family usually adds other fancy ingredients, such as thinly sliced jellyfish, abalone slices, bamboo shoots, chestnuts, and pine nuts. This dish must be prepared in advance and served well chilled. Several hours ahead of time or a day before, prepare all the ingredients, except the egg threads, pears, and seaweed. Place each component in separate airtight containers and store in the refrigerator until ready to serve.

In a saucepan, combine 4 cups of water, garlic, green onion, ch'ŏngju, and a pinch each of salt and pepper and bring to a boil over high heat. Decrease the heat to low and simmer for 15 minutes. Increase the heat to high, add the prawns, and boil for 2 to 3 minutes, or until they turn pink and are barely done. Let the prawns cool in the stock. Drain, reserving the stock for other uses. Store the prawns in a container and refrigerate.

Slice the nokdumuk into thin strips and place in a bowl. Add 1/2 tablespoon sesame oil and a pinch each of salt and pepper and toss well. Transfer to a plastic container and refrigerate.

Put the mung bean sprouts in a pot and add 1 cup of water. Cover, bring to a boil, and cook for 1 minute. Plunge into ice water to stop the cooking. Drain the sprouts in a colander, wrap in a paper towel, and squeeze out as much liquid as possible. Transfer to a bowl, add 1/2 tablespoon sesame oil and a pinch each of salt and pepper, and toss well. Transfer to a container and refrigerate.

Pour out the water from the pot and add 4 cups of fresh water. Bring to a boil over high heat. Add the watercress and blanch for 30 seconds. Plunge into ice water to stop the cooking. Drain in a colander, wrap in a paper towel, and squeeze out as much liquid as possible. Cut into 2 1/2-inch pieces. Transfer the watercress to a bowl, add 1/2 tablespoon sesame oil and a pinch each of salt and pepper, and toss well. Transfer to a container and refrigerate.

In a skillet, heat the vegetable oil over medium heat until hot. Add the mushrooms and sauté for 5 minutes, or until barely wilted. Season with 1/2 tablespoon sesame oil and a pinch each of salt and pepper. Transfer to a container and refrigerate. Up to this point, all the preparations can be done several hours or a day in advance.

Growing Up in a Korean Kitchen

In a bowl, combine the spicy mustard sauce ingredients and mix well. Set aside.

A few minutes before serving, brush one side of the kim with the remaining 1 tablespoon of sesame oil. Quickly toast the kim over medium heat for a couple of seconds (page 135) and cut into threads. Place in a dry container and set aside. (Do not refrigerate.) Peel and core the pear and cut it into quarters. Then slice it into thin matchsticks. Remove the prawns from the refrigerator and peel and devein them. Cut the prawns into thin slices. Take out all the other containers from the refrigerator and assemble on a work surface.

On a glass or ceramic serving plate, arrange the prawns, bean curd, bean sprouts, watercress, mushrooms, kim, pear, and egg threads in a fan pattern with space between each. Garnish with the parsley sprigs. Serve as an elegant appetizer with the spicy mustard sauce on the side.

Note: In the traditional recipe, this salad is lightly tossed with Vinegar Soy Sauce (page 28) just before serving.

Throughout Korean history there were endless factional struggles among the ruling elite. However, the reign of King Yŏngjo (1724–1776) is considered to have been the most peaceful in the entire Yi Dynasty (1392–1910) because of his policy of employing men from all factions, a policy called *t'angpyŏng ch'aek*. One day, King Yŏngjo is said to have eyed the peaceful arrangement of the cool royal salad in front of him and to have suddenly lamented, "Ah! Why can't we live together in harmony like this salad?" Hence the name of this dish.

Stuffed Fish Fillet, Royal Style

Ŏ Mandu

Serves 4

20 minutes to prepare
and 20 minutes to cook

1¹/₂ pounds white fish fillets, such as cod, croaker, or flounder

Salt

Freshly ground black pepper

¹/₂ pound napa cabbage, leafy part only

6 ounces fresh oyster mushrooms or white button mushrooms

6 ounces spinach, leafy part only

8 ounces medium-firm bean curd

6 ounces boneless, skinless chicken breast, coarsely ground

1 tablespoon ch'ŏngju (rice wine) or vermouth

2 cloves garlic, crushed and finely chopped

2 large sweet green onions, or 4 green onions, finely minced

2 eggs, lightly beaten

¹/₂ cup cornstarch

4 cups Clear Chicken Stock (page 59)

4 small whole green onions, for garnish

8 leaves crown daisy or parsley, for garnish

¹/₂ tablespoon sil koch'u (hot red pepper threads) or hot red pepper flakes, for garnish

4 lemon slices, for garnish

The recipe for this extraordinary and elegant dish is our casual family version, modified from a more stylized royal recipe that calls for uniform shapes and sizes. Our version may look different, but the delicate and delicious flavor remains the same. In this recipe, the fish is poached in chicken stock, whereas in the royal version the fish is steamed. Any firm and succulent white fish can be used.

❁ ❁ ❁

Cut the fillets into 4 sheets, each 6 inches square. In a large colander, spread the fillets in 1 layer and pat dry with a paper towel. Season lightly with salt and pepper and set aside.

In a stockpot, make 2 quarts of acidulated water (page 10) and bring to a boil. Add the cabbage and blanch for 5 minutes, then plunge into ice water to stop the cooking. Drain in a colander, wrap in a paper towel, and squeeze out as much liquid as possible. Finely chop the cabbage and transfer to a large bowl. Using the same acidulated water, repeat with the mushrooms and spinach, blanching each separately for less than 10 seconds. Drain, squeeze, and finely chop the mushrooms and spinach and add them to the bowl. Wrap the bean curd in a paper towel and squeeze out as much liquid as possible. Add it to the bowl. Add the chicken, ch'ŏngju, garlic, green onions, 1 egg, and a pinch each of salt and pepper to the bowl. Mix well and form into 4 balls.

In a small bowl, lightly beat the remaining egg. Spread the cornstarch on a plate. To stuff the fish, spread 1 fish fillet on a work surface and place 1 ball of stuffing in the middle of the fillet. Lightly brush the edges of the fillet with egg, fold it in half, and seal. Trim the edges with scissors, shaping each into a half moon. Discard the leftover pieces of fish or reserve for other use. Dredge the shaped fish in cornstarch and set aside. Repeat with the remaining ingredients, making 4 half moons. In a skillet, add the stock and bring to a boil over high heat. Decrease the heat to medium-high and add all the stuffed fish in one layer. Bring to a gentle boil, decrease the heat to medium, cover, and simmer for 5 minutes, or until cooked through.

To serve, with a slotted spoon, transfer the fish to 4 individual plates. Spoon some pan juices over each, and garnish each with 1 green onion, 2 crown daisy leaves, a pinch of sil koch'u, and 1 lemon slice. Serve with Vinegar Soy Sauce (page 28) and Spicy Hot Yellow Mustard Sauce (page 196) on the side. This is good with rice and delicate cooked vegetables, such as Seasoned Spinach (page 125) or Seasoned Mung Bean Sprouts (page 123), and Whole Cabbage Kimchi (page 97).

Variation: In the royal version, the stuffing is spread on the fillet, which is rolled up and steamed for about 8 minutes. The roll is sliced in half and served cut side up, showing its colorful pinwheel pattern.

Stuffed Squid

Ojingŏ Sundae

Serves 4 to 6
30 minutes to prepare
and 20 minutes to cook

6 squid, each about 6 inches long (about 1 pound), cleaned

8 ounces medium-firm bean curd

2 ounces oyster mushrooms

2 ounces spinach, leafy part only

4 ounces ground chicken breast

1/2 cup cooked sweet rice

1 tablespoon ch'ŏngju (rice wine) or vermouth

1 green onion, white and pale green part only, finely minced

1 clove garlic, crushed and finely chopped

2 walnut halves, finely chopped

1 egg, slightly beaten

1/2 tablespoon soy sauce

1/2 tablespoon koch'ujang (hot red pepper paste)

1/2 tablespoon sugar

1 tablespoon sesame oil

This recipe is based on one that comes from family friends who lived in Sokch'o, a small fishing village on Korea's northeast coast. Korean and foreign tourists alike love to visit this village to enjoy their famous fresh seafood. Among the specialties are raw seafood platters and fish stews. And, of course, this dish has to be mentioned among them.

❀ ❀ ❀

Remove the head and tentacles of the squid, and reserve them for other uses, or finely chop and add them to the stuffing. Pat the tubular body dry, inside and out, and set aside.

Wrap the bean curd in a paper towel and squeeze out as much liquid as possible. Transfer to a large bowl. In a saucepan, make 4 cups of acidulated water (page 10) and bring to a boil over high heat. Add the mushrooms and blanch for less than 10 seconds, or until barely wilted, then plunge into ice water to stop the cooking. Drain in a colander, wrap in a paper towel, and squeeze out as much liquid as possible. Finely chop and transfer to the bowl. Using the same acidulated water, blanch the spinach for less than 10 seconds, then plunge in ice water. Drain, squeeze, and finely chop the spinach and add it to the bowl.

Add the remaining ingredients to the bowl, mix thoroughly, and divide into 6 portions. Loosely stuff each squid with stuffing (if the squid is packed too tightly, it may burst during cooking). Secure the openings with toothpicks. Place the stuffed squid in a steamer and steam for 7 minutes. Transfer to a cutting board and let the squid cool enough to handle. Slice into 1/2-inch rings.

To serve, arrange the squid slices on a serving platter to resemble whole squids. Serve as an appetizer or side dish with Vinegar Soy Sauce (page 28) on the side.

Note: Native fishermen's recipes seem to include almost anything at hand, including carrots, beef, pork, mung bean noodles, chopped hot red peppers, and even wild sesame leaves.

Korean Sausage

Sundae

Serves 6 to 8
1 hour to prepare
and 20 minutes to cook

---

2 pounds not-so-lean ground pork

3 tablespoons ch'ŏngju (rice wine)
or vermouth

4 tablespoons sesame oil

1 tablespoon freshly squeezed
ginger juice

2 cups Whole Cabbage Kimchi
(page 97), without stuffing,
finely chopped

6 green onions, white and pale
green part only, finely minced

10 cloves garlic, crushed and
finely chopped

Pinch of salt

Pinch of freshly ground black
pepper

1 pound medium-firm bean curd

1 pound pork small intestine
casings

When I eat haphazardly stuffed sausage made with blood and noodles in Korean open market stalls, my mouth waters for the sausage my mother used to make in our family kitchen. Like other sausages around the world, Korean sausage has its own personality, shape, and flavor. Polish kielbasa may be its closest cousin.

Chopped whole cabbage kimchi was my mother's secret ingredient. Without it, sausage would not be sausage to me. Today's cook can buy sausage casings at the market, but Mother had to laboriously scrub and wash the messy casings herself. The only times I ever saw our menfolk stride in and out of the kitchen door to taste a work in progress was during sundae and pure bean curd–making sessions.

In a large bowl, combine the pork, ch'ŏngju, sesame oil, ginger juice, kimchi, green onions, garlic, salt, and pepper. Wrap the bean curd in a paper towel and squeeze out as much liquid as possible; add it to the bowl. Mix well to make a soft, dough-like mixture.

Put the mixture into a pastry bag and pipe the stuffing into the casing, tightly filling the casing. About every 5 inches, tie a tight knot with kitchen thread to form the sausages. Using a pin, prick the sausages, to prevent them from bursting while boiling. In a large stockpot, bring 5 quarts of water to a boil. Add all the sausage links and boil, covered, for about 20 minutes. Slice into bite-size pieces. Arrange on a tray and serve with Vinegar Soy Sauce (page 28).

Growing Up in a Korean Kitchen

Beef Tenderloin Tartare

Yukhoe

Serves 4
20 minutes to prepare

- 1 pound highest-quality lean beef tenderloin

- 1 tablespoon ch'ŏngju (rice wine) or vermouth

- 2 thread green onions, or 1 green onion, white and pale green part only, finely minced

- 1 teaspoon freshly squeezed garlic juice

- 2 tablespoons sugar

- 1 teaspoon freshly squeezed ginger juice

- 2 tablespoons sesame oil

- 1 tablespoon toasted sesame seeds

- Pinch of salt

- Pinch of freshly ground black pepper

- 1 Korean or Asian pear, chilled

- 1 egg (optional)

- 2 tablespoons pine nuts, finely chopped, for garnish

This dish is made from the leanest and most expensive beef tenderloin, cut into thread-thin strips. As one of the most prized appetizers, it is served well chilled with shredded pears. In my childhood home, yukhoe was reserved exclusively for our grandmother, father, and precious houseguests. It should be prepared several hours ahead, to allow time to chill.

❁ ❁ ❁

Cut the beef with the grain into very thin threads. In a large bowl, combine the ch'ŏngju, green onions, garlic juice, sugar, ginger juice, sesame oil, sesame seeds, salt, and pepper; mix well. Add the beef and, with your fingers, massage the seasoning into the meat. Wrap the bowl tightly with plastic wrap and refrigerate for several hours.

Just before serving, peel and core the pear and cut it into matchsticks. Add the egg to the meat and mix well. Divide into 4 individual bowls and garnish each with $1/2$ tablespoon pine nuts and pear slices. Sprinkle with a little additional freshly ground black pepper and serve.

Raw Seafood Platter

Haemul Hoe

Serves 4

45 minutes to prepare and several hours to chill

---

4 ounces fresh red snapper fillet, about 1 inch thick and 2 inches wide

$1/2$ teaspoon salt

$1/4$ teaspoon freshly ground black pepper

1 lobster tail in shell

8 medium shrimp in shell

20 medium wild sesame leaves (perilla)

1 bunch crown daisies (about 12 ounces), leaves only

4 green onions, white and pale green part only, cut into $1^1/2$-inch threads

2 lemons, cut into wedges

2 tablespoons pine nuts, finely chopped, for garnish

2 tablespoons sil koch'u (hot red pepper threads), snipped into 1-inch threads, for garnish

Squid is the most popular raw fish among Koreans, probably because they are the cheapest. They are caught in abundance along the Korean shore, especially on the east coast and off Ulnŏng Island. Some are sun-dried to become ojingŏ po, a popular snack food. They look like thousands of pairs of socks strung up on clotheslines. The freshest squid are eaten as the fishmongers slice them up into threads. Squid lovers say that the short-tempered squid begins to spoil even as they are reeled onto the boat.

This is an extraordinary and sumptuous appetizer or side dish. Sea bream, flounder, and other delicate and succulent fish are favored for this dish, which usually also includes squid, shrimp, lobster, octopus, clams, and other popular shellfish. Among the countless other candidates are cod, carp, trout, salmon, eel, scallops, oysters, jellyfish, abalone, sea cucumbers, conch, and sea skirt. Fresh seafood is an absolute must for this dish, so in the old days it was rarely served beyond the seashore restaurants that had holding tanks for live fish and shellfish.

In this recipe, I limit the main ingredients to three: red snapper, lobster tail, and shrimp. Red snapper is no match for the rare sea bream, the queen of fish, but it is almost as good and more available. Select fish with bouncy flesh, lustrous scales, and bright eyes and gills. The chores of scaling, gutting, and filleting can be left to your reliable fishmonger.

🌸 🌸 🌸

Clean the fish under running water and pat dry. Using a pincer, check carefully for any tiny bones. Put the fillet in a strainer set in a bowl and sprinkle both sides with half of the salt and pepper. Cover tightly with plastic wrap and refrigerate. In a stockpot, bring 2 quarts of water seasoned with the remaining salt and pepper to a vigorous boil over high heat. Add the lobster and blanch for about 1 minute, or until the shell turns pink. With a slotted spoon, remove the lobster and plunge into ice water to cool; drain. Using the same water, repeat with the shrimp. Pat dry with a paper towel and let cool. Place the lobster and shrimp in separate, tightly sealed containers and chill in the refrigerator.

On a large serving platter, arrange the greens in a fan pattern. Shell the shrimp, then butterfly and devein them, leaving the tails intact. Arrange the shrimp on the platter. Cut open the lobster belly with a pair of scissors. On separate cutting boards, place the lobster and snapper skin side up. Resting the fingers of one hand on the tail side, slice each into uniform, paper-thin pieces. The knife should be almost horizontal. Arrange the slices on the platter. Decorate with the lobster shell and lemon wedges. In the center of the tray, place a small bowl of Vinegar and Hot Red Pepper Sauce (page 29) or the robust Hot Red Pepper Sauce (page 30). Place the platter on a tray of crushed ice, wrap tightly with plastic wrap, and refrigerate for several hours.

To serve, sprinkle the pine nuts and sil koch'u over the seafood and give each guest a small plate with which to assemble their own bites: inside a sesame leaf, place a crown daisy, a piece of fish, and a pinch of green onions, pine nuts, and sil koch'u. Roll into a tiny bundle and dip into the sauce.

Growing Up in a Korean Kitchen

Jellied Ox Hoof

Chok P'yŏn

Serves 12 to 14
1 hour to prepare
and 6 hours to cook

---

2 ox hooves, cut into 2-inch chunks

1 pound beef shin

10 cloves garlic, crushed

3 tablespoons ch'ŏngju (rice wine) or vermouth

1 teaspoon salt

1/2 teaspoon freshly ground black pepper

2 hard-boiled eggs, sliced into 1/4-inch rings

1 tablespoon pine nuts

1 tablespoon black peppercorns, crushed with a rolling pin

1 recipe Egg Threads (page 34), cut into 1/8-inch threads

5 pieces dried stone-ear mushrooms, rehydrated (page 22) and slivered

1 tablespoon sil koch'u (hot red pepper threads), snipped into 1/2-inch pieces

I doubt if anyone today bothers to make this labor-intensive dish, since it is available in the market. Of course, commercially made is not like homemade. I remember watching my grandmother at the all-day project of making this transparent gelatin cake. I have had countless chances to taste this dish since, but it is never the same as our grandmother's. She took it seriously and always saw to it herself, perhaps because it was her favorite, but also because it was an important dish for ancestral ceremonies.

Whenever I visit Korea, I love to browse around Tondaemun Sijang (East Gate Market) and Namdaemun Sijang (South Gate Market), where I always end up sitting on a plank at a hawker's makeshift lunch counter, munching on a slice or two of this wonderful dish. I love looking at the stacks of down-home treats: pig's trotters, headcheese, pig's ears, jellied ox hooves, innards, steaming sausage links, and smiling pig's heads (somehow, Korean butchers know how to put a broad grin on a pig's face; in Korea, this smile is a sign of good fortune). It is the jellied ox hooves that always draw my special attention, however. This Korean aspic delicacy is a much loved stamina-builder and appetizer. When buying the ox hooves, be sure to have your butcher take care of cutting them up.

In a large bowl, soak the bones and meat in ice cold water for 2 hours. Drain and put them in a stockpot. Add enough water to completely cover and bring to a full boil over high heat. Boil for 5 minutes, skimming off the impurities. Drain and rinse in cold water a few times. Return the bones and meat to the pot and add the garlic, ch'ŏngju, salt, and pepper. Cover with cold water and bring to a boil over high heat, skimming off any remaining impurities. Decrease the heat to low and simmer for 6 hours, partially covered.

Lift out the bones and meat with a slotted spoon and transfer to a cutting board. Collect all the meat and discard the bones. Chop the meat into a fine dice and set aside. Pour the stock through a strainer lined with cheesecloth and into a bowl. Let cool and skim off any fat. Line the inside of a 9 by 14 by 2-inch cake pan or wooden tray with a damp hemp cloth. Carefully pour the stock into the pan, wrap tightly with plastic wrap, and refrigerate. After a few hours, when the jelly is half set, scatter the diced meat and egg rings on the surface, and push them gently into the gelatin. Sprinkle the pine nuts, peppercorns, egg threads, mushrooms, and sil koch'u on top, and gently push them between the meat and eggs. Cover and refrigerate overnight, or until firm.

To serve, slice into bite-size squares. Serve as an appetizer with Vinegar Soy Sauce (page 28) as the dipping sauce.

Celestial Hot Pot

Sinsŏnlo

Serves 4 to 6
1 hour to prepare
and 20 minutes to cook

½ recipe Fired Beef (page 179)

½ recipe Fired Chicken (page 182)

1 recipe Pan-Fried Fish Fillets
(page 174)

6 large sweet green onions, or 10
green onions, halved lengthwise

5 hot red Korean peppers, or
1 red bell pepper, seeded and
deribbed

5 hot green Korean peppers or
jalapeño peppers, seeded and
deribbed

½ pound napa cabbage, firm stem
part only

1 recipe Egg Ribbons (page 34),
cut into 1½ by 3-inch ribbons

1 recipe Bean Curd Chorim (page
217)

1 recipe meatballs from Royal
Meatball Soup (page 63)

1 ounce dried stone-ear
mushrooms, rehydrated (page
22) and slivered

20 ginkgo nuts, shelled and
toasted (page 22) (optional)

10 walnut halves, blanched and
skinned

2 tablespoons pine nuts, brown
tips removed

1 tablespoon sil koch'u (hot red
pepper threads), snipped into
3-inch pieces

3 cups Beef Stock (page 58)

Salt

Freshly ground black pepper

This royal recipe is a magnificent culinary orchestration of forms, colors, and flavors. At first glance, the thought of preparing such a dish may be overwhelming, but with a closer look, it is merely an assembly of dishes mastered individually elsewhere in this book. Nevertheless, it requires extensive resources, preparation, and time to achieve the stunning grand finale. It begs for your patience, devotion, and love of cooking. Sinsŏnlo heralds a very special occasion and special guests. This is why, if you have been treated to this dish at a Korean home, you know that your host must have thought you were truly royal.

The ingredients are exactingly cut to fit the circular pot surrounding the burner, each piece about the size of a lottery ticket and laid out according to strict rules—packed face up and sideways, alternately. As seen through the hot aromatic broth, the final presentation looks like a mini wheel-of-fortune in gorgeous rainbow colors. This dish is always expected to sit high on a feast table amidst a lavish spread of countless dishes. Koreans love to describe this as *sangdariga hwidorok ch'arin chanch'isang* (a feast table so heavily loaded that its legs are bending). The following recipe is my modified version—a presumptuous act that may not please die-hard traditionalists.

Almost all the cooking can be done a day or two ahead: meat first, then fish, and then vegetables. Wait until serving day to prepare the egg ribbons. Cutting and assembly should be done several hours ahead of serving time.

Cut the meats and vegetables into uniform strips 1½ inches wide and 3 inches long. In the sinsŏnlo pot or chafing dish, arrange the strips, alternately face up and sideways, in a circular pattern. Begin with 2 strips each of beef, chicken, and fish. Follow with 2 yellow egg ribbons, a few strips of green onions and red and green peppers, and 2 white egg ribbons. Place a bundle each of cabbage and bean curd into the pot. Repeat until the pot is full. Scatter the meatballs, mushrooms, and nuts. Top with the sil koch'u.

Shortly before serving, in a saucepan, add the stock and bring to a boil. Place the pot at the center of the table. Before the guests sit down, carefully add the gently boiling stock without disturbing the arrangement. Taste the stock and adjust with salt and pepper. Occasionally baste with hot broth to distribute the flavors.

To serve, spoon a few slices of each meat and vegetable into individual bowls, ladle in some hot broth, and top with a few meatballs. Serve with steamed rice. Leaf Lettuce Salad (page 116) and White Cabbage Kimchi (page 99) make wonderful side dishes.

Note: The egg ribbons and stone-ear mushrooms are major players in this recipe, not taking their usual role as mere garnishes. The traditional and authentic recipe always includes Pan-Fried Beef Liver (page 172), pan-fried tripe, pan-fried lung, and other beef innards.

The Chinese characters for sinsŏnlo mean "God's ambrosia," which may give an indication of its lofty standing in the panoply of royal dishes. In the old days, only the royal family and a few fortunate aristocrats ever enjoyed it, and therefore it was a symbol of wealth, power, and status. It has been said that this dish began in the royal kitchen as a way to intelligently use leftovers. They must have found it so delicious that it was developed and perfected into a stylish royal dish.

Sinsŏnlo is always served in a sinsŏnlo pot, an impressive-looking Korean chafing dish made of brass, nickel, or silver. This special vessel resembles a brass incense burner on a cone-shaped base with a mini charcoal-burning chimney at the center. Mongolian hot pots and Cantonese hot pots may be made in similar vessels. The dish is also called sinsŏllo (new hot pot), or yŏlgujat'ang (palate-pleasing hot pot for the gods).

✳ Preserved Dishes

Preserved dishes (chaban) play a wonderfully versatile role in Korean cooking. They are appetizers, side dishes, flavor enhancers, and garnishes. Chaban are made from grains, meats, vegetables, nuts, seeds, fish, anchovies, fish roe, clams, seaweed, and many other ingredients. Preserving is achieved either by salting and sun-drying (called *marŭn panch'an*) or by cooking slowly in spicy sauces until all the liquid is absorbed and the ingredients are caramelized (called *chorim*). The shelf life of preserved dishes ranges from a few weeks to a few months, depending on their saltiness and storage temperature. Traditional recipes demanded heavy salting, as chaban were stored in cool, dark pantries. Today, of course, since chaban are kept in the refrigerator, the recipes in this chapter call for much less salt.

Korean meal tables, whether small or large, always include one, two, or even more chaban tidbits among the side dishes, adding lively flavors to an ordinary meal. Chaban add zest to any dish, especially noodle and rice dishes. For busy cooks, they are an easy yet invaluable resource for making tasty one-dish meals. As garnishes, chaban are both tasty and pleasing to look at.

Once made only in family kitchens or produced in limited quantities in small mom-and-pop shops, a parade of colorful, pungent, and aromatic chaban are now available at Korean market deli counters everywhere. A variety of commercially canned chaban are also found on supermarket shelves, but there is nothing like homemade. Chaban-making remains an active part of Korean home cooking, where they are usually prepared in large quantities and served in small portions. All are economical and easy to prepare.

(above) Tubs of pollack roe

(opposite) Salted yellow corvina, Kyŏngdong Market, Seoul

Seaweed Chaban

Kim Chaban

Serves 4 to 6
10 minutes to prepare
and 20 minutes to cook

4 tablespoons soy sauce

2 tablespoons ch'ŏngju (rice wine)
or vermouth

1 tablespoon sugar

2 tablespoons sesame oil

1 teaspoon freshly ground black
pepper

2 cloves garlic, crushed and finely
chopped

1 tablespoon koch'u karu (hot red
pepper powder) or hot red
pepper flakes

12 sheets kim (laver), about
8 inches square

1/4 cup toasted sesame seeds

This spicy treat is one of the many ways in which laver is prepared in the Korean kitchen. In this recipe, the flat sheets of seaweed are seasoned and briefly toasted in the oven, resulting in a tasty snack that crumbles in your mouth like potato chips. This is a perfect way to restore kim that is not perfectly fresh, and it is simple to prepare.

❁ ❁ ❁

Preheat the oven to 175°. In a bowl, combine the soy sauce, ch'ŏngju, sugar, sesame oil, black pepper, garlic, and koch'u karu and mix well. Place 1 sheet of kim on a tray. Using a pastry brush, lightly coat the kim with the soy sauce mixture. Generously top with some sesame seeds. Repeat with the other sheets of kim, and stack them up.

Using two 17 by 11-inch baking sheet pans, place 2 sheets of seasoned kim on each sheet pan. Bake for 8 to 10 minutes, or until the kim becomes crisp to the touch. Be careful not to burn. Repeat with the remaining kim. Place all the baked kim in a serving bowl and break into potato chip–size pieces. Serve as a side dish or appetizer. Or, break into smaller pieces to use as a garnish on steamed rice, fried rice, or noodles. Place the leftovers in an airtight container or plastic bag and store in the refrigerator; they will stay fresh and crisp for a month.

Kelp Chaban

Miyŏk Chaban

Serves 10 to 12
10 minutes to prepare and cook

- 2 ounces sil miyŏk (dried seaweed threads)
- 3 tablespoons vegetable oil
- 2 tablespoons sugar
- 2 tablespoons toasted sesame seeds

Sweet and salty miyŏk chaban has a unique, almost licorice-like taste. These crispy-crunchy tidbits are simple to make.

✿ ✿ ✿

Place the sil miyŏk in a large, deep bowl. (Parchment-dry seaweed scatters when cut.) Using a pair of sharp scissors, snip into 1-inch pieces. In a 14-inch skillet, heat the vegetable oil over medium-high heat until almost smoking. Toast the sil miyŏk all at once, constantly tossing with a pair of wooden chopsticks, for 5 to 7 minutes, or until it begins to turn dark green and fragrant. Remove the skillet from the heat and immediately sprinkle the sugar and sesame seeds on top; toss well. Transfer to a serving bowl and serve as a side dish or appetizer. Or, sprinkle on steamed rice, fried rice, or noodles. Place the leftovers in an airtight container or plastic bag and store in the refrigerator; they will stay fresh and crisp for a month.

Deep-Fried Kelp

T'wigak

Serves 4
10 minutes to prepare and cook

---

4 ounces miyŏk (kelp) strips

1 cup olive oil or vegetable oil

2 tablespoons sugar

In Korean cooking, frying refers strictly to pan-frying with a drop of oil, but there are a few exceptions. Crunchy, nutty t'wigak is one of them. It is a favorite with children and adults alike. Among seaweed varieties, kelp is rather expensive. One or two dark, dried kelp pieces are folded into thin, 18-inch bundles and sold at Korean and Asian markets. Simply unfold them and cut them into the desired size and shape.

❁ ❁ ❁

Using a damp kitchen towel, wipe the powdery salt from the surface of the miyŏk, making it damp and pliable. Using a pair of sharp scissors, snip the miyŏk into $1/2$ by 4-inch strips Tie each strip into a knot. Divide into 4 batches.

In a skillet, heat the olive oil over high heat until very hot. Quickly drop the first batch into the hot oil in one layer. (Kelp cooks fast, within several seconds, puffing up like potato chips.) Turn the pieces over and cook until they turn olive green and puff up. Do not burn. (Burned kelp is very bitter and there is no way to mend it.) Transfer to a flat basket or tray lined with a paper towel, to blot the oil. Repeat with the remaining batches.

Place the crunchy t'wigak in a serving bowl and serve as a side dish. Or, it can be crumbled and used to garnish Rice with Vegetables and Meat (page 50) or fried rice. Place the leftovers in an airtight container or plastic bag and store in the refrigerator; they will stay fresh and crisp for a month.

Variations: Wild sesame leaves (also called perilla) and dried baby green peppers are also prepared in this way and make delightful side dishes and garnishes.

Cod Chorim

Taegu Chorim

Serves 4

10 minutes to prepare
and 55 minutes to cook

---

2 pounds whole fresh cod, head
and tail intact, scaled, gutted,
and gills removed

1 teaspoon salt

1 teaspoon freshly ground black
pepper

1/2 cup cornstarch or all-purpose
wheat flour

Seasoning for Fish

12 ounces Korean radish or
daikon, peeled and grated

3 ounces fresh ginger, peeled and
grated

5 cloves garlic, peeled and grated

3 fresh hot green Korean peppers
or jalapeño peppers, sliced into
rings

1/2 cup soy sauce

1 cup ch'ŏngju (rice wine) or
vermouth

1/2 cup honey or corn syrup

2 tablespoons sugar

1 tablespoon koch'ujang (hot red
pepper paste)

1 tablespoon koch'u karu (hot red
pepper powder)

2 tablespoons freshly squeezed
lemon juice

1 teaspoon freshly ground black
pepper

3 large sweet green onions, or
6 green onions, sliced into thin
rings

1 tablespoon sil koch'u (hot red
pepper threads), snipped into
2 1/2-inch pieces

2 tablespoons vegetable oil

1/2 tablespoon toasted sesame
seeds, for garnish

This is one of the many glorious culinary offerings from the Korean kitchen. It is similar to Braised Fish (page 148) in flavor, appearance, and cooking technique, but in this recipe the liquid is reduced to almost nothing and the fish is caramelized. The final result is a sweet, spicy, gelatinous glazed fish entree or side dish, fit for any occasion.

For ordinary meals, our mother used to cook this dish with inexpensive fish, such as mackerel, herring, or pollack, but for special occasions, she always used a more succulent fish, such as cod, red snapper, or sea bream. In Korea, fish chorim is as popular as Fired Beef (page 179).

Cut the fish into 2 by 2-inch chunks, including the head and tail and cutting through the bones. Pat dry, place in a colander, and season with salt and 1 teaspoon of the black pepper. Sprinkle the cornstarch on all sides and set aside. In a bowl, add the seasoning ingredients for the fish, reserving some of the green onions and sil koch'u for garnish, and mix well. Set aside.

Heat the vegetable oil in a 14-inch skillet over medium-high heat until very hot, but not smoking. Place the fish chunks in one layer in the skillet and sear for 5 minutes per side, or until the skin is browned. Transfer the fish to a heavy stockpot in one layer and add the seasoning sauce. Cover and bring to a boil over medium-high heat. Boil for 20 minutes, occasionally basting the fish with sauce. Decrease the heat to medium and cook for 20 minutes, continuing to baste the fish. Carefully transfer the fish to a saucepan and keep warm. Pass the liquid through a fine strainer into another saucepan, and discard the solids. Boil the liquid over medium-high heat for 15 minutes, or until it is reduced to a lustrous and gelatinous consistency. Carefully spoon the sauce over the fish.

To serve, reheat the fish until it is heated through. Divide into individual serving dishes and garnish with the reserved green onion rings, sil koch'u, and sesame seeds. Serve hot with steamed rice and Seasoned Spinach (page 125).

Note: This is one of those ideal dishes that can be cooked 2 to 3 days ahead and stored in the refrigerator; just reheat and serve.

Variations: Other seafood, such as whole baby squid, mussels, clams, and shrimp can be prepared in the same way.

Salted Yellow Corvina Chaban

Kulbi Chaban

Serves 4
10 minutes to cook

1½ pounds kulbi (salted yellow corvina), head and tail intact, scaled

3 tablespoons sesame oil or vegetable oil

1 tablespoon toasted sesame seeds, for garnish

1 green onion, sliced into thin rings, for garnish

1 teaspoon sil koch'u (hot red pepper threads), for garnish

Just the thought of salted kulbi makes generations of Koreans salivate and think of the old folktale about a man named Charingobi. A poor and thrifty man, with a brood of hungry mouths to feed, he was lucky just to be able to provide them with some rice. One day, he brought home the precious kulbi as a treat. He hung the fish from the ceiling on a straw rope, where it dangled above the meal table. Charingobi instructed his children that as their side dish, they could take a look at the salted fish as they ate. When one child sneaked a second peek at the fish, the father scolded him. "Didn't I tell you? Only one look per spoonful!" Henceforth, Charingobi has been ever connected to kulbi, and his name has become synonymous with "skinflint."

Salted yellow corvina (kulbi) is regarded as a delicacy, on the same level as pine mushrooms and rare fish roe. Korean gourmands covet it for its exquisite flavor. Genuine kulbi is sold briefly during summer in Korean markets in the U.S. As a child, I would see salted yellow corvina braided on straw ropes and hanging on display in the marketplace or sun-drying in our backyard. Kulbi was never cheap, but it was affordable when I was young because it was caught in abundance. It is a shame that corvina is somewhat rare today and usually appears only in gourmet shops. Salted cod or salted yellow croaker are good substitutes.

Traditionally, only a small morsel of kulbi chaban is eaten with a spoonful of rice because it is so heavily salted. In this simple recipe, the fish is soaked overnight to tone down the saltiness.

Soak the fish in water overnight; pat dry. In a skillet, heat the sesame oil over medium-high heat until hot. Sear the fish for 5 to 7 minutes per side, or until it is nicely browned. Transfer to a serving platter. Garnish with the sesame seeds, green onion rings, and sil koch'u. Serve hot.

Bean Chaban

K'ong Chaban

Serves 4
1¹/₂ hours to prepare and cook

- 2 cups dried black, white, or yellow beans
- 1 cup soy sauce
- ¹/₂ cup corn syrup or sugar
- 2 tablespoons freshly squeezed ginger juice

Nutritious, tasty, and simple to prepare, k'ong chaban complements any main dish. It also makes an interesting garnish.

❀ ❀ ❀

Soak the beans in water overnight; drain. In a heavy stockpot, add the soy sauce, corn syrup, and ginger juice and stir until the corn syrup is dissolved and the consistency is uniform. Add the beans and bring to a boil. Boil over medium heat for 30 minutes, to soften the beans. Decrease the heat to low and simmer for 1 hour, until all the liquid is absorbed and the beans are lustrous and look like raisins. Check on the mixture from time to time: if the liquid is being absorbed too quickly, add more soy sauce or water to prevent scorching. Serve in a small bowl as a side dish, or add to fried rice for extra flavor. Place the leftovers in an airtight container and store in the refrigerator; they will stay fresh for a few months.

Beef Chorim

Chang Chorim

Serves 6 to 8
1¹/₂ hours to cook

---

2 pounds beef brisket or beef shin

³/₄ cup soy sauce

3 tablespoons corn syrup, or
2 tablespoons sugar

2 tablespoons ch'ŏngju (rice wine)
or vermouth

6 cloves garlic, peeled and left
whole

2 large sweet green onions, or
4 green onions, cut into 2-inch
pieces

Chang chorim is a soy sauce–braised beef brisket, somewhat resembling corned beef. A popular side dish on its own, it is also used as a flavoring in clear broths or soups, diced in fried rice, or shredded in noodles. It is easy to prepare, and a little goes a long way!

Soak the beef in ice cold water for 1 hour; drain. Place the beef in a stockpot and add 4 cups of water. Bring to a boil over medium heat and boil for 15 minutes, skimming off the impurities with a slotted spoon. Decrease the heat to medium-low and simmer for 45 minutes. Add the remaining ingredients and gently cook over medium heat for 30 minutes. Increase the heat to medium-high and boil rapidly for 15 minutes more, or until the liquid is reduced to a thin sauce. Baste often with a spoon. Let the meat cool in its broth.

Transfer the beef and broth to a wide-mouth 2-quart jar with a tight-fitting lid and refrigerate overnight. The next day, remove and discard the solidified fat on the surface. Serve at room temperature as a side dish. It can be stored in the refrigerator and will stay fresh for several months.

Variations: Braised Pork (Toaeji Chang Chorim) or Braised Crabs (Kye Chang) are cooked in a similar way. However, for the braised pork, add all the ingredients, including 1 ounce of sliced ginger, to the stockpot and cook for a total of 45 minutes over medium heat. Store the crabs or pork, tightly covered, in the refrigerator. They will stay fresh for a few months.

Anchovy and Green Pepper Chorim

Myŏlch'i Koch'u Chorim

Serves 4 to 6
20 minutes to prepare
and 20 minutes to cook

6 ounces dried anchovies, small or medium-sized, deveined and heads removed

1 pound kkoari koch'u (mild green Korean peppers) or green bell peppers

1/2 cup soy sauce

3 tablespoons sugar

3 tablespoons ch'ŏngju (rice wine) or vermouth

3 tablespoons vegetable oil

5 cloves garlic, crushed and finely chopped

2 green onions, white and pale green part only, finely minced

1 tablespoon toasted sesame seeds

1 tablespoon sesame oil

1/2 teaspoon salt

1/2 teaspoon freshly ground black pepper

This sweet, nutty dish lives in my memory because it was always in my lunch box. After all these years, it remains a favorite. The main ingredient is the mild and sweet variety of Korean pepper called kkoari koch'u. Compared to the hot Korean pepper, these mild peppers are short and wrinkly skinned. They appear in the markets in early summer.

In a bowl, soak the anchovies in 1/2 cup cold water for 15 minutes, to soften. Drain through a colander into a small bowl, reserving both the water and the anchovies. Meanwhile, wash the kkoari koch'u, pat dry, and cut into a 1-inch dice.

Add the soy sauce, sugar, and ch'ŏngju to the reserved anchovy water and mix well. Heat the vegetable oil in a skillet over medium heat until very hot. Add the garlic and green onions and sauté for 2 minutes. Increase the heat to medium-high and add the anchovies and soy sauce mixture. Cook for 10 minutes, stirring occasionally with a wooden spoon. Add the kkoari koch'u and cook for 5 minutes, or until they turn bright green and fragrant. Add the sesame seeds and sesame oil and immediately remove from the heat. Lightly toss and season with the salt and pepper.

Serve warm or cold as a side dish. Place leftovers in a tightly closed container and store in the refrigerator; they will stay fresh for a few months. To serve leftovers, reheating is not necessary—just add green onion rings, chopped nuts, and hot red pepper flakes.

Potato and Anchovy Chorim

Kamja Chorim

Serves 6 to 8
15 minutes to prepare
and 25 minutes to cook

4 ounces dried anchovies, small or medium size, deveined and heads removed

3 tablespoons soy sauce

2 tablespoons corn syrup, or 1 tablespoon sugar

2 tablespoons ch'ŏngju (rice wine) or vermouth

1 tablespoon vegetable oil

5 cloves garlic, crushed and finely chopped

3 green onions, cut into 1-inch pieces

3 pounds russet or other firm potatoes, peeled and cut into 1-inch dice

1 tablespoon sesame oil

1/2 teaspoon salt

1/2 teaspoon freshly ground black pepper

1 tablespoon toasted sesame seeds, for garnish

Kamja chorim is a very popular side dish, and it usually appears at the table paired with Anchovy and Green Pepper Chorim (page 215).

❀ ❀ ❀

Soak the anchovies in $1/2$ cup cold water for 15 minutes, to soften. Drain through a colander into a small bowl, reserving both the water and the anchovies. Add the soy sauce, corn syrup, and ch'ŏngju to the reserved anchovy water and mix well.

In a skillet, heat the vegetable oil over medium heat until very hot. Add the garlic and half of the green onions and sauté for 2 minutes. Add the potatoes, anchovies, and soy sauce mixture. Cook, partially covered, for 12 minutes, until the potatoes are done, stirring occasionally with a wooden spoon. Increase the heat to medium-high and cook, uncovered, for 10 minutes, until all the liquid is gone. Add the remaining green onions and sesame oil and immediately remove from the heat. Lightly toss and season with the salt and pepper.

Transfer to a serving bowl and garnish with the sesame seeds. Serve as a side dish. Place leftovers in a tightly closed container in the refrigerator; they will stay fresh for a week.

Variations: Sweet Potato Chorim (Koguma Chorim) is cooked in the same way. Substitute an equal amount of sweet potatoes for the russet potatoes.

         Growing Up in a Korean Kitchen

Bean Curd Chorim

Tubu Chorim

Serves 4
10 minutes to prepare
and 15 minutes to cook

---

1 pound medium-firm bean curd, cut into 2 inch by 3 inch by ½-inch dominoes

¼ cup soy sauce

3 tablespoons ch'ŏngju (rice wine) or vermouth

3 cloves garlic, crushed and finely chopped

1 green onion, green and pale white part only, finely minced

Pinch of salt

1 teaspoon freshly ground black pepper

1 tablespoon toasted sesame seeds, plus extra for garnish

¼ tablespoon sil koch'u (hot red pepper threads) or hot red pepper flakes, plus extra for garnish

2 tablespoons vegetable oil

Cooking bean curd when it is at its freshest is probably the best way to capture and preserve its flavor and goodness. In this recipe, the bean curd is transformed into a deliciously sweet and spicy side dish.

❀ ❀ ❀

With a clean, dry kitchen towel, pat the bean curd dry and place in a colander. In a bowl, combine the soy sauce, ch'ŏngju, garlic, green onion, salt, pepper, sesame seeds, and sil koch'u; mix well. Set aside

In a 14-inch nonstick skillet, heat 1 tablespoon vegetable oil over medium-high heat until hot, but not smoking. Add half of the bean curd and pan-fry for about 3 minutes per side, until the edges turn golden. Turn only once. Transfer to a flat basket and repeat with the remaining bean curd. Return all the bean curd to the skillet in one layer and spoon the soy sauce mixture over it. Cover and cook over medium heat for 15 minutes, until the bean curd absorbs most of the liquid and the sauce is reduced to a syrup.

Transfer to a serving bowl and garnish with the sesame seeds and sil koch'u. Serve warm as a side dish. Or, slice the bean curd into strips and use as a topping on noodles, or dice and add to fried rice dishes. The bean curd can be stored in a container in the refrigerator; it will stay fresh for 1 week.

Lotus Root Chorim

Yŏnkŭn Corim

Serves 4 to 6

15 minutes to prepare
and 1 hour to cook

1 pound lotus roots, scrubbed,
peeled, and sliced crosswise
into $1/4$-inch rounds

$1/2$ cup soy sauce

1 tablespoon sugar, or 2
tablespoons corn syrup

1 tablespoon toasted sesame
seeds or coarsely chopped pine
nuts, for garnish

As in other parts of Asia, Koreans admire and make use of every part of the lotus plant: its wide leaves for wrapping beautiful flower bouquets, its showerhead-looking pod for herbal medicine, and the root as a food source. In summer, lotus roots are sold in local markets, either in bulbous pieces or in slices submerged in water to prevent discoloring. Their skins are mud brown, the flesh a sandy white, and their texture is water chestnut–crunchy. When the roots are sliced, they reveal a very attractive pinwheel pattern, making them a favorite decorative food.

In a heavy stockpot, make 4 cups of acidulated water (page 10) and bring to a boil. Add the lotus roots and blanch for 1 minute (blanching extracts bitterness while retaining color and crispness). Rinse the lotus roots in ice cold water to stop the cooking. Drain in a colander and set aside.

In a stockpot, add the soy sauce and $1/2$ cup water and bring to a boil over high heat. Decrease the heat to medium-high and add the lotus roots. Boil for 15 minutes, or until the liquid is reduced by half. Decrease the heat to low and add the sugar. Simmer, basting occasionally with a wooden spoon, for 45 minutes, or until the liquid becomes syrupy and the lotus slices are well caramelized.

Transfer to a serving bowl and garnish with sesame seeds. Serve as a side dish. Or, the lotus roots may also be used as a garnish. Leftovers can be placed in an airtight container and stored in the refrigerator; they will stay fresh for several months.

Variations: Other roots, such as aralia, burdock, and radishes, can be cooked in the same way.

Steamed Pollack Roe

Myŏngran Tchim

Serves 4
10 minutes to prepare and cook

---

4 sacs pollack roe, each 2 to 3 inches long

1 clove garlic, crushed and finely chopped

2 green onions, white and pale green part only, finely minced

1/2 tablespoon sesame oil

1/4 teaspoon freshly squeezed ginger juice

1/2 tablespoon toasted sesame seeds, for garnish

Pinch of koch'u karu (hot red pepper powder), for garnish

In Korea, fishermen gut pollack on their boats and separate each part for sale to the wholesale markets. The dried skin (ogari) is used for making a clear and tasty traditional soup. Its innards make salted ch'angran chot for winter kimchi or a plain side dish. At the same time, the roe is collected and salted. (The pollack has her eggs from November through March.) Pollack roe is sold in miniature wooden containers. Fresh, uncooked pollack roe is a good companion relish, like caviar, to any national or international dish.

From the humble and abundant female pollack comes myŏngran, a precious roe comparable to salmon roe. In Korea, it is the most popular among the salted fish roe. The mere thought of the tiny pink pollack roe in its clear membrane sac always makes my mouth water. To me, it is just as tasty as the expensive sturgeon's caviar I have tasted in foreign lands. This dish of lightly seasoned and steamed pollack roe is simple to cook and a joy to eat.

Place the roe in a ceramic bowl that can be used for both cooking and serving. Sprinkle with garlic and green onions, reserving some of the green onions for garnish. In another small bowl, combine the sesame oil, ginger juice, and 2 tablespoons of water and mix well. Drizzle this mixture onto the roe.

Place the bowl in a steamer and steam for 5 minutes, until the roe turns opaque. If you do not have a steamer, place the bowl in the center of a stockpot, add 1 cup of water to the stockpot, bring to a boil, and steam for 5 minutes. Garnish with the reserved green onion rings, sesame seeds, and koch'u karu. Serve one piece each in 4 small, individual bowls.

Note: Two other dishes using pollack roe are spiced pollack roe (myŏngran chŏt), in which hot red pepper powder, minced green onions, and sesame oil are mixed with the roe and served without cooking, and roe stew (myŏngran tchigae), in which shredded radish, salted shrimp, and a beaten egg are sprinkled on top of the roe and briefly steamed.

Desserts and Drinks

✿ Desserts and Confections

Many very elaborate Korean desserts, called *husik* (after-dinner food) originated and were perfected in the royal and upper-class kitchens. While these sophisticated recipes often require somewhat rare and expensive ingredients and complicated preparations, even ordinary households make the desserts on special occasions, such as ancestral ceremonies and Korea's four great folk-festival days: New Year's Day (Sŏl Nal), the first full moon of the first month (Tae Borŭm Nal), the fifth day of the fifth month (Tano Nal), and the August full moon (Chusŏk Nal), all according to the lunar calendar. Traditional desserts are also prominent on feast tables at weddings and birthday parties, especially if the celebrations mark the first, sixty-first, or seventy-first birthday, which are considered milestones in a person's life.

There are many delicious and easy recipes among traditional Korean desserts. They tend to be semisweet and are almost always scented with medicinal herbs and spices. Included here are recipes for some of the simpler traditional Korean desserts.

(above) Golden rice crust

(opposite) Soft persimmons

Korean Fruit Soup

Hwach'ae

Serves 4 to 6
20 minutes to prepare

$^1/_2$ cup honey

1 ounce ginger, peeled and grated

2 tablespoons freshly squeezed lemon juice

3 cups grapefruit juice

2 tablespoons ch'ŏngju (rice wine) or vermouth

1 apple, peeled, cored, quartered, and cut into $^1/_2$-inch dice

1 Korean or Asian pear, peeled, cored, quartered, and cut into $^1/_2$-inch dice

15 seedless grapes

1 peach, peeled, pitted, and cut into $^1/_2$-inch dice

1 cup diced seeded watermelon

1 cup strawberries, halved

1 orange, peeled and sectioned

1 tablespoon pine nuts

1 teaspoon ground cinnamon

6 sprigs mint leaves, for garnish

This fruit soup is a gorgeous feast of colors, fragrance, and flavors. The fruit is laced with essences of aromatic herbs, spices, and nuts. It should be prepared several hours ahead, or even the day before.

❁ ❁ ❁

To make the soup base, in a large nonreactive bowl, combine 3 cups of water with the honey, ginger, lemon juice, grapefruit juice, and chŏngju. Stir, blending well. In a punch bowl, add the apple, pear, grapes, peach, watermelon, strawberries, and orange and toss lightly to mix. Add the soup and stir lightly with a wooden spoon. Wrap the bowl with plastic wrap and refrigerate to chill.

Just before serving, sprinkle the pine nuts and cinnamon over the soup. Garnish with the mint leaves. Serve at the center of the table or in individual bowls.

Variations: To give the fruit soup a traditional color, herbal aroma, and taste, add 3 gardenia berries (ch'ija) for a yellow soup or $^1/_2$ tablespoon schisandra berries (omija) for a pink soup. Soak the berries for a few hours in a small bowl and strain, making about $^1/_2$ cup liquid; add to the soup. For extra flavor, add 1 tablespoon each of shredded mung bean curd (nokdumuk ch'ae), toasted grain powder (misu karu), or cooked barley. On top, float pink azaleas in spring or white and golden chrysanthemums in autumn. To make even more fragrant, add pomegranates and a few drops of citrus syrup (yuja chŏng).

Pears Poached in Rice Wine

Paesuk

Serves 4

15 minutes to prepare
and 1 1/2 hours to cook

---

4 ounces ginger, peeled and thinly slivered

4 cinnamon sticks

1 cup ch'ŏngju (rice wine) or vermouth

3 tablespoons honey

1/2 cup light brown sugar

2 Korean pears or other Asian variety, about 10 ounces each

60 whole black peppercorns, or to taste

1 tablespoon pine nuts

4 mint sprigs, for garnish

Naju pae, the Korean variety of pear, hails from the city of the same name in southwest Korea. Unlike other pears, its mottled skin is olive green and it is perfectly round, more like an apple. When it was first introduced to the Western world, it was called an apple-pear or pear-apple. Simmered in rice wine, herbal spices, and honey, paesuk may remind some of the French poires Hélène, but compared to its sweet and silky bites, the pears are not that sweet but are refreshingly spicy and delightfully crunchy. This is one of the most elegant desserts in the Korean classic repertoire.

Put the ginger in a small nonreactive saucepan, add 1 cup of water, and bring to a boil. Gently boil over medium heat for 15 minutes, skimming off the impurities. Pour out the water and add 1 cup of fresh water. Simmer for another 15 minutes. In a strainer lined with cheesecloth, strain the liquid into a 3- or 4-cup measure. Reserve the ginger slices for other uses; for example, they can be used to make Candied Ginger (page 235).

Put the cinnamon sticks in a heavy nonreactive saucepan, add 2 cups of water, and bring to a boil. Decrease the heat to low and simmer for 15 minutes. Remove and discard the cinnamon sticks, and strain the liquid into the cup with the ginger-infused water. Return all the liquid to the same saucepan, add the chŏngju, and simmer over low heat for 5 minutes. Add the honey and sugar and stir to dissolve. Set aside.

Cut the pears in half and core them, then cut each half into 3 wedges, making a total of 12 wedges. Work quickly, to keep the pears from discoloring. Peel the wedges, and firmly press 5 black peppercorns into each one.

Return the saucepan with the honey liquid to a medium-low heat. Carefully add the pears and simmer for 15 minutes. Decrease the heat to low and simmer gently for 25 to 30 minutes, or until the pears turn a reddish brown and become clear. Let cool, then store the saucepan in the refrigerator for 2 to 3 hours, or as long as overnight.

To serve, place 3 pear wedges each in 4 individual glass bowls and ladle in the poaching liquid. Garnish with the pine nuts and mint sprigs. It may also be served warm, before refrigerating.

Variations: Instead of the traditional thin soup, paesuk may also be served in a rich, syrupy sauce. After cooking the pears, with a slotted spoon carefully transfer them to a bowl. Strain the liquid into a saucepan and boil over high heat until it is reduced to the desired consistency. Ladle the syrup over the pears and serve. As a modern variation, serve with a scoop of ice cream.

Sweet Rice Cake

Injŏlmi

Serves 4
15 minutes to prepare
and 1 hour to cook

5 cups sweet rice

1 tablespoon salt

1 tablespoon sugar

1 cup k'ong komul (toasted soybean powder)

This is the basic recipe for all the chewy, sticky rice cakes made with sweet rice or sweet rice flour.

❁ ❁ ❁

Soak the sweet rice in lukewarm water for 1 hour. Drain in a colander. Steam the rice in a steamer for 45 minutes (see note below). Meanwhile, in a small bowl, dissolve the salt and sugar in 1 cup of cold water and set it aside. During the last 15 minutes of steaming, sprinkle this solution over the rice (this seasons and hastens the cooking).

Transfer the hot rice to a work surface. Using a mallet, pound it into a dough. Flatten the dough into a $^1/_2$-inch-thick sheet, then slice it into 1 by $1^1/_2$-inch pieces. Coat all sides with the k'ong komul. Serve as a dessert or snack with a bowl of honey or syrup on the side.

Note: The Four-Piece Multi-Cooker described on page 16 is ideal for steaming sweet rice. Whatever type of steamer is used, wrap the lid completely in a large cotton cloth, to catch the rising steam and keep the rice from getting soggy.

Variations: Injŏlmi are often coated with other ingredients to make a variety of colorful cakes. Popular coatings include jujube slivers, citrus zest, red bean paste, and coarsely chopped nuts, such as pine nuts, gingko nuts, and walnuts.

Sweet Rice Fruit Cake

Yaksik or Yakbap

Serves 8 to 10
15 minutes to prepare
and 1 hour to cook

---

2 cups sweet rice

1 tablespoon soy sauce

2 tablespoons corn syrup or honey

2 tablespoons ch'ŏngju (rice wine)
or vermouth

2 tablespoons sesame oil

1 cup walnuts, skinned, or 10
chestnuts, shelled and skinned

1 cup pitted jujubes or raisins

2 tablespoons pine nuts, skinned
and brown tips removed

½ cup dark brown sugar

1 tablespoon ground cinnamon

Yaksik, a sweet and chewy rice dish, tastes somewhat like a Western fruitcake. According to Korean folklore, it originated in the Silla Dynasty, more than 1,500 years ago. It is said that King Soji (479–500) ordered the dessert to be created to honor a crow that had warned the country of a pending calamity. It is a Korean favorite. Literally translated, yaksik means "medicinal food," probably because the dish always includes ingredients that are said to be especially good for one's health.

Soak the rice in warm water for 1 hour; drain in a colander. Steam the rice in a steamer for 30 minutes (see note on page 226). Meanwhile, in a large bowl, combine the soy sauce, corn syrup, ch'ŏngju, and 1 tablespoon of sesame oil, and mix well. Set aside some walnuts, jujubes, and pine nuts for garnish, and add the rest to the bowl. Add the brown sugar and cinnamon and mix well. Add the hot rice to the bowl and mix thoroughly with a wooden spoon, fluffing the rice lightly.

Brush the inside of a bread pan with the remaining 1 tablespoon of sesame oil. Transfer the mixture to the pan and pack in well. Place the pan in a large stockpot or Dutch oven. Add enough cold water to reach halfway up the sides of the pan. Bring to a gentle boil over medium heat, cover, and let steam for 1 hour. Let sit for 15 minutes.

Spoon into individual custard bowls and garnish each with the reserved walnuts, jujubes, and pine nuts. Serve warm as a dessert or snack. Leftovers can be stored in the refrigerator and will stay fresh for 1 week. Reheat leftovers by steaming.

Flower Pancakes

Kkot'jŏn or Hwajŏn

Serves 10 to 12
15 minutes to prepare
and 20 minutes to cook

2 cups sweet rice flour

Pinch of salt

1 cup hot water

32 dried jujubes, pitted and cut into slivers

32 crown daisy leaves or parsley leaves

4 tablespoons sesame oil

5 tablespoons pine nuts, finely chopped, for garnish

1/4 cup honey or corn syrup

The name of this elegant and sweet dessert originates from the fresh flower petals and leaves that are often used to decorate it. Traditionally, azalea, chrysanthemum, and nasturtium petals were used and, on rare occasions, rose petals. In my nostalgia, I recall that the sweet rice medallion cakes were always adorned with pretty flower patterns made with jujube slivers and stone-ear mushrooms glistening through a honey glaze. This family recipe is made with jujube and crown daisy leaves in place of live flowers.

✿ ✿ ✿

In a bowl, combine the sweet rice flour and salt and mix well. Add the hot water, 1 spoonful at time, stirring constantly to make a cornmeal-like consistency. (Uncooked sweet rice flour is very stiff, and hot water makes the dough more pliable.) Knead by hand into a soft dough.

On a work surface, roll out the dough into 2 ropes. Cover 1 rope with a damp kitchen towel. Divide the other rope into 4 pieces, then divide each piece into 4 walnut-size balls. Flatten each ball into a pancake, 2 1/2 inches in diameter. Keep the finished pancakes moist under the damp towel. Repeat with the other rope, making a total of 32 pancakes.

In a nonstick skillet, heat 1 tablespoon of sesame oil over medium heat. Place 8 pancakes in the skillet and, working quickly, decorate each pancake with 6 jujube slivers and 1 crown daisy leaf in a flower design. Keep the pancakes separate. Cook for 2 1/2 minutes per side, or until they puff up, subside, and turn golden. Turn only once. Transfer to a bamboo tray to cool. Repeat three times.

To serve, place 2 to 3 pancakes in small individual dishes. Garnish with the pine nuts. Drizzle a spoonful of honey on top.

Note: Sticky Indian millet powder can also be used to make pancakes. These pancakes—a regional dish from Kangwŏn province called pukkŭmi—are folded over like crepes, with jujubes, nuts, or sesame seeds as a filling.

Sweet Rice Balls

Kyŏngdan

Makes 16 rice balls

25 minutes to prepare and cook

---

1 cup sweet rice flour

Pinch of salt

⅓ cup hot water

½ cup ground cinnamon or k'ong komul (toasted soybean powder), or finely slivered jujubes, or toasted black sesame seeds

Sweet rice balls make a delicious dessert. They can be coated in cinnamon, toasted soybean powder, jujube slivers, or toasted sesame seeds. Plain miniature rice balls, without the coatings, are often floated in soups or porridges.

In a bowl, combine the sweet rice flour and salt and mix well. Add the hot water, 1 spoonful at a time, stirring constantly to make a cornmeal-like consistency. Knead by hand into a soft dough, and divide it into 16 hazelnut-size balls.

In a saucepan, bring 8 cups of water to a boil over high heat. Drop the balls in one by one and boil for 6 to 7 minutes, until the balls float to the surface and become clear. Remove them with a slotted spoon, then plunge them in ice water to stop the cooking. Roll the balls in cinnamon to coat thoroughly. Serve with a bowl of honey or sugar.

Snow White Rice Cakes

Paeksŏlgi or Hŭin Ttŏk

Serves 4

15 minutes to prepare and cook

---

3 tablespoons sugar

Pinch of salt

2 cups short-grain rice flour

Strange as it may seem, golden rice crust (nurŭngji), the scorched rice at the bottom of the pot, has long been the number one dessert in Korea, especially among the older generation. After our mother scooped out the steaming rice from our huge cast-iron cauldron, a golden brown sheet was left there for us. There was always a scramble among us kids over the last piece of crust. These days, the electric rice cooker does its job too perfectly, to the dismay of all nurŭngji-loving Koreans, young and old. But fear not, we can always return to the conventional method! Here's how: Cook rice in a heavy-bottom pot. When the rice is done, turn down the heat as low as possible and let the rice cook for about 20 minutes more. Scoop out the rice. At the bottom is a crusty layer in beautiful shades of color ranging from light eggshell to light chocolate brown. That is nurŭngji. Of course, packaged nurŭngji is now available in Korean markets—always displayed at a prominent spot near the cashier's counter, seducing the children in us.

Snow white rice cake is made with short-grain rice flour. The flour is steamed and made into a flat rice cake. It has a soft, chewy, bagel-like texture and is usually cut into squares and served plain or with honey or sugar. In my memory, paeksŏlgi was always made by our mother and came out of a steaming gray earthenware cake pot called *siru*. But today, everyone conveniently buys them at *ttŏk chip* (cake houses).

❀ ❀ ❀

In a small bowl, combine the sugar and salt with 3 tablespoons of water, and stir to dissolve. Place the rice flour in another bowl. Add the sugar water and mix with your hands to make a cornmeal-like texture. Strain through a medium-fine strainer into a cheesecloth-lined steamer, sprinkling it evenly, layer by layer. Cover the steamer with a dampened cheesecloth. Steam for 15 minutes to make 1 round rice cake, about 6 inches wide and 1¹/₂ inches high. Transfer to a cutting board and let cool. Slice into wedges or squares. Serve with sugar or honey.

Variations: Snow white rice cake is also made with a variety of fillings between the layers, such as blanched mugwort, sugar, stone-ear mushroom slivers, chestnut slices, jujube slivers, or pine nuts. Honey, caramel sauce, and dark soy sauce can be mixed in with the flour before steaming to make honey brown cake (kkul pyŏn).

Pine Needle–Scented Rice Cakes

Song P'yŏn

Makes about 14 rice cakes
20 minutes to prepare
and 15 minutes to cook

3 tablespoons toasted sesame
seeds

2 tablespoons honey or corn syrup

1½ cups short-grain rice flour

Pinch of salt

¼ cup hot water

2 cups pine needles, freshly
picked, washed, and patted dry

½ tablespoon sesame oil

This traditional dessert is eaten on Korea's harvest festival, Ch'usŏk Nal, the fifteenth day of August by the lunar calendar. Children love to bite into the chewy skin of the half-moon-shaped rice cakes to discover the semisweet filling inside. There is a great variety of tasty fillings, such as red bean paste, cooked or toasted soybeans, chestnuts, jujubes, and toasted sesame seeds. Every family takes pride in their own recipes. Whenever I think of this rice cake of my childhood, the fragrance of pine needles always floats past my nose. They are steamed in a bed of freshly picked pine needles. The most memorable one is mugwort-scented ssuk song p'yŏn.

In a small bowl, combine the sesame seeds and honey, mixing it into a paste. Set aside. Combine the rice flour and salt in a bowl and mix thoroughly. Add the hot water, 1 spoonful at a time, stirring constantly to make a cornmeal-like consistency. Knead into a soft, marshmallow-like dough. Cover the dough with a clean, damp kitchen cloth, to keep it moist and pliable.

Pinch out a walnut-size piece of dough and knead it into a ball. With your finger, form a pouch in the ball and fill it with about ½ teaspoon of the honey paste. Seal it back up and mold into a plump half-moon shape, about 2 inches long. Set it aside under a damp cloth. Repeat with the remaining dough, making about 14 cakes. Cook these as soon as possible, as they dry out quickly.

Spread half the pine needles in a steamer lined with muslin, and place the cakes on top of them, set ½ inch apart in a single layer. Cover with the remaining pine needles and steam for 12 minutes. Discard the pine needles and transfer the cakes to a bowl. Add the sesame oil and toss to coat the cakes. Serve warm with additional honey, for dipping.

Honey-Coated Cookies

Yakgwa or Yugwa

Makes about 20 cookies
30 minutes to prepare
and 20 minutes to cook

---

2 cups all-purpose wheat flour

2 tablespoons sesame oil

1 egg yolk

Pinch of salt

Pinch of freshly ground black
pepper

1 tablespoon freshly squeezed
ginger juice

2 tablespoons ch'ŏngju (rice wine)
or vermouth

3 tablespoons honey, plus 1 cup
honey or corn syrup

1 cup olive oil or vegetable oil

$^1/_2$ tablespoon ground cinnamon

4 tablespoons pine nuts, coarsely
chopped, or toasted sesame
seeds

One of the most traditional desserts are sweet rice cookies (sanja or kanjŏng), but making them was no simple matter: Sweet rice was steamed and pounded into a chewy, soft dough, then rolled out and cut into squares, rectangles, or ribbons. After drying, the pieces were dropped into a shallow pan of hot sesame oil and immediately ballooned into crispy, airy cookies. Then they were dipped in melted sugar or honey and rolled in sesame seeds, puffed rice, or chopped pine nuts. Fortunately, these days excellent sweet rice cookies are commercially available.

The closest translation of yakgwa is "medicinal cookies," so named because the list of beneficial ingredients includes ginger, cinnamon, honey, and ch'ŏngju. Yakgwa is a deep-fried cookie richly flavored in sesame oil and honey, somewhat like the Middle Eastern baklava. It is always deep-fried in oil, hence its other name, yugwa, which means "deep-fried cookies." Every traditional Korean kitchen had several wooden molds called *yakgwa tŭl*. They were used to stamp flower motifs on the dough, especially chrysanthemums, the Chinese character for longevity, and geometrical designs. Today, for special occasions, people usually buy these cookies at traditional pastry shops, although they are not difficult to make.

❀ ❀ ❀

Sift the flour into a large bowl, and make a well in the center. Add the sesame oil and egg yolk to the well and mix into a cornmeal-like consistency. Add the salt and pepper and sift once more. In a small bowl, combine the ginger juice, ch'ŏngju, and 3 tablespoons honey. Mix well and stir into the flour mixture, 1 spoonful at a time. Knead lightly into a soft dough. Do not knead too much, to keep the cookie's light and crunchy texture (similar to a piecrust).

Form the dough into the size of golf balls, making a total of about 20 balls, each about $1^3/_4$ inches in diameter. Press each ball lightly into a decorative mold, to form an impression on the surface. Using a fork, poke several holes in the dough (this allows more uniform cooking). In a deep frying pan, heat the vegetable oil over high heat until very hot, then decrease the heat to medium. Drop the balls, 5 to 6 at a time, into the oil. Fry for about $2^1/_2$ minutes, turn them once, and fry for about $2^1/_2$ minutes more, or until the balls are golden brown and crispy. Transfer to a paper towel to absorb the oil. Repeat with the remaining balls.

In a small saucepan, add the remaining 1 cup honey and heat over medium-low heat. Using chopsticks, dip each cookie in the hot honey, coating it all over. Drain and cool on a rack. Transfer the cookies to a plate in one layer. Sprinkle the cinnamon and pine nuts on top.

Black Sesame Seed Cookies

Kŏmŭnkkae Tasik

Makes about 12 cookies
30 minutes to prepare

1 cup black sesame seeds
3 tablespoons honey

The traditional tasik mold is a wooden pallet, usually about 15 inches long and 2 inches wide, with five intricate designs carved into it, each about 1 inch in diameter. Of course, you may make your own design by hand.

This soft cookie can be made with one of many, various ingredients, such as mung beans, soybeans, ginger starch, chestnuts, and even sweet rice flour and wheat flour. One of the most admired and exotic tasik is made from pale yellow pine flower pollen (songhwa). In this recipe, black sesame seeds are the main ingredient, but you can also make it with white sesame seeds. Tasik may be ordered from most Korean markets.

Wash the sesame seeds several times and drain in a fine-mesh strainer. In a skillet, carefully toast the sesame seeds over medium heat for 15 minutes, or until fragrant. Stir constantly, and be careful not to burn them. Transfer the seeds into a mortar and pound the seeds into a paste. It will be very oily. Add the honey and mix well, to make a soft, marzipan-like dough. Divide the dough into 12 chestnut-size balls. One at a time, press a ball into a mold, packing it in tightly. Pop out the tasik and transfer to a tray. This dessert goes well with tea.

Puffed Rice and Sesame Seed Cookies

Kkaeyŏt Kanjŏng

Makes 24 cookies
35 minutes to prepare

$^1/_2$ cup white, black, or brown
  sesame seeds

$^1/_2$ cup sugar

$^1/_2$ cup corn syrup

1 cup puffed rice

1 tablespoon pine nuts

2 tablespoons raisins, coarsely
  chopped

1 tablespoon sesame oil

There is one cookie among all the delicious Korean cookies that lives in my heart. Not even my grandmother could make it. Only P'al-se, our neighborhood cookie maker, made kŏbuk kwaja, or "turtle cookies" as we called them, because of the turtle-shell design stamped on them. I remember P'al-se's crumbling thatched-roofed shack, where his grilling irons were lined up above a makeshift oven fashioned out of an old gasoline drum. He would pour his magic mix into one side of a hot iron and deftly snap it shut. In that incredible moment, one of the most wonderful aromas would rise and float throughout the neighborhood. Then, in no time, there they were—thin, round, and golden brown—his batter transformed into crispy curved turtleback cookies.

This dessert is easy to make. Toasted sesame seeds and puffed rice are coated in syrup, rolled out into sheets, and cut into bars. Sesame seeds of various colors and flavors, plus pine nuts and raisins, make wonderful, brittle dessert bars.

Wash the sesame seeds and drain in a fine-mesh strainer. In a skillet, carefully toast them over medium-low heat for about 15 minutes, or until fragrant. Stir constantly, and be careful not to burn them. Set aside and let cool.

In a nonreactive saucepan, stir the sugar and corn syrup together with a few drops of water. Boil over medium-low heat for about 5 minutes, or until it caramelizes and coats the back of a spoon. Add the sesame seeds, puffed rice, pine nuts, and raisins and mix into a soft dough. Line a baking sheet with plastic wrap and brush with the oil. Spread the puffed rice mixture onto the baking sheet into an 8 by 12-inch rectangle about $^1/_4$-inch-thick. It hardens quickly and baking is not required. Using a pizza cutter, cut into 1 inch by 4-inch bars. Serve as a snack.

Candied Ginger

Saenggang Chŏnggwa

Makes 1¹/₂ cups
1¹/₂ hours to prepare

---

8 ounces ginger, peeled and thinly sliced

1 cup sugar

¹/₂ cup honey

1 tablespoon corn syrup

There is a more complicated candied ginger dish called saengran ch'o or saengran chŏnggwa, which calls for ginger starch extracted from grated ginger cooked a short time and caramelized in sugar and honey. It is then formed by hand into ginger root shapes.

Candied desserts are among the sweetest of all the Korean desserts and are usually served in small portions. They are also used in making tea (although fresh ingredients of course make the best tea). These sweets are made from fruits (citrus, jujubes, and pears), dried vegetables (radishes and pumpkin strings), and herbal roots (ginseng and bellflower roots). Candied ginger, lotus, and citrus are three of the most candied desserts.

In a nonreactive saucepan, add the ginger and 2 cups water and bring to a boil. Decrease the heat to medium-low and simmer for 15 minutes. Pour out the water and repeat 3 times (this removes the bitterness). Drain in a colander and set aside. The ginger will still be quite spicy.

In the same pan, combine the sugar, honey, corn syrup, and 1¹/₂ cups of fresh water and bring to a boil. Decrease the heat to medium-low and add the ginger. Simmer, occasionally stirring with a wooden spoon, for 30 minutes, or until the ginger turns transparent and is caramelized. Adjust the cooking time, for either a chewy or a crispy texture (the longer the cooking time, the crispier). With a fork, spread the ginger on cookie sheets to cool. Serve as a snack or use it to make ginger tea. Crumbled, it can be used as an ice cream topping.

Note: The bitter ginger water is reserved and used as a Korean cold medicine, with a drop of honey.

Candied Lotus Roots

Yŏngǔn Chŏnggwa

Serves 8 to 10
About 1¹/₂ hours to prepare

1 pound lotus roots

1 cup sugar or honey

1 tablespoon corn syrup

Candied lotus roots, with their attractive wagon wheel pattern, are one of the most gracious sweets among Korean desserts. The preparation is similar to Candied Ginger (page 235). Be sure to use fresh lotus roots with unblemished skin.

Scrub the lotus roots with a brush and peel them with a stainless steel knife or peeler, to avoid discoloration. Cut them crosswise into ¹/₄-inch slices. Drop the slices into cold water immediately, or they will oxidize and turn dark brown. Let soak for 30 minutes. In a nonreactive saucepan, make 4 cups acidulated water (see page 10) and bring to a boil. Add the lotus roots and cook gently over medium heat for 15 minutes. Rinse a few times in cold water (this removes the bitterness). Drain in a colander and set aside.

In the same saucepan, combine the sugar, corn syrup, and 2 cups of water and bring to a boil. Decrease the heat to medium-low and add the lotus root. Simmer for 45 minutes, or until the lotus slices are transparent and caramelized into a shiny dark brown. At this point, the lotus slices will have absorbed most of the syrup. Be careful not to burn.

Transfer each slice to a cake rack and cool completely. Store in a plastic bag, being careful not to disturb their neat appearance. Serve as sweet tidbits, as garnish for other desserts, or as a crumbled ice cream topping. Freeze leftovers for later use.

Variations: Fresh ginseng, broad bellflower roots, aralia roots, sun-dried radish, and gourd strings are among the good candidates for this recipe. Use them in place of the lotus roots.

Candied Quince

Mogwa Chŏnggwa

Makes 2 cups
30 minutes to prepare
and 15 minutes to cook

---

1 pound quince, halved, cored,
and sliced paper-thin

1 cup sugar or honey

1 tablespoon corn syrup

1 tablespoon ground cinnamon

Korean quince is famous for its unsightly bumpy look. It is so irritating that there is a Korean proverb, *Sagwa mangsinŭn mogwaga sikinda* ("The quince gives apples a bad reputation"). At the same time, quince is widely recognized for its nutritional value. In my childhood home, before the advent of refrigerators, quince was picked in the fall, candied, placed in an earthenware pot, and buried in the backyard for 5 to 6 months. The clear, sweet syrup, mogwa ch'ŏng, was used as a sweetener on special occasions, for ancestral ceremonials, and for making a fragrant citrus tea.

In a steamer, steam the quince for 30 minutes. Meanwhile, in a non-reactive saucepan, combine the sugar, corn syrup, cinnamon, and 2 tablespoons of water and bring to a boil. Decrease the heat to low and simmer for about 15 minutes, or until the liquid looks like thick honey.

In a sterilized 1-pint wide-mouth glass jar with a tight lid, arrange a layer of quince slices in a fan pattern. Drizzle a spoonful of the sugar mixture over the quince. Repeat until all the quince are placed, packing each layer well. Serve as a snack. Stored in the refrigerator, it will keep almost indefinitely.

Variations: This recipe can be used to make Asian Citrus Peel Preserves (Yuja Chŏnggwa or Yuja Ch'ŏng).

Rice Punch

Sikhye

**Makes about 3 quarts;
serves 8 to 10**
1¹/₂ days to prepare and cook

1¹/₂ cups barley malt powder

1 cup sweet rice

1 tablespoon pine nuts

2 tablespoons raisins, chopped
(traditionally jujube)

When preparing the barley malt, a residue settles on the bottom while a clear liquid remains on top. The remaining residue was used to boil cooked rice to make kamju, a murky, sweet, but crude drink that was reserved for us kids. The clear liquid—a less sweet, but more refined juice—was used to make the sikhye that went to the adults and precious guests via the ancestral ceremonial altars.

This is a refreshing nonalcoholic drink made from rice and barley malt. Koreans call it *ipgasim*, a palette-cleansing drink. It is a sheer delight after spicy food, a refreshing dessert drink that will be enjoyed by both young and old. It is a customary offering at ancestral altars. Our mother still makes it in a huge pot-bellied crock. It is best to prepare and refrigerate the punch a few days before serving.

❀ ❀ ❀

In a heavy nonreactive stockpot, bring 6 cups of water to a boil and let cool. Dissolve the malt in the water and let sit for about 6 hours. Strain the milky liquid into a bowl, pressing hard with a wooden spoon to squeeze out as much liquid as possible. When the residue settles, carefully pour off the clear, dark brown liquid at the top into a pan. Discard the residue at the bottom.

Soak the rice in lukewarm water for 1 hour and drain. In a steamer, steam the rice for 15 minutes (see note on page 226). Place the hot rice in a 4-quart earthenware pot. Add the clear malt liquid and cover. Preheat the oven to 200°. Place the pot in the oven and let sit for about 5 hours, to let the yeast develop. (Our mother now uses an electric rice cooker-steamer for this purpose.) The rice kernels will ferment and float to the surface. Lift them out with a slotted spoon or a flat sieve; reserve the remaining liquid. Rinse the rice in cold water and drain. Keep in a covered bowl and chill. You should have about 1¹/₂ cups of rice.

Pour the reserved liquid into the stockpot and add 8 cups of fresh water. Bring to a boil, skimming the impurities rising to the top. Boil just once and cool. (If you continue simmering and stirring at this point, it will turn into syrup, one step in making Korean taffy, kaeng yŏt.) This liquid can be used immediately, while still warm. Or, return it to the earthenware pot and chill in the refrigerator.

To serve as a dessert, ladle the punch into individual glass custard bowls and float 1 or 2 spoonfuls of rice, some pine nuts, and a few chopped raisins on top. Or, serve as a refreshing drink. Stored in the refrigerator, it will stay fresh for 1 month.

Persimmon Punch

Sujŏnggwa

Serves 4
1 hour to prepare

---

2 ounces ginger, peeled and thinly sliced

2 cinnamon sticks

2 cups sugar

½ cup honey

½ cup ch'ŏngju (rice wine) or vermouth

4 dried persimmons, stemmed and seeded

2 tablespoons pine nuts

This Korean punch is made with dried persimmons (kkot'kam) and a spicy syrup. This traditional punch is as popular as Rice Punch (page 238). Persimmons are plentiful in Korea; a persimmon tree is growing in the yard of practically every home. In the fall, the countryside is dotted with flaming yellow persimmons skewered like beads on a string, drying in the sun. When a ripe persimmon is peeled and dried, its hard and bitter pulp turns chewy and sugary like a raisin, and its surface is coated with sugar dust. This recipe is somewhat similar to Pears Poached in Rice Wine (page 225), but with less wine and a good deal more sugar. For best results, make a day ahead so the punch has time to chill.

In a 4-quart nonreactive saucepan, add the ginger and 5 cups of water. Bring to a boil and cook over medium heat for 15 minutes (this removes the bitterness). Strain the liquid into a 3- or 4-quart measure and set aside. Reserve the ginger for other uses; for example, it can be used to make Candied Ginger (page 235). In the same saucepan, add the cinnamon sticks and 5 cups of fresh water. Bring to a boil and cook gently over medium heat for 30 minutes, to extract the essence. Remove the cinnamon sticks and strain the liquid into the measure with the ginger-infused water. Discard the cinnamon sticks, or reserve for other uses. Return all the liquid to the saucepan. Add the sugar, honey, and ch'ŏngju and stir to dissolve. Bring to a boil once, then allow it to cool. Cover and chill in the refrigerator.

About 1 hour before serving, put the dried persimmons in the punch to soften. Serve in 4 individual glass bowls. Place a softened persimmon in each bowl and add ¾ cup of punch. Float a few pine nuts in each and serve. It will stay fresh in the refrigerator for 2 weeks.

Note: Traditionally, a persimmon is studded with a walnut at its center.

❂ Teas

In the sixteenth century, Hŏ Chun, a Korean medical scholar, set forth the basic tenets of healthy living, and they are observed in Korea to this day. His twenty-volume work, *Tongŭi Pogam (The Theory and Practice of Oriental Medicine)*, dealt with the treatment of all manner of illnesses and outlined methods to maintain good health. To fortify the immune system, he said, good food and a balanced diet are essential and are the ultimate preventive medicine. The prescribed diet included teas, tonics, wines, and spirits. According to Korean tradition, teas (ch'a) and spirits (sul) should be imbibed not simply for enjoyment, but also for the more serious purpose of sustaining healthy bodies and souls.

The tea our grandmother brewed for our family and her guests was minsok ch'a (folk tea), or as it is also called, taeyong ch'a (substitute tea). The simplest tea of all was sungnyung, a rice tea made by adding boiling water to the crust of rice at the bottom of the rice pot. It was our habit to drink this during and after all our meals. Other folk teas were made with fruits, herbs, seeds, roots, and leaves other than traditional tea leaves. As the seasons turned, our grandmother collected from her garden ginger, citrus, mint, persimmon leaves, and anything else that could be concocted into refreshing and mind-soothing ch'a. Many of these were kept as standbys in her medicine cabinet in case any of us children fell ill. The popular folk teas introduced in this chapter are the ones our grandmother used to make. Today, all are commercially available in packets and jars at Korean markets.

Shin family medicinal earthenware pot on brass brazier

(above) Shin family medicinal mortar and pestle

(opposite) Lantern at a traditional drinking house

Here are some hints on brewing tea:

❂ Ceramicware is best for brewing tea. Avoid metal.

❂ The quality of the water is very important. Use spring water or filtered water.

❂ Most teas are not sweetened, although honey (never sugar) can be added to minsok ch'a.

❂ Grain teas, like iced tea, will stay fresh in the refrigerator for a week. Most others should be brewed fresh.

Korean Ginseng (Insam)

Koreans religiously believe in their ancient folk medicines and the mysterious healing power of the herbs that grow in abundance throughout the land. Of all these plants, ginseng (insam), the root that resembles a human figure, is undoubtedly the most highly revered. For centuries, Koreans have regarded it with awe as an elixir of longevity, if not the fountain of eternal youth. They say that four or five thousand years ago, wild ginseng (sansam) thrived in the deep forests and mountainous regions of the Korean peninsula. About one thousand years ago, our ancestors began pioneering methods of cultivating ginseng. Today, wild ginseng is extremely rare, and the supply of ginseng comes almost totally from commercial farms.

Korean Spirits (Sul)

Korea has a long history of making wines and spirits. It is believed that prior to 1910, more than 300 varieties were being produced in Korea, but during the Japanese colonial rule (1910–1945), all Korean wine making was outlawed. Sadly, most of the recipes were lost during this period, but a few hyangt'o myŏngju (folk-distilled wine and spirits) survived.

Soju, a whiskey-like spirit, is distilled from sweet rice, barley, wheat, millet, potatoes, and other grains and is 40 to 45 percent alcohol by volume. There are several grades of rice wine. Makgŏlli (t'akju) is the easiest to make at home and the least expensive; it has 6 to 8 percent alcohol by volume. Following in alcohol content and quality are yakju, tongdongju, ch'ŏngju, and ch'ŏngjong. These everyday, table rice wines are used in cooking or drinking and have 10 to 16 percent alcohol by volume.

Our grandmother also used to make yaksul, homemade medicinal wines for folk remedies. To make these compounds, the herbs, flowers, or fruits are coated with honey or sugar, macerated in soju diluted with water, then matured for a few months. Almost everything that grew in her garden and orchard, it seemed, went into her yaksul: garlic, hot peppers, pomegranates, aralia roots, cinnamon, licorice, pine cones and needles, schisandra berries, gardenia berries, azalea flowers, mint—and the list goes on. They were all there, ready to cure our aching tummies, colds, or headaches.

Barley Tea

Pori Ch'a

Serves 4
10 minutes to prepare
and 1 hour to brew

1 cup unhulled barley

2 quarts spring water

ccording to *The Nine Virtues of Tea*, tea is good for clearing the mind, the ears, and the eyes. It stimulates the appetite, quenches thirst, reduces fatigue, and prevents drowsiness. Tea wards off the discomforts of extreme weather and helps sober up the intoxicated.

In Korean homes, restaurants, and tearooms, barley tea and brown rice tea (see below) are provided in the same way as a glass of water would be in America. Barley tea is such a mainstay that in tearooms even an order of coffee is served with a cup of barley tea to the side.

Wash the barley and drain in a colander. In a skillet, add the barley and toast over medium-low heat for 3 minutes, or until fragrant, stirring often with a wooden spoon (be careful not to burn the barley). Let cool.

Put the water and the barley in a heavy ceramic teapot. Bring to a boil over high heat and immediately decrease the heat to low. Simmer for 1 hour. Serve warm or cold. Leftovers may be stored in the refrigerator for a few days.

Note: It is customary to serve these healthy folk teas unsweetened.

Variation: To make Brown Rice Tea (Hyŏnmi Ch'a), use the same amount of brown rice instead of barley. Follow the directions above, but simmer the rice tea for only 20 minutes.

Five-Grain Tea

Ogok Ch'a

Serves 4
10 minutes to prepare
and 1 hour to brew

3 tablespoons unhulled barley

2 tablespoons brown rice

1 tablespoon unhulled wheat

1 tablespoon millet

1 tablespoon Indian millet

2 quarts spring water

This tea's earthy flavor and healthy ingredients make it an invigorating drink, especially at breakfast. Premixed and powdered ogok ch'a is available in many Korean markets.

Wash the grains and drain in a colander. In a skillet, add the grains and toast over medium-low heat for 3 minutes, or until fragrant, stirring often with a wooden spoon (be careful not to burn). Let cool.

Put the water and the grains in a heavy ceramic teapot. Bring to a boil over high heat and immediately decrease the heat to low. Simmer for 1 hour. Serve warm or cold. Leftovers may be stored in the refrigerator for a few days.

Note: It is customary to serve this healthy folk tea unsweetened.

Variation: Each grain may also be brewed separately, or in any combination you like.

Wild Sesame Tea

Tulkkae Ch'a

Serves 4
5 minutes to prepare

4 tablespoons wild sesame seed
powder

4 cups spring water

This tea is known for its healthy and nutritious qualities. It is an old Korean custom for parents to give tŭlkkae ch'a to a daughter who is about to marry, believing that wild sesame seeds possess an essence that promotes healthy skin, clears the mind, and retards graying hair. Making this tea is simplicity itself.

❀ ❀ ❀

Put the spring water in a nonmetallic teapot and bring to a boil. Spoon in 1 tablespoon powder into each of 4 cups and add the boiling water. Stir to dissolve. Serve with honey.

Yuja Tea

Yuja Ch'a

Serves 4
2 minutes to brew

8 slices candied yuja

4 cups spring water

½ tablespoon pine nuts,
for garnish

This beautiful amber-hued and vitamin C–rich minsok ch'a is brewed with candied Asian citrus, yuja. One of the most beloved of all the teas, it has an explosive and exhilarating citrus fragrance. This recipe calls for candied yuja, which is easily obtainable, though the tea can also be made with fresh yuja (see below).

❀ ❀ ❀

Put the yuja and water in a nonmetallic teapot. Bring to a boil over high heat. Decrease the heat to very low and simmer for 2 minutes. Pour into warm porcelain teacups and garnish with slivers of yuja peel and a few of the pine nuts floating on top. Serve either hot or chilled. This tea goes well with Korean rice cakes and other desserts.

Variations: To make the tea with fresh yuja, use the peel from 1 yuja. Brew for 5 minutes and serve with honey or sugar on the side. Tea made with fresh yuja will have a heightened citrus fragrance.

Follow the base recipe for brewing Candied Quince Tea (Mogwa Ch'a) or Candied Tangerine Tea (Kamgyul Ch'a).

To make Jujube Tea (Taech'u Ch'a), use 2 ounces pitted jujube and simmer for 15 minutes; serve plain. According to Korean folklore, tea, wine, or soup made of jujube has a depressant quality and is a kind of tranquilizer. There is a saying that it is good for oppressed and stressed-out daughters-in-law.

Growing Up in a Korean Kitchen

Ginger Tea

Saenggang Ch'a

Serves 4 to 6
15 minutes to brew

4 ounces ginger, peeled
  and thinly sliced

5 jujubes, pitted (optional)

6 cups spring water

Honey to taste

1/2 tablespoon pine nuts,
  for garnish

1/2 tablespoon ground cinnamon,
  for garnish

Spiked with the essences of ginger and cinnamon, this tea is very spicy, peppery, and aromatic. This tea pairs wonderfully with sweet desserts.

✿ ✿ ✿

Place the ginger, jujubes, and water in a nonmetallic teapot. Bring to a boil over high heat. Decrease the heat to low and simmer for 10 minutes. Pour through a strainer, reserving the ginger. (The ginger can be brewed for a second and even a third time. It will retain its spicy and peppery flavor, although its intensity will diminish.) Sweeten with honey, to ease the strong spiscy flavor, and pour into 4 to 6 porcelain cups. Garnish each with the pine nuts and a pinch of cinnamon. Serve very hot.

Note: To make a strong dose of folk medicine, reduce the amount of water to 4 cups and simmer for 15 minutes. In Korean homes, the ginger is often brewed with large sweet green onions (bulb portion only) and jujube as a cure for common colds. Our grandmother always did this for us. For a severe cold she added grated garlic. As an adult, I always rush to my cupboard and make this concoction as soon as any member of my family has a hint of a cold coming on.

Variations: Follow the above recipe to make Cinnamon Tea (Kyep'i Ch'a) or Kudzu Vine Root Tea (Ch'ik Ch'a). For Licorice Tea (Kamch'o Ch'a), use dried licorice roots and brew for 40 minutes. Both licorice tea and kudzu vine root tea are dark brown, with a bittersweet taste.

In Korea, vendors sell raw ch'ik ch'a along most roadsides and in every open market. The raw drink is freshly pressed in front of customers. This inexpensive tea is believed to quench thirst and invigorate the fatigued.

Schisandra (or Five-Flavor) Tea

Omija Ch'a

Serves 4
5 minutes to brew

¼ cup schisandra berries

4 cups spring water

Honey to taste

As the name implies, this tea has a combination of five different flavors. It is made with schisandra berries (omija), which are sweet, salty, spicy, bitter, and very sour. Its sourness is so dominant that some chefs in Seoul use omija juice instead of vinegar. Because of its complex flavor, pleasant pink color, and medicinal qualities, omija is a favorite herb in Korean cooking.

Put the berries and spring water in a nonmetallic teapot. Bring to a boil over high heat. Decrease the heat to low and simmer for no more than 5 minutes, or the berries will become bitter. Sweeten with honey and serve hot in warm cups. Store the leftovers in the refrigerator. It will stay fresh for a couple of days.

Variations: Two other popular teas are brewed in much the same way. Orange-red and vitamin C–rich Chinese Matrimony Vine Tea (Kugija Ch'a) is made with kugija berries and simmered for 15 minutes. Dark caramel-colored Kyŏlmyŏngja Ch'a is made with tiny kyŏlmyŏngja beans. Toast 4 tablespoons of beans first and then brew for 20 minutes.

Persimmon Leaf Tea

Kamip Ch'a

Serves 4
10 minutes to brew

---

4 cups spring water

4 tablespoons dried persimmon leaf tea

Honey to taste (optional)

There is no lack of ingredients for this tea in Korea, as persimmon trees are ubiquitous there. The leaves are picked in July when they are young and tender, then they are shredded, steamed, and sun-dried. According to the drinkers, this tea is packed with vitamin C. They say it is good for diabetics and also helps lower high blood pressure. With its pleasant leafy flavor, this leaf tea is a Korean favorite.

Bring the water to boil in a nonmetallic teapot, add the tea leaves, and let steep for 10 minutes. Sweeten with honey, if desired, and serve as an invigorating tea.

Variations: Use the same procedure for making other leaf teas, such as Green Tea (Nok Ch'a), Chrysanthemum Tea (Kukhwa Ch'a), and Mint Tea (Pakha Ch'a).

Growing Up in a Korean Kitchen

Korean Ginseng Tea

Insam Ch'a

Serves 4
1 to 2 hours to brew

---

2 ounces Koryo hongsam (red ginseng)

6 cups spring water

It is surprisingly simple to brew ginseng tea or tonic, but not the way our grandmother went about it in my childhood home. She would approach each preparation session with great ceremony. There would be a few different kinds of teas and tonics made in combination with ginseng. A pasty, chutney-like tonic made with a whole mountain goat was one I remember most. All brand-new utensils, except for the same old clay medicinal pot, would be ready, including a new wooden spoon that she herself carved with a pocketknife. In my memory, that stained pot and mud brazier is always at the same spot outside the kitchen door, and the tea is brewing away over a weak charcoal fire with the bitter smell of ginseng seeping through the mulberry paper cover, permeating our backyard.

Today, ginseng is relatively easy to obtain, although it may be quite expensive, especially if it is of a very high grade. Ginseng tea bags and other elaborately prepared ginseng extracts are sold at all Korean markets in America, and you can purchase the roots to brew insam ch'a. This recipe calls for red ginseng. This first-rate modern ginseng is not exactly red, but it has a faint red tint, the result of a special steaming process. The straw-colored infusion is moderate in strength and makes a mild and invigorating tea.

❁ ❁ ❁

Slice the bone-dry ginseng into pieces with a very sharp knife or *chakdo* (herb chopper). Put the ginseng and water in a nonmetallic teapot and bring to a boil. Decrease the heat to low and simmer for 1 to 2 hours (the longer the brewing time, the stronger the tea). Strain through a hemp bag and extract as much juice as possible. Reserve the residue for later use (see below). Pour the tea into ceramic cups and serve very hot. In the strict manner, ginseng tea is savored alone without any sweetener, but in this moderate concoction, some honey may be added to tone down the bitterness. Insam ch'a cannot be reheated.

Note: The ginseng residue left in the hemp bag can usually be brewed once or twice more. When I was little, our mother sweetened the crumbled residue for us to eat.

Variation: Mushroom Tea (Yongji Ch'a) is brewed similarly. Cut dried yongji mushrooms into shreds, place in a muslin pouch, brew for 1 1/2 to 2 hours, and strain. This rare, powerful medicinal ingredient is very hard to obtain. In any case, it is recommended that no more than 1 small cup be consumed in a day. Recently a so-called combination ginseng and yongji tea has appeared in stores. In spite of what the label says, each teabag probably contains a mere hint of the mystical yongji mushroom, known as the mushroom for eternal youth.

Acknowledgments

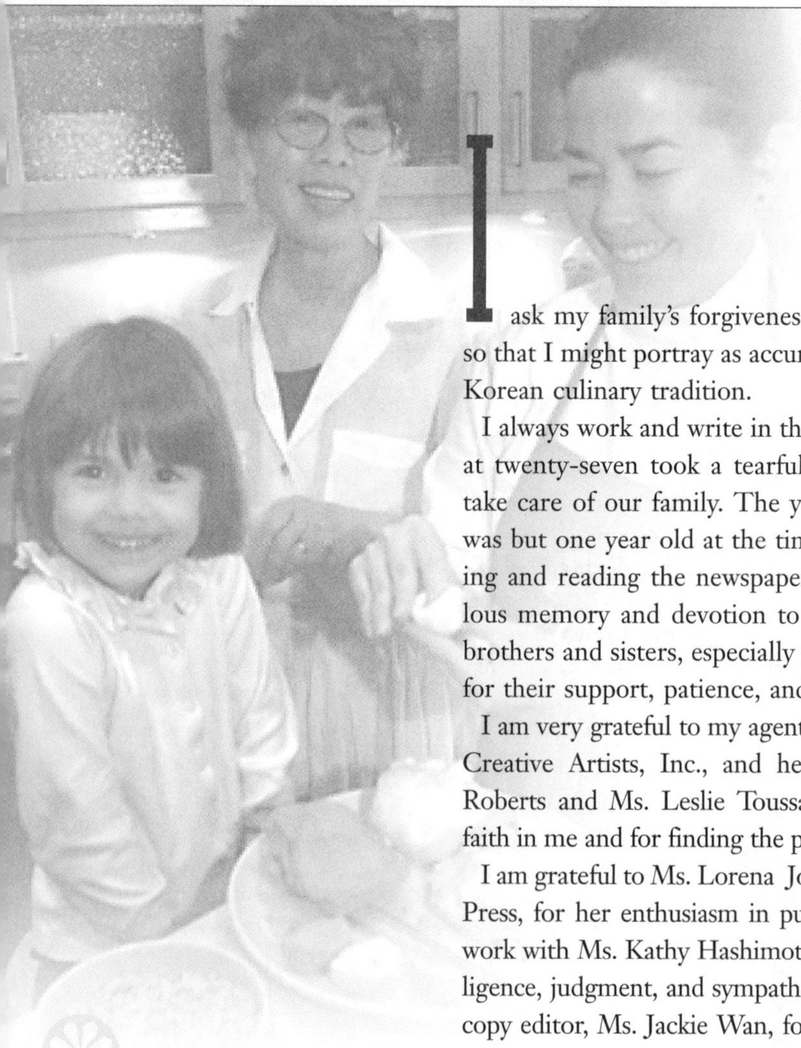

I ask my family's forgiveness for putting them at center stage so that I might portray as accurately as I could the richness of the Korean culinary tradition.

I always work and write in the memory of our big brother, who at twenty-seven took a tearful oath at our father's deathbed to take care of our family. The youngest of our fourteen members was but one year old at the time. I thank our mother, still cooking and reading the newspapers at ninety-nine, for her miraculous memory and devotion to her family. I am indebted to my brothers and sisters, especially to my second brother and his wife for their support, patience, and generosity.

I am very grateful to my agent, Ms. Muriel Nellis of Literary and Creative Artists, Inc., and her thoughtful assistants, Ms. Jane Roberts and Ms. Leslie Toussaint, for their encouragement and faith in me and for finding the perfect publisher for my manuscript.

I am grateful to Ms. Lorena Jones, editorial director at Ten Speed Press, for her enthusiasm in publishing this book. It was a joy to work with Ms. Kathy Hashimoto, my editor. I appreciate her intelligence, judgment, and sympathetic understanding. I also thank my copy editor, Ms. Jackie Wan, for her hard work, invaluable advice, and judicious editing. I thank the art director, Ms. Nancy Austin, for her insight and direction. I am stunned and pleased by the artistry and sensitivity of our book designer, Mr. Jeff Puda.

I owe thanks to University of Maryland University College administrators and faculty in Europe and Asia for their erudite knowledge of the art of eating and upon whom I perfected my recipes.

I thank Larry, my partner in our life-long adventure. Without him, this book could never have seen the light of day. I thank Sonya and Steve for their loving friendship, for allowing us to be a part of their lives, and for giving us two wonderful grandchildren, Samantha and Oscar.

✿ Index